Praise for

D0299810

"Robert L. Leahy, one of America's most respected self-help psychologists, treats us to a tour de force in how to help soothe our anxious minds. With the most ancient and up-to-date wisdom and self-help techniques, Dr. Leahy is an expert guide and coach."

— **Paul Gilbert, Ph.D.**, author of *Overcoming Depression: A Step-by-Step Approach to Gaining Control Over Depression*

*"**Anxiety Free**, by the internationally renowned Dr. Robert L. Leahy, provides us with a state-of-the art guide to overcoming anxiety. Written in his trademark accessible style, Dr. Leahy's new book will help you develop your own self-help program, using the latest and most powerful techniques of cognitive therapy. His ingenious use of 'rule-books' immediately empowers you to know why you feel anxious and what you can do right now to overcome your fears. I highly recommend this excellent book."*

— **Aaron T. Beck, M.D.**, Professor of Psychiatry, University of Pennsylvania

"If you have a problem with anxiety, this is the book for you. **Anxiety Free** *provides detailed practical guidelines for understanding and overcoming all types of anxiety problems. You can trust this book."*

— **Christopher G. Fairburn, M.D.**, Professor of Psychiatry, University of Oxford

"Robert L. Leahy has written a comprehensive and vital primer which offers hope for recovery to even the most severe cases of fear and anxiety. This well-crafted book is replete with self-diagnostic tools and easy-to-use, step-by-step scientific procedures for freeing oneself from the pain of anxiety. **Anxiety Free** *is a pleasure to read and is full of many helpful case examples. It offers reassurance and hope to the millions who struggle with this crippling ailment. A must read for anyone who has ever experienced debilitating fear or anxiety."*

— **Frank M. Dattilio, Ph.D.**, ABPP, Department of Psychiatry, Harvard Medical School

"Dr. Leahy has done it again. Drawing from recent and well-supported research findings, Leahy, speaking in understandable and appealing language, offers powerful suggestions for addressing myriad anxiety problems. Sufferers of chronic and debilitating anxiety can take heart in a uniquely helpful resource."

— **Douglas Mennin, Ph.D.**, Director, Yale Anxiety and Mood Services, Department of Psychology, Yale University

ANXIETY FREE

ANXIETY FREE

UNRAVEL **YOUR** FEARS
BEFORE THEY UNRAVEL YOU

ROBERT L. LEAHY PhD

HAY HOUSE

Carlsbad, California • New York City • London • Sydney
Johannesburg • Vancouver • Hong Kong • New Delhi

Published and distributed in the United Kingdom by:
Hay House UK Ltd, 292B Kensal Rd, London W10 5BE. Tel.: (44) 20 8962 1230;
Fax: (44) 20 8962 1239. www.hayhouse.co.uk

Published and distributed in the United States of America by:
Hay House, Inc., PO Box 5100, Carlsbad, CA 92018-5100. Tel.: (1) 760 431 7695
or (800) 654 5126; Fax: (1) 760 431 6948 or (800) 650 5115. www.hayhouse.com

Published and distributed in Australia by:
Hay House Australia Ltd, 18/36 Ralph St, Alexandria NSW 2015.
Tel.: (61) 2 9669 4299; Fax: (61) 2 9669 4144. www.hayhouse.com.au

Published and distributed in the Republic of South Africa by:
Hay House SA (Pty), Ltd, PO Box 990, Witkoppen 2068.
Tel./Fax: (27) 11 467 8904. www.hayhouse.co.za

Published and distributed in India by:
Hay House Publishers India, Muskaan Complex, Plot No.3, B-2, Vasant Kunj,
New Delhi – 110 070. Tel.: (91) 11 4176 1620; Fax: (91) 11 4176 1630.
www.hayhouse.co.in

Distributed in Canada by:
Raincoast, 9050 Shaughnessy St, Vancouver, BC V6P 6E5. Tel.: (1) 604 323 7100;
Fax: (1) 604 323 2600

© Robert Leahy, 2009

The moral rights of the author have been asserted.

The author of this book does not dispense medical advice or prescribe the use of any technique as a form of treatment for physical or medical problems without the advice of a physician, either directly or indirectly. The intent of the author is only to offer information of a general nature to help you in your quest for emotional and spiritual wellbeing. In the event you use any of the information in this book for yourself, which is your constitutional right, the author and the publisher assume no responsibility for your actions.

A catalogue record for this book is available from the British Library.

ISBN 978-1-84850-031-0

For Helen

CONTENTS

CHAPTER 1

Understanding Anxiety

The woman came into my office looking slightly haggard. She was well dressed and her features well formed, but a certain tenseness around the eyes and mouth kept her from seeming really attractive. She didn't smile but glanced at me nervously, not quite meeting my gaze as she entered the room. She sat awkwardly on the edge of her chair, constantly shifting her position as she spoke, while her eyes darted around the room. I had the impression she was expecting something awful to happen.

"So, Carolyn," I said, when we had finished our introductions. "How can I help you?"

She paused a long moment. "I . . . I think I'm going crazy."

"Really. What makes you think so?" I asked.

"I keep having these anxiety attacks. I . . . I've actually had them for years. I don't know what's wrong with me. There's no reason for them." She went on to describe the attacks: sudden terror at being outdoors or in a shopping mall or looking out from a tall building. Total, unreasonable, suffocating panic, accompanied by a pounding heart and shortness of breath. The attacks would strike without warning and, when they did, she would rush home and close herself inside the house for several days.

"I think I know what's happening to you," I said. "But first why don't you tell me a little about your life?"

She hesitated, as though frightened by the prospect. But after a bit of encouragement she launched into her story. It turned out her relationship had recently fallen apart: her boyfriend had decided he couldn't live with her anymore. The issue wasn't so much her anxiety attacks as it was all her other fears and phobias. And there were many, as even I, who'd seen quite a few in my patients, had to admit. Not only was she afraid of flying, she could barely ride in a car without tensing at every intersection. She avoided elevators. She abhorred crowds but also open spaces. She was painfully uncomfortable being with others at a dinner or party, which put

1

a real crimp in her social life. At work she found meetings excruciating, especially if she was called on to speak, and even had trouble making phone calls. And she was a chronic worrier; for years she'd suffered from insomnia because she couldn't shut her mind off enough to get to sleep.

At a certain point in the story, she burst into tears. "I'm so miserable," she said. "I think I'd like to die." After a few minutes of applying tissue, she pulled herself together enough to tell me what had brought her to me—which, incredibly enough, was *not* her anxieties! She'd always accepted those as just part of life! It was her growing depression. Since the breakup, she'd started drinking more heavily. She'd cut herself off from her friends, convinced they all despised her. She wasn't doing well at work and was in danger of losing her job. As she grew more lonely and isolated, she became more and more depressed. She told me she had been contemplating suicide.

"Carolyn," I said finally. "Have you ever sought help with this before?"

"No," she admitted.

"Any particular reason?" I asked. "I mean, I'm a little surprised, someone who's been having as tough a time as you have."

"Well," she said, "I guess I never thought anyone *could* help me. I've just always been this way." Then she met my eyes for the first time. "I guess I don't really believe you can help me either."

Fortunately, Carolyn was wrong on both counts. Help *is* available—and not just from me. It's true that anxiety can be a crippling ailment. It can limit you in every area of your life. It can lead to depression and even suicide. It's the most common psychological condition we have. And it can last for years if it's not treated. Yet the somewhat surprising good news is that anxiety disorders *can* be treated—often very effectively. Carolyn's proved to be quite treatable—and she was an extreme case. If you suffer from any of her symptoms, there's a good chance you can overcome them enough to live a perfectly normal, satisfying, and complete life. You can make the journey from that bleak territory of fear to the other shore, where your anxiety no longer controls you, destroys your sense of pleasure, or impinges on your health and well-being. How to begin that journey is the subject of this book. And we'll start by looking at some of the factors—historical, biological, psychological—that lie behind Carolyn's condition and are in many ways the key to understanding it.

A MODERN AFFLICTION

We live in the Age of Anxiety.

In any given year, about 18 percent of Americans will suffer from an anxiety disorder. This is twice the rate as that for depression—though the latter seems to receive more attention. Over the course of a lifetime, the number who will suffer from anxiety rises to close to 30 percent. These are remarkable statistics. Just as clinical depression is a lot more severe a problem than people just feeling "down" now and then, clinical anxiety is a lot more severe than being subject to everyday worries. The fact is, a real anxiety disorder is a serious thing. If you suffer from one, chances are it has a major impact on your life. People with anxiety disorders often find themselves unable to work effectively, to socialize, to travel, or to maintain stable relationships. They may go through all sorts of contortions to avoid certain people, places, or activities, including driving, flying, and riding in elevators. They may be unable to endure crowds, social gatherings, open spaces, or small amounts of dirt. They often have trouble sleeping. Some become socially reclusive or housebound. In extreme cases, an anxiety disorder will require hospitalization. For real sufferers, the condition goes well beyond fretting over income taxes or feeling jumpy around spiders. It's a real and lasting affliction with life-impacting consequences.

Nor does it end there. Those who suffer from anxiety disorder are far more likely to become clinically depressed, giving many the dubious distinction of suffering from two debilitating conditions at once. They're also far more likely to be substance abusers, especially alcoholics. And there's little doubt that having an anxiety disorder is bad for your health. It's been linked to cardiac problems, hypertension, gastrointestinal distress, respiratory illness, diabetes, asthma, arthritis, skin problems, fatigue, and a host of other conditions. It affects about 16 percent of children with significant impact on their future development. Children with anxiety disorders have more problems in school (both academic and social) and far more chance of growing up to be psychologically impaired or disabled. Anxiety, unlike some more discreet ailments, is one of those conditions that severely impacts overall health and well-being.

All this is costly to society as well as to individuals. The cost of treating anxiety disorders runs to many billions of dollars; about a third of medical costs for *all* psychiatric problems is for treatment of anxiety. People with anxiety disorders are less productive at work and more likely to use medical services or visit emergency rooms. People with panic disorder are *five times* more likely than average to receive disability payments. Quite outside official statistics, millions of people who suffer from symptoms of anxiety—whether diagnosed as "disorders" or not—consult medical practitioners of all sorts with anxiety-related complaints. How much of a burden this places on the health care system no one can say for sure. But there's no doubt that the stress many of us feel as individuals is being felt as a collective stress on society at large.

IS ANXIETY GROWING?

One thing about all this that's hard to ignore is that it seems to have gotten worse. Rates of overall anxiety have increased dramatically during the last fifty years. The most striking increase occurred between 1952 and 1967, but numbers have continued to rise ever since. In fact, the average *child* today exhibits the same level of anxiety as the average *psychiatric patient* in the 1950s.

Why such an increase? Aren't most of us better off than we used to be? Don't people live longer, have better medical care than they used to? Haven't many of the common risks of life been eliminated or dramatically reduced: child mortality, malnutrition, smallpox? Aren't we better protected against the ravages of weather and climate? Aren't our houses bigger and more comfortable, filled with conveniences that bring ease to our lives and spare us the rigors of hard, dangerous work? Don't more of us retire earlier, play golf, take tropical vacations? Don't we have unemployment insurance, bike helmets, reliable police forces, better teeth? Few of us ever have to go out in a snowstorm, cross a raging brook, or go out in the woods to find food or gather fuel. One would think that since our society keeps us, on the whole, safer from catastrophe than it used to, that our overall level of anxiety as a people would have subsided. Instead, it's risen. We've become a nation of nervous wrecks. What explains that?

Apparently there are factors other than material comfort and security. One of them seems to be the level of "social connectedness" we experience in our lives. Over the last half-century our ties to other people have grown less stable and predictable. Divorce is far more common, with families broken apart and scattered. Extended families living close together are now rare. Local communities have become far less cohesive, dispersed by economic mobility, roads and automobiles, and faraway shopping and entertainment centers. Participation in community activities is a shadow of what it once was. Cities and suburbs have supplanted small towns;

people are more isolated from their neighbors. More and more of us now live alone. In many places, crime has risen; streets no longer feel like safe public areas. Terrorism now seems like a real threat. As globalization and economic competition have intensified, job security has declined; people are laid off from jobs in ways that would have seemed unthinkable a generation ago. Many of us can no longer count on pensions or adequate social security in our old age. All these factors contribute to a feeling that life is not quite as secure as it once was. The support from "the tribe" that evolution has accustomed us to depend on simply isn't there the way it used to be.

These changes have also been accompanied by changes in the way we think about our lives. Our sense of self-reliance has given way to a feeling of being controlled by large, distant forces whose workings are only dimly known to us. At the same time, our expectations of material comfort have been raised by affluence, by our newfound identities as consumers rather than citizens or members of a community. We're better off materially than our parents and grandparents, but feel even more that we don't have enough. This feeling is reinforced by a barrage of TV and magazine ads that demonstrate how idyllic our lives would be if only we bought the right products, ate the right foods, wore the right clothes. The more plugged in to a vast consumer network we are, the more solitary we feel. As the economy offers us more and more choices, we become less and less content, wondering nervously if our choices were the right ones. Our standards of beauty, our expectations of success, our demand for continual, unrelenting happiness leave us dissatisfied with a world in which we are getting fatter on junk food and labor-saving devices, where our leisure time feels more and more empty, and where we desperately purchase one self-help book after another in the search for meaning and happiness.

IS THERE HOPE?

Is there something we can do about all this?

As individuals we have choices as to *how* we deal with it. We also have opportunities we didn't used to have. Modern psychology has learned a great deal about anxiety in the last few decades. We know much more than we once did about where it comes from, how it operates on the mind, the nature of the behavioral patterns it generates. All this can help us understand the role that anxiety plays in our lives. And *understanding* that role is the key to *overcoming* anxiety—not to eliminating it completely, for, as we'll see, that's not a realistic goal. But we'll learn to neutralize it, control it, and keep it from being a debilitating force that restricts our health and freedom. Understanding anxiety, in short, is the way to escape its tyranny.

The first thing to understand about anxiety is that it's part of our biological heritage. Long before any recorded human history, our ancestors lived in a world filled with life-threatening dangers: predators, starvation, toxic plants, hostile neighbors, heights, disease, drowning. It was in the face of these dangers that the human psyche evolved. The qualities necessary to avoid danger were the qualities that evolution bred into us as human beings. A good many of those qualities amounted simply to different forms of caution. Fear was protective; one had to be wary of many things to survive. This wariness persists in our present psychological makeup in the form of some of our deepest aversions and phobias. These fears were *adaptive*—they are really survival instincts left over from a primitive era. In our next chapter we'll talk in more detail about how these fears came to be programmed into us and what some of the implications for us are.

The next thing to understand is that, since we no longer live in that primitive world, the fears we carry from it are no longer adaptive. Thanks largely to the effects of language and civilization, the challenges we encounter in our lives are quite different from the ones our ancestors faced on the savanna or in the jungle. Yet our brains continue to operate as though nothing has changed. We're driven by the instinct to run from a hungry jaguar when all we may be confronting is a barking dog. We're afraid to touch a plate someone has used because our ancestors had a healthy aversion to contaminated food. We feel pathologically shy because, in another era, a stranger could easily kill us; even a member of our own tribe might do harm to us if offended. When it comes to our deepest instincts, we act as though we are still in the Stone Age, facing Stone Age conditions.

We are, in short, operating on an outmoded set of "rules." Evolution has programmed these rules into us as a way of protecting us from risk. They're like a kind of software installed in our heads—software that's millions of years old. Every instinct we have tells us that obeying the rules will keep us safe, when, in fact, just the opposite may be true. Our method of breaking free from the tyranny of anxiety will be to challenge these rules—in effect to rewrite them. This will involve examining the irrational beliefs that the rules are based on. For these beliefs, when unquestioned, exert a hidden but enormously powerful influence over our thoughts and behavior.

Once we challenge these beliefs, we can begin revising the rules governing anxiety, even though the latter are embedded deeply in our mind. Why are we able to do this? Because nature, in addition to providing us with certain instincts, has also given us the ability—located for the most part in a different part of our brain, the part we call rational—to modify those instincts on the basis of our experience. This is the key to treating anxiety. It is not the same as "being rational" about our fears. This does *not* work: knowing or being told that a fear is irrational does not make it go away. But if we can actually *experience* a seemingly dangerous situation over and over again, but *without* harmful consequences, our brains *learn* to be more rational and less fearful. It happens all the time in life. All it takes is to set up a program in which we can have a certain fearful experience regularly but *in a context that teaches us it is safe.* Thus over time we learn to lessen our fear. In the chapters that follow we will apply this principle to a number of different anxiety disorders, replacing the rules that govern them with a new, far more workable set. We'll be doing what evolution has not had time to do—adapting the rules to our present-day circumstances.

DO YOU HAVE AN ANXIETY DISORDER?

There are six common recognized anxiety disorders, each with its own particular group of symptoms. They all come from the same kind of basic survival instinct. Despite the names given to them, they are not so much separate disorders as they are simply our fundamental human anxiety manifesting in different ways around different stimuli or situations. People who have one of these disorders frequently have more than one—occasionally an individual will have most, if not all of them. But each disorder does have its own characteristics and challenges, which means that the techniques we use to treat it will be somewhat customized. The most effective treatments are tailored to the specific anxiety disorder.

This should not dissuade you from using this book as a whole or from developing an overall understanding of the subject. Even if you suffer from a particular disorder, you may learn something useful reading about the rest. The skillful treatment of anxiety in all its forms is, to some extent, a single art, an art you can learn and practice in many ways on your own.

The six recognized anxiety disorders are:

1. *Specific Phobia.* This is a fear of a specific stimulus or situation: planes, elevators, deep water, certain animals, etc. Your underlying belief is that the thing is actually dangerous in itself (the plane may crash, the dog may bite). About 12 percent of us have specific phobia, though a much larger proportion may have particular fears around one or more of the stimuli.

2. *Panic Disorder.* This is a fear of your own physiological and psychological reactions to fearful stimuli—in essence, fear of a panic attack. Any abnormalities, such as altered breathing or heart rate, vertigo, sweating, or tremors, are seen as signs of impending collapse, insanity, or death. The accompanying avoidance of situations that could trigger these reactions is known as *agoraphobia,* and often limits mobility severely. About 3 percent of us have the disorder, often linked to depression.

3. *Obsessive-Compulsive Disorder (OCD).* You have recurring thoughts or images (obsessions) that you find distressing—for example, thoughts of being contaminated, losing control, making a mistake, or behaving inappropriately. You have the overwhelming urge to perform certain actions (compulsions) that will neutralize these images: washing, arbitrary rituals, constant checking, etc. This disorder often leads to depression and affects about 3 percent of the population.

4. *Generalized Anxiety Disorder (GAD).* This is essentially a tendency to worry continually about a lot of things. One's thoughts are devoted to imagining all possible negative consequences and imagining ways to prevent them. The disorder is often accompanied by physical symptoms of stress: insomnia, muscle tension, gastrointestinal problems, etc. About 9 percent of us have it.

5. *Social Anxiety Disorder (SAD).* A fear of being judged by others, especially in social situations. These may include presentations, parties, meetings, using public eating or restroom facilities, or simply encounters with new acquaintances. Symptoms include extreme tension or "freezing up," obsessive

worry over social interactions, and a tendency toward isolation and loneliness. This disorder is often accompanied by drug and alcohol abuse. About 14 percent of us have it in some form.

6. ***Post-Traumatic Stress Disorder (PTSD).*** This involves excessive fear caused by previous exposure to a threat or injury. Typical traumas include rape, physical violence, severe accidents, and exposure to warfare. Sufferers often reexperience their traumas in the form of nightmares or flashbacks and avoid situations that bring back disturbing memories. They may exhibit irritability, tension, and hypervigilance. Alcohol and drug abuse among sufferers is endemic, as are feelings of depression and hopelessness. About 14 percent of us suffer from this disorder.

It's obvious from a glance at this list that a major anxiety disorder is quite a difficult thing. Any of the above conditions can dramatically affect the quality of your life. All of them can foster depression, impair your physical health, reduce your effectiveness in the world, and damage your relationships. In addition, each one can limit or disrupt your life in its own special way. *Specific phobia* can keep you from traveling, being close to nature, leaving the ground floor, or doing whatever specific thing it is you fear. *Panic disorder* may keep you frightened of your own breath or heartbeat, and prevent you from going just about anywhere. *Obsessive-compulsive disorder* can consume you with meaningless precautions and rituals and oppress you with the sense of things amiss or out-of-kilter. *Generalized anxiety disorder* may keep your mind constantly agitated with worries and prevent you from relaxing. *Social anxiety disorder* can paralyze you in front of others, limit your activities, and condemn you to loneliness. *Post-traumatic stress disorder* can turn your life into a recurring nightmare, increase alcohol or drug abuse, and impair your ability to function. The cost of an anxiety disorder, in just about any terms, is considerable. Freeing yourself from one would seem to be one of the kindest and most rewarding things you could do for yourself.

CAN ANXIETY BE TREATED?

What can be done to treat anxiety disorders? Unfortunately, many people assume that the answer is little or nothing. They see their disorder as the expression of some fundamental flaw in their character. Or they've lived with it for so long they've gotten used to it. Or they've tried certain kinds of therapy (usually the kind that tries to unravel your deep personal "issues") and found them ineffective. Or—and this is usually at least part of the problem—the thought of facing your anxiety is just too scary. Studies have shown that around 70 percent of anxiety sufferers receive either no treatment or inadequate treatment. As a result, many tend to have ongoing problems for years, if not a lifetime. These problems can become severely debilitating, leading to alcoholism or drug abuse, depression, and functional disability. Left untreated, an anxiety disorder can be one of the most devastating conditions an individual can suffer.

This is truly unfortunate because indications are that anxiety is now highly treatable. Newer forms of cognitive-behavioral therapy have repeatedly proven effective in addressing major anxiety disorders. These treatments do not rely on medication. They do not take years and years to work; patients often show significant improvement right from the start and many are able to bring their disorder under control within months or even weeks of initiation. Most are able to maintain improvement indefinitely through increased awareness and practice of self-help skills. The self-help techniques offered in this book are based on up-to-date clinical research, as well as on the experience I've had personally working with hundreds of anxiety sufferers. There's no question in my mind that the great majority of people can be significantly helped. It merely takes an awareness of what the resources are, an openness to new approaches, and the determination to change one's life for the better.

WHAT THIS BOOK OFFERS

This book can serve as a guide to the process. It will outline the basic steps of treatment and show you what lies ahead. In Chapter 2 ("Anxiety as Adaptation"), we'll take a look at the evolutionary basis of anxiety in order to understand how it comes to be part of our human makeup. We'll see what function your anxiety served in a primitive environment—that is, how it was adaptive—and how those adaptive mechanisms survive in your current psychological makeup. Chapter 3 ("The Anxiety Rule Book") will examine the basic "rules" that evolution has written into your brain to help you deal with risk. We'll see how those rules no longer apply to the conditions of modern life—how they tend to focus on nonexistent dangers while ignoring more pressing concerns. We'll uncover some of the beliefs the rules are based on—and how you can begin to challenge them. This will enable you to start rewriting the rules, revising your assessments of what is safe and what is not by subjecting them to actual experience rather than leaving them to irrational thoughts and atavistic habits. This is the key to overcoming anxiety: actually *experiencing* it in a safe context. No matter how deeply your fears are embedded in your mind, you have the ability to *learn* the lesson of safety.

In the six subsequent chapters—4 through 9—we'll explore ways you can put these ideas to the test. We'll go through each of the six recognized anxiety disorders, explaining what they are, how they work, and what particular form the rules of anxiety take. Each of the six chapters offers step-by-step techniques for confronting your anxieties—first in imagined situations and then in real ones.

In the Appendix to this book, I have provided a number of self-report diagnostic tests, examples of how to categorize your anxious thoughts and how to change them, how to assure a balanced diet and sufficient exercise, information on depression and suicidal risk, medication guidelines, and information on insomnia, relaxation, and mindfulness. You may want to go through the relevant parts of the Appendix to learn more about specific techniques and treatments. Practicing these techniques will allow you to reverse your anxieties—but not by battling against them or trying to eliminate them. You'll instead find that the key to success is to distance yourself from your fears—to alter your perspective so that you are no longer a victim of your own mind. There's one great guiding principle: your fear level is determined not by the situation you find yourself in but by your *interpretation* of that situation. When the interpretation changes, your whole sense of what is fearful and what is not changes with it. Once the ogres, demons, and specters your mind has created finally vanish, the path to the shining castle lies open before you.

We've now seen how the path begins. Let's proceed on the journey.

CHAPTER 2

Anxiety as Adaptation

WHAT CAN EVOLUTION TEACH US ABOUT ANXIETY?

Why are we so anxious?

We are (or so we like to think) the most intelligent of species. More than any other animal, we have the capacity for rational thought—for assessing a situation realistically and deciding on the best course of action. Why, then, are we so controlled by anxieties that are plainly irrational? Why can't we use our marvelous human intelligence to simply see that things, for the most part, are going to be okay? Our friends and partners seem able to assess our anxieties pretty clearly. They seem to know when we're going off the deep end. "You don't need to be so anxious," they reassure us. "There's really nothing to worry about." It almost never helps. At some level we know they are right—that their picture of the situation is more realistic than our own, but we simply don't feel any less anxious. It's as if our brains are wired to override rational or logical truth.

In fact, our intelligence always seems to be busy coming up with *new* things to be anxious about. We ingeniously develop scenarios of disaster: embarrassing ourselves in public, not living up to our standards, getting sick, failing exams, collapsing, catching diseases, making mistakes, and— well—just about anything we can think of. It's as if we are too smart for our own good. We keep peering into the future, imagining what people might think, what could possibly go wrong—risks that we alone seem to appreciate. Carried far enough, it all makes us wonder whether we are really insane. *Am I going crazy?* is a thought that often pops up, sometimes followed by *Would I know if I were?*

One of the striking features of this process is that it seems relentless. When we are dominated by anxiety, our mind seems to operate 24/7, never taking time out to rest. We can't turn off the thinking process. It simply generates more and more anxiety, like a machine whose switch is stuck on "go." The mind chatters away even when we wish to sleep or relax or simply do nothing. It creates enough anxiety to blot out the most pleasant surroundings. No matter how well things are going, no matter what blessings life is offering us at the moment, we are too preoccupied with anxieties over the past and future to take them in.

At some level we believe all this worrying is important, that we *need* to do it. We give it all our energy and focus. Because we can think of so many possible problems—and possible solutions to each of them—we take the need to figure it all out very seriously. We think we need to pay attention to what our minds are telling us, so that we can avoid catastrophes and grab more of life's goodies. Unfortunately, this idea seems to be mostly an illusion. Our anxieties never seem to steer us toward a better, more rewarding existence. They're never the reliable navigation system we want them to be. Instead, all they seem to do is make our behavior less appropriate, to disrupt our sleep, to put us in conflict with others, to limit our options in life, to continually darken our perspective—in short, to make us suffer.

What would it be like for all this to stop? What would it be like to be serene, at peace with ourselves, content with what life brings us?

To answer this question, I turned to my cat.

My cat seems to live a rather worry-free life. He eats, sleeps, plays, and lies in the sun with what appears to be unbroken equanimity. He doesn't suffer from insomnia. He doesn't lie in bed thinking about all the work he has to do the next day or if he left the oven on. He doesn't ruminate about his interactions with humans or other cats, or wonder if he behaved inappropriately the other day. He certainly doesn't seem to worry about my (or anyone else's) expectations. As long as he's comfortable right now, he's happy. At times it's hard not to envy this blissful serenity.

It's also obvious that my cat has been perfectly fitted by evolution for the life he leads. Cats have been around for about 12 million years without any significant change in their form or function. (After all, how would you improve on the design of a cat?) They are well adapted to a simple life of preying on other animals and reproducing. The evolutionary instructions for a cat consist of some pretty simple thoughts—none of which would easily lead to anxiety: *This feels good, this doesn't feel good, that's mine, and what's next.* Cats have a simple formula: "Find prey, kill, and eat." Or, "Find other cats, decide if they're friendly, then either fight them or play with them, and maybe have sex with them." Or, "Locate human beings, rub up against them, and purr till they feed you." Life is pretty simple. If you just act on instinct in the moment, you'll probably come out all right. Zen cats.

Humans, of course, are another story.

We are neurotic—and have been for quite a while. Thanks to our advanced conceptual and language skills, we have the ability to remember the past and anticipate the future. We can think about things that have not happened and may never happen—but could happen. We can imagine what other people think of us and how that might impact our future success. We can wonder whether we offended someone last week. We can worry about not being prepared, about making mistakes, about leaving things undone. We lie in bed (next to our cat who is sound asleep) thinking *Why can't I get to sleep?* or *What did Susan mean when she said that?* or *Will I ever be able to get all this work done on time?* We dwell on the meaning of life, the specter of death, the opinions of others, and whether we have the right clothes for the party tomorrow. There is virtually no end to the things that can cause us anxiety.

What good is all this thinking? Why aren't we more like cats? Why can't we just put ourselves down on a nice warm blanket, close our eyes, start purring, and fall asleep?

The answer is that evolution has not treated us the same as it has treated cats. It has left cats pretty much in tune with their present-day environment. They are as well-fitted as ever for eating, sleeping, hunting, and begging for food. Our own evolution, however, was pretty much finished up back in the days of primitive hunter-gatherer societies. The abilities and tendencies it left our ancestors with are those that were necessary for survival in that environment. But things have changed fast in the last ten or twenty thousand years—well beyond the pace of evolution. Modern civilization has altered our circumstances far too rapidly for our evolutionary biology to catch up. So we're left with the kind of hardwired biological apparatus whose "software" no longer fits the circumstances we actually live in.

It's important to remember that evolution is not about being happy, relaxed, or guilt-free. It's about survival. And survival depends on only one thing: passing on your genes to your progeny. It's the genes that need to survive, even if the individual is sacrificed in the process. It's plain that we humans have been incredibly successful as a species (whether we'll continue to be, of course, is another question). We've done so by successfully passing on, through millions of years of evolution, the genes that allow us to adapt to our environment. This didn't make us the "strongest" species—after all, you're not going to win a fight with a gorilla or a tiger. Nor did it necessarily reward sheer aggressiveness—other humans could always gang up on you and throw you off the prehistoric cliff if they didn't like you. It wasn't even about having as many babies as possible, since your genes don't survive if all the babies die.

What are the characteristics, then, that have assisted humans in passing on their genes?

There's no precise answer, but our knowledge of evolutionary biology and psychology gives us a rough picture. Most obviously, the humans who successfully passed on their genes were the ones able to attract other humans of the opposite sex and have babies with them—probably those who were generally attractive and somewhat dominant physically. But there's another major factor: the social unit. We humans are perhaps not as mindlessly devoted to the welfare of the colony as bees or ants. But our survival as a species does depend to a large extent on cooperation, and thus the individual skills we developed tended largely to be social ones. Our prehistoric ancestors evolved in groups that hunted and gathered together. The ability to get along with and exert influence over others would have been favored by natural selection. Communication would have played a central role (hence the development of language), while general intelligence would become an increasingly valued asset. The sheer ability to learn and remember the properties and nutritional values of thousands of plant and animal food sources (including which ones were poisonous) would have been highly useful for survival. So would the ability to figure out how to trap and kill much larger animals or start a fire or drive predators off or care for children or keep the tribe from running out of food. All these individual capacities conferred enormous benefits upon the group.

We can recognize the same qualities in modern-day humanity. Even in our society, they are all adaptive to some extent. But what about anxiety? How do our irrational fears fit into the evolutionary picture? Why should we be hardwired to toss and turn all night? To worry about things we can do nothing about, to brood over past mistakes, to obsess about what other people think of us, to set standards for ourselves that make us miserable, to create terrifying future scenarios out of nothing, to paralyze ourselves through our own fears so that we cannot think or act effectively? Why are our personal lives so often a mess even as our efficiency as a species gives us unprecedented dominance over nature?

A Visit with Stone Age Stanley

I recently wanted to find out what life was like 100,000 years ago so I got into my imaginary time machine and traveled back in time to interview Stanley, the prehistoric neurotic.

"Hey, Stanley, I'm Bob—and I'm new around here. Do you have some time to talk?"

"Can't you see I'm busy? I'm in a rush. I think it's going to rain, and I don't have my lion skin. I mean, I could catch a cold, develop a fever. So, what's on your mind?"

"Well, I wanted to find out a little about you."

"Have I done something wrong? I thought I put the fire out last week—did something burn down? I try to be careful, but I can never be sure."

"No, Stanley. I wanted to find out about what your life is like."

"My life? Well, first, I can't sleep. Up all night. Worrying about the tigers and wolves in the forest. They tell me it's safe around here, but I've heard stories that would make your hair stand on end."

"So you have insomnia?"

"Not all the time. But it really drives me nuts. I can't sleep—I keep telling myself, Stanley, get some sleep! You'll be good for nothing if you don't get some sleep."

"Tell me, Stanley. What's this area like?"

"Dangerous. Be careful on the bridge. I don't know what klutz strung that thing up, but you could fall with one false step. And then try to get a doctor!"

"So, you're afraid of heights?"

"Hey, you'd have to be an idiot not to be afraid of heights. They can kill you. And, if it's not the falling that kills you, it's the drowning. Last month a couple of guys who thought they were macho took some wood they strung together. They tried to float it to get to the other island. They drowned. I warned them. But, no—they thought they knew it all. They said, 'Stanley, you're always worried—so negative. It's bad for your digestion to think this way.' Well, they're at the bottom of the ocean, and I'm talking to you. So, who's the smart one?"

"I guess you are, Stanley."

"Yeah, but I have this indigestion. I hope it's nothing serious. I went to the doctor—maybe you've seen him—the old guy with the snake around his head."

"I just got here. I haven't seen him."

"Well, he gave me this disgusting drink—for my stomach. It's supposed to calm me. It made me throw up. I'm just worried I have something serious. Why, just last year a whole tribe south of here died from food poisoning. I wash everything—everything—before I eat it. But I'm not sure that the water is safe to drink, either. Ever since this place has gotten more crowded—I think it's contaminated. People think I'm a fanatic, but I haven't gotten food poisoning."

"Yep, you're still alive, Stanley. How do you feel about these strangers coming into the area?"

"I don't trust them. I mean, who knows. They could attack me, they might take my Sara and my kids, drive me out. So I try to maintain a low profile. I don't look them in the eye. I speak softly. I try not to make a scene. What's that old saying, 'No one kicks a sleeping dog'? Low profile, soft voice. I'm a bit shy, you could say."

"What are you afraid of?"

"Well, besides everything. I'm afraid of being killed. That's what it comes down to."

"Has anything happened?"

"Last month—I can't get this out of my mind—I saw some strangers—foreigners. They had different animal skins, their hair was different. It was frightening. I saw them take my uncle Harry and string him up, and then they boiled him and ate him. It was a terrible scene. Thank God, for me, that I was running like hell at the time—but I can't get the image out of my mind. I wake up in the middle of the night hearing his screams. I could be next."

"Sounds terrible. So, you're afraid that what happened to Uncle Harry could happen to you?"

"Yeah—but if I say so myself—I'm a bit wiser than he was. Uncle Harry—always the big mouth—always saying, 'Stanley, you're such a pessimist. What are you so worried about?' With all due respect for my late uncle—he's lunch and all I have is indigestion."

"It must be hard for you to be so anxious so much of the time."

"Hard for me? It's terrible. Two years ago I developed these 'attacks.' I would be walking outside—out in the fields—and I could feel my heart beating rapidly. It was sunny outside, no lions walking around. I suddenly got so afraid I was going to have a heart attack that I got dizzy. I couldn't catch my breath."

"What happened next?"

"Lucky for me Sara was there—God bless her soul. She took me by the arm and got me to the nearest cave. I was so dizzy. But for the next three months I was afraid to go out to the field. I thought I'd have another attack."

"So how did you get over it?"

"Well, I'm not over it—although I haven't had any attacks recently. I think what helped is that Sara absolutely insisted—and she can be pushy, if you ask me—but she insisted that we pick the strawberries in the field before the birds got them. I was hungry, and I thought, *As long as Sara is with me, if I have an attack, I'll be able to get away with her.* But I think it helped to pick the strawberries. But I still worry I'll have another attack."

"Are you a worrier?"

"All the time. I worry about whether we'll have enough food, whether Sara will run off with someone stronger than me. I worry about the kids—if they'll get into trouble. I always worry about my health."

"It must be hard."

"Watch out!"

"What is it, Stanley?"

"Oh—it's okay. I thought that branch was a snake. Snakes are poisonous, so be careful around here."

"Thanks for taking the time to talk with me, Stanley."

"You're welcome. I hope I didn't sound too negative. Everyone is saying, 'Stanley, you're such a negative person. Always afraid. Always thinking the worst.' Maybe they have a point. Maybe I'm losing my head. Wait, let me think, did I put the stone over the food in the hole? What if someone comes along—what if a bear comes into the cave, finds the food—what if the bear is drawn to the cave because of the food—because I didn't put the stone over the hole—and kills my family? It would be all my fault. I wasn't careful enough. I think I put the stone there—but I'm not sure . . . "

"Stanley, I've got to go."

"Maybe I put the stone over the hole. I should go back to check. But if I do then I'll miss the meeting with Sid. He'll be angry. If he's angry, he could tell everyone I'm unreliable. Then what?"

Okay, Stone Age Stanley is my little joke. But you can understand the point. It's about evolution, about our ancestors from hundreds of thousands of years ago—what their lives were like, what qualities they needed in order to cope with the challenges they faced, and how all of this is connected to the way we are today. For some time now, evolutionary psychology has been putting together the pieces of the puzzle. And anxiety is one of those pieces. So let's take a more serious look at how anxiety came to be part of the human condition.

WHAT IS ANXIETY GOOD FOR?

In short, why would evolution make us so neurotic?

Evolutionary psychologists answer this question by recasting it slightly: "How could anxiety have helped our ancestors survive in a primitive environment?" They look at the function of a particular fear, trying to determine how it might have served to guide or protect in certain situations. The fact is that every one of Stone Age Stanley's neuroses was adaptive. Heights were dangerous, spoiled food could be contaminated, it was risky to offend murderous strangers, you didn't want to cross an open field where lions could see you, and you might avoid starving to death by saving some food for the winter. Stanley may seem like a neurotic to you and me—but it was the Stanleys of the world who survived. They survived because of their anxieties. Those who weren't anxious enough simply *didn't survive.* In circumstances where death from starvation was always a threat, where animal attacks could happen at any moment, where precipices needed to be avoided, where strangers could kill you or your young, where your survival could depend on whether your tribe liked having you around, anxiety was one of the principal survival tools. It was simply nature's way of instilling prudence.

And yet the anxieties that once served us no longer seem to work. Instead of helping us survive, anxiety seems more often than not to "mess up" our lives. We've been handed a set of biological and psychological responses that fit us poorly for the requirements of our actual existence. In order to understand why, to see where those responses come from, to understand how our modern consciousness—with all its advantages and drawbacks—has evolved, we need to dip into our evolutionary psychology a little more deeply.

THINKING ABOUT THINKING

One of the key differences between humans and other animals is that we humans have developed what we call a theory of mind. This is not a "theory" in the sense of a scientific hypothesis. It is simply how we think about the world—more specifically, how we think about thinking itself. Thanks mostly to the development of language as a conceptual tool, we are aware that we have minds and that we are engaging in a process called thinking. We also have the ability to imagine what's going on in someone else's mind (*What are they up to?* or *What do they want?*). Animals don't seem to have this ability to conceptualize the mind-states of other beings. This doesn't mean animals don't have emotions or that they don't respond to those of other creatures. Anyone who has ever lived with a dog or cat knows that animals can be extremely sensitive in responding to emotions. But what makes humans distinctive is that we've developed a concept of how others of our species might think and feel—and how those thoughts and feelings might be analogous to our own. We have a deep-seated recognition that our fellow humans have their own wants, fears, needs, and reactions. And so in our relationships with these people (our family, our tribe, or simply other members of our species), their mental states must be taken into account.

21

The area of the brain in which this ability to understand other minds resides is the orbito-frontal cortex, a more advanced part of the brain. When people have lesions in this area of the brain they tend to lose their social judgment; they don't know quite how to act around others. When animals have lesions in the same area, they tend to lose social status. In neither animals nor small children is the orbito-frontal cortex as well developed as it is in a normal adult. This is especially true in those who suffer from autism: their intellectual faculties may be intact, but they have a hard time understanding the mental states of others. They have difficulty grasping concepts like intention, deception, disappointment, longing, hope, regret, or long-range motivation. In human society, these concepts form the basis of most relationships, which explains why children without autism, as they mature, normally learn to understand them, while autistic individuals often do not.

Through evolutionary psychology, we can reconstruct the way this theory of mind—our understanding of mental states—came to be programmed into us. One simple fact driving the evolutionary process was that human infants, for a variety of reasons, undergo an unusually long period (compared to other mammals) of relative helplessness. Then, as now, children did not become fully functioning adults until their teenage years. This meant that groups could provide better care, in terms of nourishment, protection, and learning opportunities, than could a single mother/father unit. (For one thing, it was probably not uncommon for a child's parents to die while the child was still young, requiring the tribe to take over the child-rearing function.) For such cooperative child rearing to take place, a great deal of what we might call social concern was required—a nurturing instinct, an interest in what others think, empathy for their feelings, care for one's reputation in the group. The necessities of child rearing made us into more socially sensitive beings.

This was only one of many things steering us in the direction of group cooperation. As early humans expanded their ecological niche, it was increasingly the tribe, not the individual, that determined success in the wild. Hunting, gathering food, avoiding poisonous plants and animals, fending off predators, seeking suitable habitat—all these activities were performed increasingly by the group, requiring greater amounts of group interaction. Individuals better suited to this cooperative life tended to survive and to pass on their genes. This had a great effect on the development of our brains—in effect, we became hardwired for cooperation. A well-functioning group was far more likely to successfully negotiate the perils of primitive existence than a tribe of warring individuals. And a sociable individual would be more useful to the tribe than one who was belligerent, antisocial, or indifferent to the general welfare. Thus our cooperative instincts were, in a sense, bred into us—they ensured our survival.

Much of this development was facilitated by language, so much so that at some point the ability to learn and use it became innate. The use of language was a great advantage in adapting to our environment. We could now efficiently share information about things like where to forage for food or how to avoid dangerous predators. Language gave us the critical tool of symbolic thinking—something our simian relatives did not possess. It gave us the ability to go beyond individual memory, to store information in the form of a group culture. This allowed us to preserve and pass on the collective knowledge essential to a planned existence—the use of tools, methods of food storage and preservation, hunting techniques, the mapping of territories, and so on. All this knowledge could now be disseminated among members of the tribe and passed on from one generation to the next. The acquisition of language was thus a major factor in our success as a species, changing forever the way we interacted with one another and our environment.

Though language may have given us the tools, emotions were still the driving force in human behavior. And anxiety was one of the principal emotions. In general, the evolutionary characteristics most reflected in present-day anxiety are the ones that tend toward caution or restraint. Humans who could show that they were not threatening to others—who were respectful or deferential—were less likely to be attacked by the more powerful. Signaling a willingness to cooperate—perhaps not unrelated to a dog's "submissive" posture toward a dominant rival—was a good way to avoid a possibly deadly confrontation. Other cautionary impulses served the same function. Fear of heights, deep water, or open spaces helped our ancestors avoid perilous situations. Wariness toward strangers was protective since a chance encounter with a hostile tribe could easily prove disastrous. A tendency to worry about the coming winter's food supply might help the tribe make it through till spring. In general, it's clear that many of the anxiety disorders we experience today have their origins in fears programmed into us by our evolutionary history.

THE RIGHT FEAR AT THE WRONG TIME

This is a critical starting point in learning to deal with anxiety: seeing that it originally had an adaptive function. All our fears—no matter how irrational they may seem to us today—are in some sense survival-based. The instinctive, cautionary behavior that underlies modern anxiety had it roots in the conditions of primitive life, especially as it was lived cooperatively by groups or tribes. It didn't matter what was being avoided; attention to the subtleties of social interaction had the same survival value as obvious protective mechanisms like fear of heights or revulsion toward rotten meat. These impulses may have helped our ancestors avoid all sorts of unfortunate consequences. But eons later, in a civilized setting, the same impulses appear somewhat neurotic. It appears that evolution has unwittingly instilled in us the capacity for anxiety disorders. It taught our ancestors, "Better safe than sorry."

What does this mean, practically speaking? Well, for one thing, it means we can take almost any modern anxiety disorder and trace it back to its origin as a survival mechanism. Take obsessive-compulsive disorder (OCD), for example. Individuals with OCD may harbor an extreme fear of germ contamination. A ridiculous phobia? Not in terms of history. Until recently, our ancestors were highly susceptible to contagious diseases that were often fatal—especially as populations became denser. Obsessive people also tend to hoard things—old newspapers, clothing, food, and other things. The impulse would be useful in a primitive environment where resources were scarce. Indeed, as recently as the Middle Ages, failing to save up enough food for winter was a significant cause of death (even animals frequently exhibit seasonal hoarding instincts). Or consider the obsessive's fear of losing control and becoming violent. In a primitive environment, this might translate as simple prudence. Such inhibitions may seem out of proportion in present-day circumstances, but it's not hard to see where they come from.

Each of the recognized anxiety disorders has similar links to evolutionary history. Agoraphobia—fear of open spaces—no doubt is related to our ancestors' vulnerability to predators in exposed, open settings. Post-traumatic stress disorder almost certainly originated as a way of keeping us away from dangers we'd already experienced as witnesses or near-victims. Generalized anxiety disorder is simply a modern version of farsightedness. The tribe's "worriers" might have simply been the ones who anticipated calamities and prepared for them.

Once we've seen and understood that our anxieties have a solid basis in our evolutionary history, we're better prepared to accept them as simply part of our biological heritage. We no longer need to view them as personal shortcomings that require us to feel guilt or embarrassment. But the really good news is that while we may have been born with these fears, they don't necessarily have to exert control over us forever. It's possible to reduce their power—especially when they're clearly out of proportion to actual dangers. In most cases we don't learn to be afraid of things—we inherit most of our fears—but we can learn to be *less* afraid. We do this simply by experiencing real life situations and finding that they are not, in fact, associated with terrible consequences. We can learn that the noise that our minds give out is simply a set of false alarms.

This is why many fears we have naturally in childhood go away as we get older. Children are often afraid of things like animals, water, the dark, or being alone. Normally as they grow up, they learn that these things are usually survived, that they do not pose threats. Experience teaches children to relinquish fear more than it teaches them to be afraid. Research supports this: city children are more afraid of snakes than kids in rural areas because country children come in contact with snakes more often and learn that they are not dangerous. The primal fear subsides. Many children are terrified of water, but once they learn to swim, the fear dissipates. It's easier to be gripped by a fear—particularly one that's been biologically instilled—if you're facing it for the first time.

But fears also protect us. If fears of falling were entirely learned, you would expect that kids who had fallen and gotten injured would have been more likely to be afraid of heights. But research shows that the opposite is true. Kids who initially had a fear of heights were less likely to fall at a later time.

This is no less true for adults. During the Second World War, people in cities that were bombed were less afraid of air raids than people from cities that were spared. People in the bombed cities had learned that they could survive. After the terrible events of 9/11, I noted how much more people from Connecticut and New Jersey feared coming to the city than those of us who already lived here. Apparently you need to be exposed to the thing you're afraid of in order to find out it's not as frightening or dangerous as you thought. The key to reducing fear is to see that the fear you are experiencing does not apply to the reality you are facing. And the way to see this is to actually experience that reality in a context of safety. You need to practice your fears.

Evolution, admittedly, has made it difficult to do this. It is normally not possible to simply give up your fear just because something you were afraid of didn't come to pass. This is because evolution operates on the "better safe than sorry" principle. It has a bias toward overpredicting danger. Let's say you're living in a primitive hunter-gatherer society where there are prides of lions roaming around. Safety depends on being able to spot the presence of lions in time to take protective action. What if you're an individual who's unusually nervous—who tends to see lions everywhere, even when there's no lion within miles? Would that be a problem? From an evolutionary point of view, probably not. The constant running and hiding might be a bit of an inconvenience, but it would not necessarily be a disadvantage in natural selection—that is, it wouldn't necessarily keep you from surviving and passing on your genes. On the other hand, a tendency to be casual about the danger of lions—a tendency to underpredict their presence—might be a different story. Imagining a lion in the underbrush nine times in a row might be harmless, but failing to spot the lion that all-important tenth time could be fatal. Evolution, therefore, has a bias in favor of caution: it wants us to be super-careful, to be constantly alert to danger. It instructs us not to relax our vigilance just because a certain peril we have been imagining has so far failed to materialize.

This is critical to our understanding of anxiety. What we think of as an anxiety "disorder"—a kind of quirky deviation from the norm— is really not an aberration at all but simply the natural result of our evolutionary history. Evolution has written the "software" for it in our brains as a survival mechanism. The problem is not with us but with the lives we live—the fact that they have changed so drastically from the lives we lived on the savanna or in the jungle. Ironically, the problem is that our environment is safer now, so our fears are usually unnecessary. They don't protect as much as they inhibit our enjoyment of life. It's the right fear at the wrong time. What was dangerous then may not be dangerous now, while behavior once inconsequential may now seriously impair our ability to function in our economic, social, and personal lives. Patterns that protected us in the wild no longer make sense in the workplace, the home, or the neighborhood. What we're being asked to do is to modify our primal instincts in a way that fits our present-day reality.

Is this possible? I believe it is. I believe that by examining some of the ways that anxiety limits and controls our lives, we can come to a better understanding of how to deal with it. By gaining awareness of how fear operates we begin to loosen its hold on us. We begin to work with our fear in a productive way, a way that takes advantage of our capacity to learn, to adapt to new circumstances. In the chapters to come we will look at some of the ways the anxious mind dominates our thinking—and how that dominance can be undone. We will see that no matter what the object of our anxiety—whether we fear heights, contamination, speaking in public, getting into elevators, making mistakes, meeting strangers, being stuck behind closed doors, or anything else of the kind—there is an underlying consistency to the process by which fear becomes the overriding factor. Likewise there is an underlying consistency to the process by which we can neutralize that fear.

Our minds are the filters through which we view reality. They have been programmed by our evolutionary history and our lifelong conditioning to send us constant messages, often irrational, about the nature of that reality, as well as instructions (in this book I call them "rules") on how to respond. When we experience anxiety, the message is that *nothing is safe*. The rules that go along with the message say that there's something crucial we must do (or not do) to make ourselves safe. But what if none of this is true? What if the message is false and the rules counterproductive? After all, a message is simply a message—we don't have to believe it. By challenging the message of fear, by questioning its truth, by holding it to the light of experience, we weaken its power to control our thoughts and behavior. We open ourselves to our true potential and our true freedom.

Let's take a closer look at the "rules" evolution has handed down to us. They may not be as immutable as we think.

CHAPTER 3

The Anxiety
Rule Book

IDENTIFYING THE RULES

We now know where our anxiety comes from. It doesn't just spring up in our minds for no reason. It's not the result of some mistake we made or some character defect. It wasn't generated in our messed-up childhood. When we experience an irrational fear—it could be of a plane crash, a growling dog, financial ruin, contagious disease, being rejected, or virtually anything at all—we are acting out a pattern laid down for us hundreds of thousands and even millions of years ago. That pattern may have kept our distant ancestors safe from myriad dangers, but it is not keeping us safe from anything now. Instead it is wreaking havoc in our lives.

Can we do anything about this? Is there a way to become less neurotic? If I could bring Stone Age Stanley back in my time machine with me (unfortunately it only seats one at present), would he be flexible enough to adapt to the modern era? Could he overcome his many neuroses sufficiently to lead a healthy and productive life?

My answer to this is an unequivocal *yes*. There's plenty that Stanley could do and that you can do as well. There *is* a way to treat anxiety, both through your own efforts and by getting help professionally. Moreover, it's a way that applies to any anxiety disorder, regardless of the shape it takes or the particular fears that make up its profile. The treatment methods I'll outline in subsequent chapters have proven effective for all kinds of patients with the full range of anxiety symptoms. Once you learn this approach, you'll have the basic tools you need to overcome your anxiety.

Let me explain why that's true. The six basic types of anxiety disorder listed earlier are general categories only. They aren't really distinct afflictions in the way, say, that different diseases of the body are.

Rather they're part of a general pattern of anxiety handed down to us by our evolutionary programming. For that reason, an anxiety disorder, though it may have a specific object, is usually part of a more universal condition. In fact, most people who have one of the specific anxiety disorders are likely to have some of the others as well—perhaps even most of them. That is why many psychologists now talk about general patterns of anxiety rather than trying to hone in on specific symptoms as a basis for diagnosis.

Because of their shared roots, the various patterns of anxiety tend to have certain processes in common. By understanding those common processes we can get a better handle on how our minds generate anxiety. Our evolutionary programming—the "software" in our brains—has left us with a fairly consistent set of instructions for dealing with risk. These instructions seem to govern even the minds of "normal" individuals. They become even more forceful when an individual is predisposed to extreme anxiety. They become less like cautionary signals and more like absolute rules. They take over, crowding out whatever else is going on in the mind. That is when we become seized by anxiety and our power to think and act intelligently becomes impaired.

What are these rules exactly? Human behavior is complex and (one would think) hard to reduce to simple elements. But it's interesting how broad and universal our patterns of anxiety turn out to be once we identify them. No matter how convoluted our fear-based thinking, how elaborate our strategies of reaction and avoidance, we always seem to follow certain basic tendencies, certain rules, in responding to fearful situations. It's as though nature has written a list of these rules into our brains. That list can be summarized as follows:

1. *Detect Danger.* The first rule is to identify a danger as quickly as possible so you can eliminate it or escape from it. If you fear spiders, you will be very quick to detect—or even to imagine—their presence. If you fear rejection by others, you will be quick to notice when people are frowning; ambiguous facial expressions will appear hostile. If you worry about disease, you may run from anyone who so much as coughs; the most casual item in the newspaper about an outbreak somewhere may grab your attention. When you have severe anxiety, you tend to move through the world in a constant state of alertness that hovers just this side of alarm.

2. *Catastrophize Danger.* The next step in the process is to automatically interpret the danger as an utter disaster. If someone is not friendly at a meeting, it means you are a pathetic loser. A dark spot on the skin indicates cancer. A slow or malfunctioning elevator is a sign that you will shortly be trapped inside with no way out. Nothing is a simple inconvenience; for you, a bump in the road is a land mine waiting to explode.

3. *Control the Situation.* The third step is to try to control your anxiety by controlling the things around you. If your hands have come in contact with germs, you race to the sink to wash. If you think you might have made a mistake at work, you return to the office and go over everything you did that day. If you're grappling with obsessions, you try to banish obsessive thoughts from your mind (which only makes it worse, since the attempt itself is the product of an obsessive thought).

4. *Avoid or Escape.* An alternative to step three is either to avoid the threatening situation altogether (if it hasn't yet materialized) or, if it has materialized, to remove yourself from it immediately. If you're nervous about meeting someone at a party, you simply don't go—or if you've already run into him there, you leave immediately. If you fear a panic attack, you stay out of any place that might trigger one: you refuse to get into an elevator, shop at a mall, or sit in a crowded theater. You avoid going to the zoo because you might have to look at a snake. Under no circumstances do you allow yourself to confront any of your deep-seated fears.

These are the universal rules of anxiety. I call them The Anxiety Rule Book. When we are in their grip, these rules seem to have absolute power, like inexorable laws from on high. Yet if we look more closely, we see that each of them is actually supported by certain *beliefs* we have—that give the rules much of their authority. Examining these beliefs and assumptions—holding them to the light to see whether or not they are actually true—may lend a different perspective to the question of how much we are at the mercy of our anxieties.

RULES AND BELIEFS

Let's take a closer look at the four rules listed above to see if we can identify some of the underlying beliefs that support them.

Rule 1: Detect Danger

If you're in anxiety mode, you begin with a belief that you need to predict any and all dangers. If you can, your mind tells you, then you will be able to get all possible information about what can go wrong, and thus you will be in a position to address the situation. If, say, you are going to give a talk, you should try to anticipate all the bad things that can happen—your mind might go blank, the audience could be hostile, your projector may fail, there might be something important you left out. According to your mind, the more dangers you can think of, the more prepared to deal with them—i.e., the *safer*—you will be. The reality, of course, is that the more dangers you think of, the more anxious you get and the more dysfunctional you become. In short, your very vigilance is your undoing.

Part of this belief system is the "better safe than sorry" principle; i.e., better to predict a lot of imaginary dangers, even if they don't materialize, than to miss a single real one. After all, if you don't get on a plane and it doesn't crash, no harm done—or so it would seem. By the same token, if you're already on the plane, you'll be safer if you check constantly for unusual sounds or look out the window to see if the weather is getting bad or listen for indications of turbulence in the pilot's announcement. Perhaps you'll catch something the pilot and flight crew have missed, then you'll be able to warn them and save everyone from a crash. The safest, most prudent course of action is to stay alert—to focus all your mental energy toward identifying threats. This will prepare you to deal with them effectively.

The absurdity of this is evident, yet these are the assumptions that propel us when anxiety is in the driver's seat. The problem is that the primitive brain (which we have inherited) is organized around emotions, not logic. When emotions are dominant, your ability to identify what is and what is not a danger is pretty much out the window. Once the "fear files" in the brain are opened up, it's hard to get out of them. All you find when rummaging around for information are more fear files. Every "what if" triggers a search for more "what ifs," like billiard balls hitting one another—a chain reaction of fear. Meanwhile the "rational" files, stored in the neo-cortex—the ones that contain all those boring tables and graphs that show how few planes actually crash or the overwhelming percentage of people with headaches who need an aspirin rather than a brain scan—are forgotten or ignored.

All this can seem perfectly rational. The mind is supposedly engaged in "reasoning," in looking for evidence, but the only evidence it sees—the only evidence it *can* see—is evidence provided by the emotions. And the only evidence that you look for when you are anxious is that you are in danger. The more you look, the more terrifying it becomes. So when I become convinced that I've contaminated myself by touching the faucet in the bathroom, it's not that I have actually detected a danger in the faucet. It's simply my irrational *feeling* of being dirty or contaminated that seeks out further evidence of contamination—a vicious cycle of fear. Or I go to the doctor for a checkup. She tells me I'm healthy but need to reduce my cholesterol a bit. Uh-oh. High cholesterol? Am I going to have a heart attack? How can she be sure I'm not? I call her, and she tells me there are no signs—blood tests normal, no risk factors, etc. Too late: I've already begun to worry. I dismiss all her abstract information in favor of the graphic picture of myself lying on the floor, gasping for breath, clutching for the telephone. To the amygdala—the emotional part of the brain—one picture is worth a thousand charts and tables.

I have come to believe my own mind. Rather than be objective about the facts, I rely on my fear-driven mind to tell me if I am in danger.

Rule 2: Catastrophize Danger

The essential belief here is that any negative consequence you can picture coming your way will, if it arrives, be intolerable. Any burden will be beyond your capacity to endure. Being turned down for a job will ruin your career. Stepping on a nail will cause tetanus. A small weight gain will undermine your health. A failure to perform sexually means the end of your love life. There are no minor inconveniences, only disasters. Even casual events can be filled with forebodings of the worst possible scenarios. You walk by a growling dog and picture him tearing your arm off. Driving over a bridge is terrifying because you can see yourself crashing through the rail, plunging into the water, and drowning. If someone declines your dinner invitation, it confirms the fact that you're a social outcast.

A related belief, also lurking in the shadows, is the belief that all threats are imminent. There's no time to wait and see if genuine danger materializes; any situation posing a threat is a dire emergency. There's no room to reflect on the danger, to gather information, to consult others, or to formulate a prudent response. Even if the dreaded situation lies far in the future, something in you demands that it be dealt with right away. Anxiety sufferers know this feeling well. Once the future threat has been identified, there can be no rest until it has been prevented—no relaxation, no enjoyment of anything else, no attention to other (possibly more serious) matters. Rationally there is no need for any of this, but emotionally it is as though disaster were about to strike instantly, like a saber-tooth tiger leaping out of the bushes. Which, of course, is where the impulse comes from: the primitive fear-response inherited from our ancestors.

A subtle but powerful variation on these themes has to do with the way you view your own anxious thoughts. They *themselves* become part of the danger. The moment we experience an anxious thought we are already in trouble. Here we encounter the underlying belief that our thoughts themselves have the power to harm us. If this belief is accepted, it is easy to see where it leads. We must fear our own thoughts; they must be controlled or warded off to avoid catastrophe. If they persist, all is lost. Thus the notion of having a panic attack can actually become a primary object of fear, even when you're not sure what real-world event the panic attack is about. Any sign of labored breathing, sweating, or dizziness is a sure sign that you are approaching collapse, thus causing you to break out into—what else?—labored breathing, sweating, and dizziness. The panic attack, in effect, becomes self-generating.

As we shall see later, each of the anxiety disorders described in this book is, at least in part, *a fear of anxiety itself.* One develops a picture of oneself as a ticking time bomb, ready at all times to self-destruct. If one knew that one's obsessions in no way reflected the real world—if one thought of them as mere background noise that meant nothing—it would be harder to be obsessive. Sensations of shortness of breath would be simply that—sensations—with no real-world consequences. It is the belief in the catastrophic power of anxiety—its promise to spin out of control, overwhelm us, and last forever—that allows it to cast such a haunting shadow over our consciousness.

Rule 3: Control the Situation

The underlying belief here is not hard to identify. It is the belief that you have the power to keep all things bad from happening. Your mind asserts that if you do not control things they will fall apart—that your safety depends on your ability to manipulate every factor in your environment. That message, of course, is at odds with the obvious fact that you cannot possibly control all those factors. Yet the very realization of this causes you to feel even more anxious. Since your belief in the *necessity* of controlling everything persists, you merely increase your desperate efforts to control. Doing something—anything—is equated in your mind with reducing danger. *As long as I am in control, nothing can threaten me.*

One consequence of this dubious proposition is the resort to "magical thinking"—the false belief that if two things are associated in time, then one is the cause of the other. For example, the rooster's crowing "causes" the sun to rise. Anxiety sufferers often apply this kind of thinking in a desperate attempt to assert control over their environment: *As long as I keep my hands on the table, no one will laugh at me,* or *If I punch the elevator button really hard, it won't stall.* This virtually amounts to superstition, not really different from what made our ancestors don masks, paint themselves, and dance to their gods. When disasters don't strike, you thank the gods—or the medicine man. When they do, you ratchet up the level of ritual and sacrifice because obviously what you did before was not enough.

A typical example of this thinking might be, say, a woman with an intense fear of flying. She boards the plane but immediately recognizes that she has surrendered control of the situation to the pilot and the plane's inner workings. This is totally unacceptable: she has to find something that will make her feel safe—something she *can* control. She grasps the side of the seat with one hand and holds a cushion tightly with the other. It somehow makes her feel safer. She makes it through the flight; the plane does not crash. She now has the feeling that it was her little ritual that kept the plane from a wreck. From then on she has to perform that ritual every time she flies. It makes no sense, but the compulsion is irresistible. Of course if you ask her, "Will clutching the seat and holding the cushion keep the plane from crashing?" she will reply, "Of course not—that's crazy." But if you ask her why she does it, she will say, "Because it makes me feel safer." We call these "safety behaviors" because your magical thinking tells you that you are safer when you do them. Later we will see how safety behaviors are part of every anxiety disorder and that they ironically maintain your belief that you are in danger.

When anxious thoughts themselves are the source of fear, magical thinking is often turned inward. If I am horribly shy and fear making a fool out of myself on social occasions, I start watching myself like a hawk to ward off the anxious thoughts that may cause me to act foolishly. I try to suppress any signs of anxiety: shaking, sweating, or blushing. Most of all,

I try to keep the anxious thoughts from entering my mind. Of course far from giving me more control, this only increases my feeling that I am apt to go out of control at any moment. Unwanted thoughts *do* appear; I have the urge to scream or say something terrible. I'm not really about to give in to this urge, but it somehow seems crucial to keep the thoughts out of my head. The more I tell myself that I must rid myself of unwanted thoughts, the more terrified I am because I cannot. My attempts to control result in my feeling out of control.

Control of the inner and outer can become hopelessly entangled. A woman has had panic attacks over what seems like nothing. She begins to worry about having another one in public. When she goes shopping she makes sure to bring someone with her. She makes up excuses like "It's not much fun shopping alone." She starts taking her mother along, thinking that if she has an attack her mother can drive her home or call a doctor. It doesn't help. In the store she starts to feel dizzy; she presses against the counter so as not to fall. It makes her feel a little more secure. Soon she cannot enter a store without pressing against the counter. She begins to develop endless little rituals, just to be able to do the shopping. Each trip to the mall is both terrifying and exhausting. There's a curious paradox to all this: the belief in one's power to control everything is closely linked to a belief in one's *powerlessness*. It's like a kid who is afraid of drowning and slaps frantically at the water to keep himself up. He sinks. It's hard to just lie back on the water and float. Doing nothing is often the hardest thing to do when we are anxious. It's like surrendering to impending doom. We want to fight harder as we sink deeper into our anxiety.

The underlying feeling that we are helpless to solve our problems as they arise causes us to grasp at the fantasy of absolute control. The feeling is tied to a view of ourselves as incapable of tolerating discomfort, anxiety, problems, or conflicts. The anxiety sufferer may lie awake thinking about recent cutbacks at work, worrying about what he would do if he lost his job. He may not even be sure he wants to keep the job. Moreover he may be competent enough that if he lost it he would have no trouble finding another, perhaps a better one. But he doesn't believe it. If he can't foresee the outcome, if there is any uncertainty at all, he is awash in anxiety. He cannot trust in his ability to handle whatever situation comes up—even if he has always been able to do so before.

Chronic worriers may or may not be good at solving problems once they occur, but they consistently underestimate their future ability to deal with the world. They may be good at giving others useful advice, but when it comes to themselves, they are baffled. They harbor a deep-seated belief that they are incapable of handling any of life's challenges: frustration, rejection, conflict, illness, new responsibilities, loneliness, finding a new job or partner—all the problems that constitute normal life as we know it. So much of this seems beyond their control that they feel helpless. But effective control over our circumstances comes from understanding the limits to that control and being able to work within them. Imperfection, doubt, unpredictability, setbacks—these are always part of the picture. It helps to know this at a deep level and be prepared to live with it.

Rule 4: Avoid or Escape

This rule is, in a sense, an alternative to Rule 3 (Control the Situation). If total control is impossible, perhaps the way to avoid anxiety is to *avoid the situation altogether.* The belief underlying this strategy is that risks can be eliminated by refusing to face them. Safety lies in maintaining the illusion of safety.

One consequence of this rule is paralysis. We are afraid of flying, so we never make that important family visit. We're afraid we'll be turned down for the job we covet, so we never apply. Someone we don't get along with lives in the next street, so we always take the long way around so as not to have to go that way. When our underlying conviction is that we cannot endure any discomfort, our life becomes hemmed in by all sorts of boundaries that keep us frozen, passive, and cowering.

A common manifestation of paralysis is indecision. Often we refuse to act until we have what we think is sufficient information—which somehow we never manage to acquire. Fear of making the "wrong" decision (which in primitive circumstances could mean sudden and violent death) keeps us from any decision at all. When we are anxious, we are completely risk-averse. We believe that the world is dangerous, we won't be able to handle the consequences, and we need absolute certainty. And, when we are anxious, we believe that if something doesn't turn out well, we will regret it forever. We imagine ourselves regretting the worst outcome and telling ourselves, *I told you so!*

Our anxiety leads to procrastination. Our primitive brain tells us we shouldn't do anything until we *know* it's safe, until we stop feeling afraid. The message persists, so we believe it's important not to act until we're *ready.* As long as we feel anxiety around an activity, we postpone it— whether it's doing our income taxes, working on a project we're not sure we can handle, having a painful conversation, or going to the dentist.

Underlying it all is the belief that the painful consequences of decisive action are greater than those of doing nothing—that the "safest" course is to wait till anxiety is gone. Of all our illusions, this is the one perhaps most frequently exposed.

What if it's too late to avoid a situation? What if we're already immersed in it? Obviously the strategy then is to get out as soon as possible. Again, the link with primitive urges is apparent: removing oneself quickly from danger was often critical to survival. In our modern lives, we head for the exit. We cross the street to get away from crowds of strangers. We duck out of a meeting that's not going well with a lame excuse. We call in sick the day of an important exam. Removing oneself from the source of danger is such a deep and powerful instinct that it often overwhelms all other considerations, however rationally compelling. Of course by always obeying this urge we miss out on an important lesson, which is that we *do* have the ability to learn how to handle difficulty. When we resort to escape we never find that out.

In codifying these "rules" of anxiety, I've obviously simplified a great deal. In practice there's a good bit of overlap among them, not to mention many situations in which they mingle with more commonsense impulses. But each of these rules, is surely familiar to all of us, whether we're classified as anxiety sufferers or not. This is because the patterns of thinking and behavior they represent have been inextricably implanted in our psychology as a species. Our protective instincts—the true origin of the rules—are no different from what they were millions of years ago: detect, catastrophize, control, escape. Judging by our success as a species, these rules proved effective through millions of years of prehistory. But if we're still blindly following them in a modern-day environment—one in which wild animals, hostile tribes, disease, and malnutrition are no longer the principal threats—we're no longer promoting our own survival. If anything, we're doing the opposite: making ourselves confused, tentative, paralyzed, dysfunctional, incapable of effective thought or action. We're using the right rules at the wrong time. In fact, following the rules faithfully today is probably the best way of developing what our society now describes as an anxiety disorder.

HEY, WAIT A MINUTE—I NEED A SECURITY CHECK!

Overcoming your anxieties is not as complicated or mysterious as some people think. But you make a good point when you raise the questions "Is this just positive thinking?" or "Aren't there some real risks?" Good points. The goal is not to become foolhardy or take unnecessary and dangerous risks. That's even more problematic than having an anxiety problem.

But how can you decide? What is the "sensible" thing to do?

I will give you a security check. If you have any doubts, just ask yourself the following questions:

- What would most people think or do?

- What would most people think is reasonable?

- What are the probabilities that things will work out okay?

This is the reasonable person, or plausibility, rule. For example, if you have a fear of contamination, I would like you to ask, *Would most people think it's risky?* For example, if you are at a diner in a remote area of a poor country and you are thinking of drinking the water in the sink—*don't do it.* Most people would think it's contaminated. But if you are at your house in the suburbs and you want some water, you can drink the water out of the sink. Most people think it's safe . . . because it is safe.

The same thing is true with your fear of an elevator or airplane crashing. Most people think they are safe. The odds are billions to one in your favor for the elevator and millions to one for the airplane. Or the same rules apply to your fear of panic attacks—your fear that you will go insane or die because of one. I've been seeing patients for more than 25 years, and I have supervised a clinic where we have seen thousands of patients. No one has ever died or gone insane from a panic attack. Reasonable psychologists can tell you this. But there is no *guarantee.* Maybe you will be *the exception.* No absolute guarantees.

The only thing you can think about in a new game is to play the odds. If the odds are billions to one that the elevator is safe, go with those odds. If you want absolute certainty, then you will have to get used to having anxiety and depression for the rest of your life. Is that a risk worth taking?

So to apply the new rule book—which involves *breaking all the rules*—you will have to give up on certainty and perfection. But if you play by the old rules—the mind-games in your head—you are guaranteed to stay anxious.

Now, I want you to think this through. Are you willing to consider giving up on certainty? What are the advantages of demanding certainty? You might think that you will be able to get close to certainty and reduce any unnecessary risks. Have you ever been able to get any real certainty about the future? Has anyone? What are the disadvantages? You will continue procrastinating, avoiding, and holding on to your anxieties. Isn't that a risk?

And, in fact, you don't have certainty about anything that you do now. If you go to a restaurant, drive in a car, or send off a package in the mail—you don't have certainty. You don't have certainty about your friends, family, or your job. We call this "acceptable risk" because we observe that you are already doing these things and, therefore, accepting the risk. If you accept those everyday risks—and you do—then why not accept other small, insignificant risks? That's part of the reasonable person, or plausibility, rule.

The same thing is true for perfection. You've never had perfection and you never will.

There is no certainty—but you may think that you need it. Here's how you have been thinking: *If I falsely conclude that attempts to control, my avoidance, or my safety behaviors have protected me—well, how am I that much worse off? At least I have learned that doing something while living in this "dangerous environment" makes me feel better. Maybe I'll get lucky and I'll do the right thing. But even if I don't, even if I engage in absolutely absurd safety behaviors, I still may be lucky enough to find a partner—perhaps an anxious partner—who is willing to procreate a couple of anxious kids with me.*

You can't learn that the environment is *not dangerous unless you do nothing,* and *doing nothing* is the hardest thing to do.

We have been using the wrong software. The rules for being anxious make us play a game where we always lose—because we either feel anxious or we convince ourselves that we have to keep playing the anxiety game. The rules are built into our heads. We are stuck in a rut as we dig a deeper hole every time we play by the old rules.

The good news is that we can make up some new rules. And then we can break all the old rules and rid ourselves of unnecessary anxiety.

There's a new game in town.

UNRAVEL THE RULES

You've been listening to the old rule book in your head. It's all about danger, avoidance, and playing it safe. The new rule book, which reflects a different, wiser mind, allows you to give up on your old software by simply overwriting it. It's a different part of your head—one that is rational, above and beyond the primitive mind, and more in tune with the world as it really is—not as you fear it might be.

The new rules are going to say something like this: "Things are pretty safe. My thoughts, feelings, and sensations are simply my imagination and my arousal. Nothing is really happening except a lot of noise and a lot of false alarms. I don't need to control anything. In fact, I will practice letting go, surrendering, floating, observing—even having fun with—all of this anxious arousal. I can do things even when I am anxious. In fact, I will learn more and get stronger when I do things when I am anxious."

There is a new game in town. It's the game of *breaking all the rules.*

Let's now look at each of the Anxiety-Free Rules and see how you can use them.

Old Rule 1: Detect Danger

New Rule 1: See Things Realistically

When you're in a typical state of anxiety, you make decisions about what is dangerous *automatically.* You don't stop to consider whether or not a situation is actually dangerous, you simply assume that it is. A single sign of danger, however slight, is conclusive. To circumvent this mechanical thinking, you must go through a process of risk evaluation. This can be done consciously and deliberately, for example, by asking yourself a series of questions.

1. Am I using all the information at my disposal or only the negative parts?
2. Am I making predictions on the basis of facts or simply feelings?
3. Is my imagination getting the better of me?
4. Have I assessed the likelihood of the outcome I fear?

For example, if I am terrified about a talk I have to give, I am convinced it will be a disaster. I can go through the above questions in my mind (or on paper, if necessary), and answer them this way:

Actually, I have a number of things on my side. I am very well prepared. I have something to say, which is why I have been asked to talk. I have reviewed the material and practiced my delivery. I have given successful talks before. In my fretting over this, I have ignored all these considerations.

1. I have the *feeling* that I will fail, but in the past such feelings have been useless in making predictions. I fear that when I am anxious I will go blank, but, in fact, this rarely happens. Even when it does, I always manage to get through it somehow.

2. My mind can come up with all sorts of "what ifs." I am treating them as though they were real, rather than what they are: products of my imagination. None of these "what ifs" come from real-life situations. They are fantasies, with no power to harm me. People don't die from their imaginations.

3. I am assuming that the talk will be a disaster. I don't know that. There are as many reasons to think I will be successful as to think I will fail. I am equating possibility with probability. I have not assessed the outcome realistically.

We want to live in the real world so we have to use all the information— not just search for "signs of danger" and run away. Let's say that you are going to give a talk and you are anxious (who isn't?). Let's use the new rule book:

Table 3.1

Using Your Anxiety-Free Rule Book for Your Public-Speaking Anxiety: Changing Danger to Realistic Thinking

Rule 1: See Things Realistically	Examples
It's important to use all the information—including positive information.	I have given talks before. I prepared my talk, rehearsed it. I have something to say—which is why I've been asked to talk. I have my notes and I know my stuff. I know the material—I've reviewed it and practiced it.
It's better to be realistic than pessimistic.	I can expect to get through the talk because I have never been unable to get through the talk. Maybe I will feel anxious, but I've done things when I was anxious before. Being pessimistic doesn't help me get things done, it only makes me avoid what I need to do and makes me more depressed. Being realistic doesn't mean that I think everything will work out, it just means I am willing to look at some positive and neutral information—to have a balanced view of things.
Use the facts, not your feelings, to make predictions.	My feelings have been useless in making predictions. Every time I feel anxious I think I will go completely blank, but that has never happened. The facts are that I have been able to get through things—even when I am anxious.
Treat "what-ifs" as part of your imagination.	I have come up with a million "what-ifs," but they haven't come true. I simply have a wild and anxious imagination. People don't die from imagination.
Use probabilities rather than possibilities.	Anything is possible, but the probability is that I might be anxious but will get through the talk.

By using the new rule book you can recognize that your anxiety is not dangerous, your imagination is not the same thing as reality, and emotions don't predict the future. You can give up on demanding certainty—and go with probabilities. You are safer than you think you are.

The key here is to unhook from the panic state long enough to go through an evaluation of the situation. This is what anxiety sufferers fail to do or forget to do. "Being reasonable" may seem like a weak response to anxieties that seem overwhelming. But it's remarkable how easily such a simple process can pull us out of our distorted perceptions. We will explore this more in later chapters.

Old Rule 2: Catastrophize Danger

New Rule 2: Normalize Consequences

In the past you may have assumed that any setback would be catastrophic: that catching the flu would lead to your death, that a failure to perform sexually was the end of your love life, that a panic attack would cause you to die or go insane. None of this has ever materialized, but you continue to follow the old rule book and assume it will. In order to see things realistically you have to stand back from your emotions and anxieties and ask some basic questions:

1. What has actually happened in the past?
2. What is the worst that's actually *likely* to happen?
3. How bad would it be if it did happen?

For example, you've come in contact with someone who may be ill; you feel the need to scrub your hands over and over again. You might stop and ask yourself: *How often have you been exposed to germs in this way, and what has happened as a result? If other people have been exposed as much as you, are they catching the disease? What if you did catch it? Would you die? How likely is that?* The reality check questions provided can be helpful. Or say you're on a plane that's encountering turbulence. Yes, in theory, you could crash and die. But turbulence on planes is an everyday occurrence. Planes are constructed to fly in exactly those conditions. What will almost certainly happen is that the plane will shake around a bit and you'll feel a bit uncomfortable. But you will survive. You've already survived worse. Imagining the direst consequences is a hopeless game: there's a doomsday scenario to everything, including sitting comfortably in your backyard (where you could be hit by a meteor).

The only "emergency" in most cases is the one going on in your head. The message that you will die, go crazy, be humiliated, or whatever you're picturing is, in effect, a false alarm. The notion of catastrophe is a thought, not a fact. You created it. Most important of all, your *anxiety itself* is not catastrophic. To have sweaty palms or an accelerated heart rate may be unpleasant, but it won't kill you. It will shortly go away, and you'll be in a tolerable state once more. Anxiety is simply an arousal of energy. You can observe this energy moving through you, just like the energy of vigorous exercise, sex, or dancing to music. It does not foretell any particular outcome in the real world; it merely attaches itself to a picture you have constructed in your mind.

Table 3.2
Examples of How to Normalize Consequences

Rule 2: Normalize Consequences	Examples
False alarms are not the same thing as reality.	The only thing that is happening soon— or even now—is your false alarm. Your false alarm is telling you that you will get contaminated, go crazy, make a fool out of yourself, make a mistake, fall over the cliff, or get killed. These things haven't happened to you—and the false alarm is exactly that, "false"—there is no emergency, except the one going on in your head.
What will really happen is that you will feel anxious— and maybe exhausted— from your anxiety. That's all.	All the things that you describe haven't happened. And it's not so awful to look a little anxious, have a rapid heartbeat, feel light-headed, lose your erection, or feel anxious. It's unpleasant and it "feels awful." But your anxiety and your discomfort will decrease and go away.

You don't die from obsessions, panic, worry, or fear.	These are feelings—not fatalities. Your intrusive thought that you are contaminated (or any other obsession) is not dangerous. It won't kill you. It is a thought—not a fact. Your rising anxiety does not lead you to go insane, lose control, or die.

Anxiety is simply arousal. It's like observing that your energy is flowing through you and you are aware of it. It's not the same thing as a bomb going off inside you. You also have arousal when you exercise, watch an exciting movie, or have sex. These things don't harm you. Once you think of anxiety as arousal—or simply "noise"—you can let it go.

Old Rule 3: Control the Situation

New Rule 3: Let Go of Control

Like many anxious people you are always looking for some way to take control because you fear that things will go out of control. If you are a fearful passenger in the car, you clutch the side of the seat, nag the driver about danger, and pray that you will arrive safely. But the biggest area of your control is your belief that you need to control your thoughts, emotions, and sensations. You try to suppress and neutralize any obsessions you have—*Bad thought, Stop that,* or *I didn't mean that.* You perform rituals to neutralize or cancel out the thought. It won't work. You notice you are short of breath so you try to take deep breaths and you can't catch your breath. You are trying to control your breathing—it won't work.

You have insomnia and you tell yourself, *Get to sleep right now.* It fails.

You worry you won't do well on the test, so you keep scanning your mind to make sure that you cover all the bases—try to remember everything and try to see if there is something that you are overlooking. It makes you more anxious, and you feel more out of control. So you tell yourself to stop worrying, and that doesn't work.

Trying to control yourself fails. It always has, it always will.

You have been chasing after your obsessions and trying to control them. It's like chasing after your own mind. You always lose.

You've been trying to run away from your thoughts, sensations, emotions, and pain. It's like trying to run away from your hips. No matter how fast or far you go, they are always there.

46

Your Anxious Mind-Game tells you to take control, but it is the wrong message for today. There is no danger—it's your false alarm. You try to control your false alarm by trying to suppress your thoughts, neutralize things, clutch, tense your body, breathe more deeply, and eliminate your anxiety. Ironically, the more you try to control your anxiety the worse it gets.

The new Mind-Game Rule is "Let Go of Control."

By practicing letting go of control you can learn that your thoughts, sensations, and anxious emotions will decrease on their own. You will learn that there was nothing to fear—it was just another false alarm. You will find out that you can lie back, relax, observe, and gain distance from the alarm. It's the noise that bothers you—but it is noise. Letting go of control will teach you that you are safe.

Imagine you are trying to learn how to swim. At first, you are afraid that you are drowning. You thrash around, gasping for breath. And then your teacher says, "Float. Let your body go limp. Float on the surface." And you float along, peacefully. No struggle.

Rather than asking you to control your thoughts, feelings, and sensations, I am going to ask you to try two things: *observe them* or *dive into them*.

Let's take *observing*. Rather than trying to eliminate your rapid breathing or intrusive thoughts that you are contaminated or going insane or your anxious feeling that you are physically so tense you will explode, try this: *observe*. Stand back—as if you were to write a description of your heart rate—and consider what it looks like. Stand back and observe, *It's beating rapidly, a little more rapidly than before.* And observe everything else outside of you as well. *It's a bit cloudy outside. There is a lot of stuff on my desk. I can see the photograph on the wall.* Observe. Don't control.

The second part is to dive into it—go directly to the heart of it.

Have you ever stood in the shallow water at the edge of the beach when the waves were crashing in? You see some kids about twenty feet from shore jumping up and down in the waves. But you are hesitant. You don't want to get knocked down. You walk a few feet out to the water and stand firmly. A wave comes crashing against you—almost knocking you down. But then it occurs to you. You can dive *under the wave*. You dive under, holding your breath, and the wave crashes on the other side. You jump up in the water, laughing with the other kids. You became part of the wave.

The same thing is true for your anxiety symptoms. Rather than trying to control them, you can learn how to practice them intentionally to make them more intense, repeat them, and dive into them. In fact, you can learn to practice and repeat your intrusive obsessions, practice having a panic attack, try to lose your train of thought—even try to go crazy. You will become a Zen warrior of anxiety—someone who practices the fear so that you can *go with it* rather than struggle against it.

When the obsession comes, you can practice it ad nauseam. When you realize that the thoughts, sensations, and feelings don't have to be controlled, you will feel less anxious. *Your anxiety is actually your resistance to your anxiety.* Once you surrender—once you give up control, let your mind and body "lay back"—you can allow your sensations and thoughts to flow through you—and past you—without any struggle.

This is the power of surrender and letting go—the power of the Zen warrior.

Your old rule book was written to make you a control freak about yourself. You felt you had to control everything inside you—especially your mind, your sensations, and your feelings. It only made you feel less in control. Imagine that you are in deep water and feel you are drowning. You decide to lie back on the surface of the water. You have surrendered, given up control. You relax and float and feel sleepy.

A lot of what we will talk about in this book is about letting go of control—rather than trying to control your anxiety. You don't have to control it; you have to accept it. You can "receive" your anxiety as you receive and take in the fresh air. Breathe it in. It's not going to kill you.

Try this. Tense your muscles in your body, breathe rapidly, and get ready to jump. Think about all the ways you will have to control any thoughts that come into your head—because these are "bad" thoughts. You have to order yourself to feel less anxious, less tense. Think of yelling at yourself to *Stop being so anxious*. Think about performing sexually with your lover while someone stands five feet away and yells, "Relax!"

You will immediately feel more anxious—as if you are going out of your mind.

Now imagine letting go. Make yourself a fluid through which the tension flows. Your anxious tension flows through you. Rather than tensing yourself, you let your muscles droop. You are floating in your chair. Your mind does not try to control a thought—it watches and sees that the thought moves along like letters going across the page.

You exhale and let it go.

You move forward, floating, by letting go. Float.

Table 3.3 Examples of Letting Go of Control	
Rule 3: Let Go of Control	**Examples**
You don't need to control your mind or your feelings.	1. Rather than try to control your thoughts and feelings, stand back and say, *Let go* and *Let it happen.* Imagine that you are observing shallow water running over your body—it's warm and it flows over you. This can be your anxiety—whether it's the intrusive thought, the panic sensations, or your worries. Let them flow. Watch them flow along a stream—each thought, sensation, or image is on a leaf and flows gently away. Stand back. Surrender. Don't try to control. 2. Shift your attention away from things you are trying to control. Shift away from your thoughts, feelings, and sensations. Describe all the things in the room. What shape are they? What colors do you see? Now that you have given up controlling your thoughts and feelings, has anything terrible really happened?
Magical thinking maintains anxiety—give it up and think rationally.	Notice any safety behaviors—the way you breathe, things you say to yourself, clutching, tensing, asking for reassurance. Now practice giving them up. You can practice doing the opposite of some of your safety behaviors—like relaxing your muscles, slowing down your breathing, moving your eyes toward neutral things in the room, reading a book rather than asking for reassurance.
You are a problem solver in real life.	You actually can control real things in real life. List all the real problems that you have handled—in school, work, relationships, and your other activities. Don't generate new and implausible catastrophes. Just focus on the real problems that you can solve. You may deserve more credit than you think.

Old Rule 4: Avoid or Escape Your Anxiety

New Rule 4: Embrace Your Anxiety

Your old rule said to avoid anything that makes you anxious. Don't meet new people; don't be in the room with a spider; don't go to the theater or shopping mall; stay away from germs, planes, and parties. Unfortunately, obeying this rule has not lessened your anxiety or improved the quality of your life one bit. What it has done is keep you locked in your prison by reinforcing your belief that you can't handle any of these situations. The new rule says you not only *can* learn to handle them, you *must*. You can certainly learn to handle them gradually, gently, and skillfully, as succeeding chapters will show you. But it's essential that you be willing to stretch your limits, to test out your discomfort zone. Above all, you will have to learn to do things *even when they cause you anxiety*—to be afraid of doing something and yet doing it anyway. It's the only way to teach yourself that you *can* do it. In order for your emotional brain to learn how to handle anxious situations, it will have to practice *being* anxious—and surviving.

You have to go through it to get past it.

This rule will seem even more counterintuitive than the last. You're being asked to stop running away from discomfort and instead to *seek it out*. Instead of waiting till you're "ready" for something, you'll look for opportunities to confront it right away. Instead of escaping unpleasant situations at the earliest possible moment, you'll learn to wait them out. You'll welcome all this because it's a chance to challenge the belief in your own helplessness, to become stronger. Once you start in, you will find yourself developing a new relationship with your anxiety. You've always thought of it as your enemy. Now it's going to become your good friend, accompanying you wherever you go—like a pet you take for a walk. It will be your teacher, showing you what you're capable of, letting you know what works and what doesn't, telling you when you're making progress.

From all this you will learn that anxiety is not really a threat at all. Rather it's a passing phenomenon, an event in the mind, something that's not dangerous and doesn't need to be controlled or escaped from. It's more like a false alarm going off, warning you of nothing—simply an irritating noise. Once you accept that, the alarm will subside on its own—you won't need to hunt for the switch to turn it off. Your old rule told you that anxiety escalates the more you allow it in. The new rule says that if you cease to feed your anxiety, if you stop giving it energy, it runs out of steam pretty quickly. You don't need to run away from it because it poses no danger. You are safe. In fact you have been safe all along—you just haven't realized it.

Rather than running away from your anxiety, you can think of it as the experience that you practice. The more you do it, the easier it is. You learn that anxiety is simply another noise, another sound, another way of feeling. When you can do the things that make you anxious you can learn it's not dangerous, there is no catastrophe, and you don't need to control things.

The only way to learn how to swim is to get into the water. Get wet. By embracing anxiety you can learn to let it go.

Table 3.4 Examples of How to Seek Discomfort	
Rule 4: Embrace Your Anxiety	**Examples**
Seek out experiences that make you anxious.	If you fear speaking, take classes on speaking, volunteer to speak, raise your hand. If you fear using public toilets, go into a number of them every day. Let anxiety be a signal—do it now.
Do it when you are anxious and uncomfortable—don't wait to feel ready.	Use your discomfort as a sign that it is the right time to do it. Discomfort is a motivator—not a deterrent. It tells you that this is a chance to unravel your anxiety. It tells you that you can prove that your anxiety cannot stop you.
Accept reasonable risk.	Ask if most people think it's safe. Most people think that speaking is not dangerous or that you won't get contaminated by using a restroom or that you won't go crazy if you worry.

Stay in as long as possible.	The longer you stay, the stronger you get. That's because you are practicing the thing that frightens you. Stay past your anxiety, wait it out, watch it go up and then go down, make a point of staying in so long that you are bored.

The longer you stay with your fear, the less frightening it is. You learn that the alarm will subside on its own. It meant nothing. For all the different anxiety problems that we will discuss in this book, the longer and more frequently you do these anxious things, the less anxious you will get.

Sometimes discomfort is your friend. It tells you that you are making progress.

QUESTIONING YOUR BELIEFS ABOUT YOUR ANXIETY

We've now rewritten the "rules" around anxiety in ways that change our relationship to it. As we've seen, a good deal of the power that anxiety has over us lies in the way we think about it. We retain certain beliefs about our anxiety; these beliefs are what give it strength. Most of us never question the truth of these beliefs; we simply take them for granted. We allow them to control our lives, our activities, our behavior. But we don't have to. We can break their grip on us by holding them to the light of truth. They are really no more than myths, vague assumptions we have unthinkingly bought into. To challenge them is the beginning of emotional intelligence.

Here are some of the beliefs around anxiety that we tend to cling to, together with what a more intelligent perspective on each of them might look like. See if any of them resonate for you.

- *I shouldn't feel anxious.* Of course you should feel anxious. Your mind is trying to protect you by warning you of what might go wrong. That's what it's supposed to do. It's just been getting mistakenly hooked up to situations that aren't dangerous, in effect, producing a false alarm. You need to keep your anxiety around as a guide; you just need to learn when to listen to it—and when not to.

- *I should be ashamed of my anxiety.* There's nothing weak, immoral, or shameful about anxiety. It's not something you ever chose to have; it's just part of your evolutionary heritage. It actually means you have an excellent ability to detect danger and respond quickly—like a scout on patrol. These skills would be useful in a more dangerous environment. Your work is learning to adapt them to present-day circumstances.

- *My anxiety is a form of insanity.* Your anxiety is actually a form of common sense that nature has programmed into you. It's what enabled your ancestors to function and survive. When you learn to identify danger more realistically, your anxious instincts will become useful. They will then make perfect sense.

- *My anxiety is dangerous.* Your anxiety may be unpleasant at times, but it is not dangerous. It consists merely of anxious thoughts—a kind of background noise. None of these thoughts have any power over you unless you give it to them. You can have fearful thoughts and yet remain perfectly safe. Knowing the truth of this will free you from the tyranny of anxiety.

- *I need to get rid of my anxiety.* No, you don't. You can't anyway—trying to get rid of it only reinforces it. But it's not necessary to get rid of it. You can learn to live with anxiety, you can observe it calmly, and you can act productively in spite of it. When you accept it as part of your consciousness, its power to disturb you will subside *on its own*.

- *I should be rational at all times.* You are a human being, not a machine. Your emotions are *supposed* to guide you; they help you to set your goals, to chart your course. Your anxiety may be telling you what you need in your life: more assertiveness, different relationships, a new perspective, whatever. Rationality may assist you in achieving these goals, but it is only useful in the service of your feelings.

- *My anxiety is going to go out of control.* It can't, any more than it already has. Anxiety is like a headache—it lasts for a while and then goes away. You don't *need* to be in control of it; control is an illusion when it comes to anxiety. The more you try to control it, the less in control you feel. You can let your anxiety have free rein—you merely need to distance yourself from it.

SUMMARY: OUR PROGRESS SO FAR

We've taken a number of important steps in this chapter. We've examined the "rules" that govern our anxious behavior to see what they're actually telling us to do. We've seen where those rules come from—our evolutionary past—and how they came to be programmed into us. We've investigated the irrational beliefs the rules are based on to see whether or not they apply to our present-day reality. And since we've concluded they do not, we've come up with a new set of rules that fits our current reality in a more realistic and constructive way. This has led us to a whole new way of looking at anxiety—from battling it as an enemy to living with it harmoniously.

We're now prepared to move on to the next step—seeing how our new outlook and our new set of rules can be applied in practice. In the chapters to come we'll be looking at the six major categories of anxiety disorder. Though they have much in common, each one has certain characteristics that define it and set it somewhat apart. You can look through these chapters to see which type of anxiety fits your own pattern (it may well be that more than one of them does). In each chapter I've gone into some detail, outlining both the nature of that anxiety pattern, as well as some of the particular strategies that have helped others deal with it effectively. My first job is to help you understand how your anxiety pattern came to be part of your psychological makeup. Next I'll show you how a different approach to that anxiety—the approach we've already outlined—can change the picture, making it possible for you to work with your anxiety productively. Finally, I'll describe some specific practices and exercises that have proven effective for people struggling with the same general patterns. These practices will help you get to know your anxiety, to become familiar with its ways, and above all to actually experience it within a safe context. This—the *safe experience* of anxiety—is the real key. It replaces the mind-games your anxiety has forced on you with something that is real and solid, something connected with what's actually happening. It means you can stop trying to convince yourself that you're safe, and start actually *feeling* your true safety.

This approach is based on facing and accepting anxiety rather than denying it. As long as you avoid anxiety, as long as you run from it at every opportunity, you never learn to see its phantom nature. You continue to acknowledge its power over you, which is what gives it that power. The "cure" for anxiety is to experience it directly and viscerally, and at the same time to learn—equally directly and viscerally—that it is not connected with any terrible consequences. This is the difference between paralysis and freedom—between being *in control of* your anxiety and being *controlled by* it. Exchanging the one state for the other is something you can learn to do, if you have the will to try. This volume can be your textbook, but you are in charge of what goes on in the classroom. I have supplied the curriculum only; you are responsible for the program, the routine, the discipline, the daily lessons, and your own attendance.

It is time to begin the training.

Table 3.5
Your Anxiety-Free Rule Book

Rule 1: See Things Realistically

- It's important to use all the information—including positive information.
- It's better to be realistic than pessimistic.
- Use the facts, not your feelings, to make predictions.
- Treat what-ifs as part of your imagination.
- Use probabilities rather than possibilities.

Rule 2: Normalize Consequences

- False alarms are not the same thing as reality.
- What will really happen is that you will feel anxious—and maybe exhausted—from your anxiety.
- You don't die from obsessions, panic, worry, or fear.

Rule 3: Let Go of Control

- You don't need to control your mind or your feelings.
- Magical thinking maintains anxiety—give it up and think rationally.
- You are a problem solver in real life.

Rule 4: Embrace Your Anxiety

- Seek out experiences that make you anxious.
- Do it when you are anxious and uncomfortable—don't wait to feel ready.
- Accept reasonable risk.
- Stay in as long as possible.

CHAPTER 4

"That's Dangerous!"
Specific Phobia

WHAT IS SPECIFIC PHOBIA?

Betsy enjoys her job, except for the occasions when she has to fly. When she does, she worries for days beforehand. She checks the weather channel looking for signs of storms. She lies awake at night thinking about the flight, dreading it. She remembers plane crashes she's read or heard about. The day of the flight she's a wreck. As she boards the plane, she looks around for anything amiss; she listens for noises as the engines start up and the plane shudders. *Could something be coming apart?* she wonders. As the plane takes off, she shuts her eyes, grips the arm rests tightly, and holds her body rigid. Luckily, she's had two martinis in the lounge before boarding and can look forward to another couple of drinks when the plane levels off. She opens her eyes and releases the arm rests but cannot relax: at the slightest jolt she clutches them again and says another prayer. The flight seems to last forever. As the plane finally lands and taxis up to the terminal, she returns to normal, relieved but exhausted.

Betsy is not normally a fearful person. She doesn't mind insects or elevators; she doesn't worry about getting sick or not having enough money or making a fool of herself at a party. She's confident on her job and easygoing with friends. Her fear is aroused specifically by flying—by the prospect that the airplane she's on could crash. She knows her fear is irrational, but it doesn't seem to matter. She often chooses to go places by car rather than fly, even though she's well aware that driving is statistically more dangerous. As long as she doesn't have to get on an airplane, she is relatively anxiety free. On the other hand, because of the nature of her job, her flying problem does impose a serious limitation on her life.

Betsy has what is called specific phobia—a fear that attaches to a particular stimulus for no apparent reason. It is not uncommon: according to some measures, 60 percent of adults have at least some fears of this type, while 11 percent actually qualify for the diagnosis of specific phobia at some point during their lives. Females are slightly more likely than males to receive the diagnosis. The list of things that can trigger specific phobia is large and somewhat amorphous. Some of the most common ones are bugs, mice, snakes, spiders, bats, heights, water, storms, lightning, closed spaces, open spaces, the sight of blood, hypodermic needles, public transportation, tunnels, bridges, and, of course, flying.

No one can say exactly why a certain person has a particular phobia. But there are some things we know about the phenomenon in general. Virtually all specific phobias are universal—they are found in every culture. They seem, to some degree, innate rather than learned; that is, people have them when encountering the feared object for the first time. They attach consistently to certain kinds of things: for example, to animals rather than flowers. From all this we can reasonably infer that such phobias were, at some point in human history, adaptive—that is, they helped our ancestors survive in dangerous and unpredictable environments. It's fairly obvious why that's so: one has only to think of things like snakes and spiders (often poisonous) or heights or deep water, to see why avoiding such perils would be conducive to survival. Phobias around modern phenomena like tunnels or airplanes seem linked to more primitive dangers involving suffocation or dangerous heights.

One kind of specific phobia is interesting to me because it's one I have myself: blood injury injection phobia. This fear is stimulated by the sight of blood—especially one's own. It causes a person to feel queasy or faint—on the verge of collapse. It's been shown that this response is often accompanied by a drop in heart rate and blood pressure—the opposite of the adrenaline-fueled reaction that most dangerous situations produce. One theory is that this evolved to protect people from blood loss when injured; a drop in heart rate and blood pressure meant they wouldn't bleed as much. Another is that it is a strategy to mimic death or incapacity, so as to "fool" predators or enemies—the human equivalent of playing possum. In any case, the phenomenon is almost surely a survival mechanism from our ancient past.

Modern psychology can also tell us a few things about specific phobia. We know that the fears grouped under that name are located in the emotional part of the brain, which means they have little to do with the rational, risk-calculating part. We know they are maintained by avoidance; as long as the feared object is kept away from our experience, the fear is unlikely to go away. On the other hand, when the fear is confronted and linked to safe consequences, it tends to diminish. In short, activating our fear is essential for overcoming it. Clinical experience shows that almost all specific fears can be substantially altered or neutralized with proper treatment. But before we get into specifics, let's look again at the question of how specific phobia originates.

HOW ARE SPECIFIC FEARS ACQUIRED?

There are basically two main theories about how we come to have specific phobia. One theory is that our fears are learned, either directly (by experiencing painful consequences) or indirectly (from observing others showing fear or experiencing painful consequences). The second theory is that these fears are inborn. Both of these theories have merit—we are predisposed to fear certain stimuli or situations, but experience can make matters worse. However, let's briefly examine the merits of the "learned fear" theory to see if it has anything to contribute.

If you ever took a course in psychology, you may recall a famous experiment done in the early 20th century. An 11-year-old boy has a pet rabbit. The experimenter "trains" the boy to become afraid of the rabbit by first showing him the rabbit and then banging a metal bar to make a loud, frightening noise. After a while, the boy cries at the sight of the rabbit because he associates it with the fearsome sound.

This model of learning is part of what's known as Pavlovian conditioning. It's based on the pairing of a neutral stimulus with either a positive or negative experience. (Pavlov had famously trained dogs to salivate at the sound of a bell by ringing the bell every time food was offered.) A variant on this model is the notion that you can learn to be afraid by watching others be afraid: a young girl sits next to her mother on a plane, sees the mother go into panic mode, and twenty years later has a full-blown fear of flying. Whether acquired directly or indirectly, fear arises from the association of an experience with negative consequences and then persists on its own.

There's certainly evidence that something like this is possible: fear can, under certain circumstances, be learned. However, at some point, psychologists began to ask why fears generated by experience would continue to linger after the negative pairing is discontinued. If the frightened individual subsequently avoids further negative associations (i.e., the boy has no more bad experiences with rabbits), shouldn't the fear decrease over time? Why should such fear be conserved, or maintained? Why doesn't the boy "learn" to stop fearing the rabbit the same way he learned to fear it?

A later theory attempted to explain this by splitting the learning model into a two-stage process. The first stage involves *acquisition of the fear*. The second involves *maintenance of the fear*—the process by which you *stay* afraid. Once the fear is acquired, the individual proceeds to avoid the object feared. Each time the boy is around the rabbit, he feels more anxious; each time he *avoids* the rabbit, he feels *less* anxious. His fear is thus reinforced by what is called "operant conditioning." Avoiding the threat leads to a reduction of fear: in effect, avoidance is rewarded. Thus it comes to have a positive association, while fear around the primary stimulus is maintained.

This second-stage theory—how fear is maintained by avoidance or escape—does seem to have some truth to it, a truth that supplies us with significant understanding for the treatment of anxiety. If fear can be maintained through avoidance (and there is evidence that it can), then fear can be unlearned by reexperiencing the fearful object and finding it to be innocuous. The boy learns he can be around rabbits safely. This unlearning process will be an important tool later on, as we learn to cope with our anxiety.

As we've already seen, the acquired fear model has limitations as a theory: Evidence strongly suggests that many specific fears are innate and predisposed—we are prepared (by evolution) to be more afraid of certain stimuli (e.g., heights, snakes, bugs, rats) than others (e.g., flowers). These fears are common to all cultures, and they almost always relate to situations that would be dangerous in a primitive environment. If we are in doubt as to any of this, we have only to consider some of the relevant data:

1. 77 percent of mothers with five-year-old children who had fear of water claimed their children feared it the first time they encountered it.

2. 56 percent of adults who feared dogs claimed to recall an unpleasant experience with a dog. However 66 percent—an even *higher* percentage—of adults *without* fear of dogs also recalled such an experience. This is the opposite of what we would expect if the fear were learned.

3. Experiments show that humans will, to some extent, learn to fear any stimulus that's paired with an electric shock. However they will learn to fear a spider in this manner far more readily and strongly than a flower. This implies that the former is inherently more fearful than the latter.

4. When a person gets indigestion, he will link it automatically to something he has eaten, rather than to any other event or circumstance that was present. We tend to connect intestinal discomfort specifically with food consumed; i.e., with being "poisoned."

Here are some of the dangers that would have been prevalent in a primitive environment, together with some of the adaptations, or responses, that many of us deal with today:

Table 4.1 Fears and Adaptations	
Fear	**Adaptation**
Starvation	Binge eating, preference for sweet or high-calorie foods, carbohydrate craving, hoarding of food, excessive weight gain, somnolence, reduced metabolic rate and inactivity during winter months
Predators	Avoid animals, avoid crossing open fields, fear of the dark (nighttime predators), group yourself with others when crossing fields as protection against predators
Attack by strangers	Fear of strangers, protect one's territory, allegiance to one's family and tribe, use of appeasement gestures to show that one is not hostile, submissiveness to stronger and more threatening figures
Natural Danger	Fear of heights, water, lightning; hesitancy in moving forward
Death of Children	Attachment of parent (especially mother) to child. Parent responds to infant crying, clings to infant, soothes infant. Infant and young child fear abandonment, maintain closeness to parents, fear being left alone, the dark, and animals.
Poison	Avoid any smells or tastes associated with bacteria or toxins. Quickly learn that some foods are poisonous.

Even a cursory list such as this provides clues as to the origin of most fears grouped under specific phobia. They reflect the major hazards that would have been prevalent in a primitive environment. If you suffer from a specific fear—that is, one not linked to a general pattern of anxiety but attached principally to a specific thing or situation—you will probably be able to place it somewhere on this list.

THE RULES FOR BEING AFRAID—AND STAYING AFRAID

Let's write out some of the rules that you can follow to make sure that you are afraid and that you stay afraid:

1. If you feel afraid, then it must be dangerous.
2. The danger is approaching rapidly. Don't rely on probabilities; you could be the one who gets hurt.
3. You must have absolute certainty or it is dangerous.
4. It will be catastrophic; it could kill you.
5. Focus on the threat; this will save you.
6. Look for clues that it is dangerous.
7. You will not be able to cope; you are potentially helpless.
8. Ignore anyone who tells you it's safe; you could get overconfident.
9. You must get out or avoid immediately.
10. Use safety behaviors to tolerate the discomfort.
11. If you survive, it's because your safety behaviors helped you.
12. Always avoid anything that makes you anxious.
13. Anxiety is always bad.

This phobia rule book will lead anyone to develop and maintain a phobia. The phobia rule book is built in to the way we think when we are afraid of heights, flying in airplanes, insects, snakes, or being trapped in closed spaces. We rely on our emotions to tell us that it is dangerous, we reject evidence based on probabilities, we look for sounds or clues of danger, we comfort ourselves with superstitious safety behaviors, and we think we have to get out immediately. By following this rule book we increase our fears and limit our behavior. The good news is that by following the advice in this chapter you can rewrite this rule book.

Take a look at Figures 4.1 and 4.2 to understand the origins and maintenance of your fear and how your thinking makes you fearful.

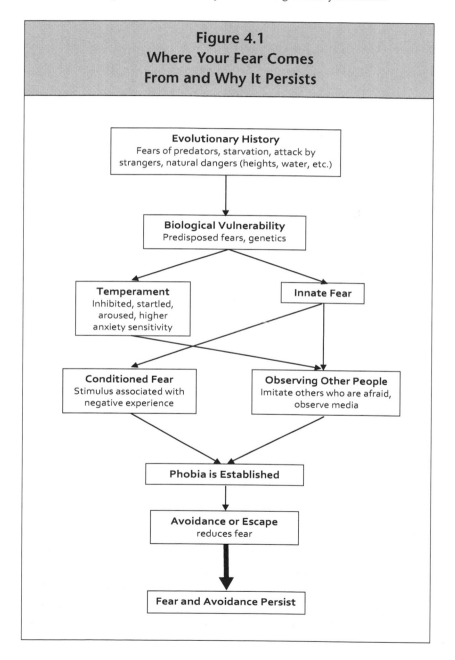

Figure 4.1
Where Your Fear Comes From and Why It Persists

Evolutionary History
Fears of predators, starvation, attack by strangers, natural dangers (heights, water, etc.)

Biological Vulnerability
Predisposed fears, genetics

Temperament
Inhibited, startled, aroused, higher anxiety sensitivity

Innate Fear

Conditioned Fear
Stimulus associated with negative experience

Observing Other People
Imitate others who are afraid, observe media

Phobia is Established

Avoidance or Escape
reduces fear

Fear and Avoidance Persist

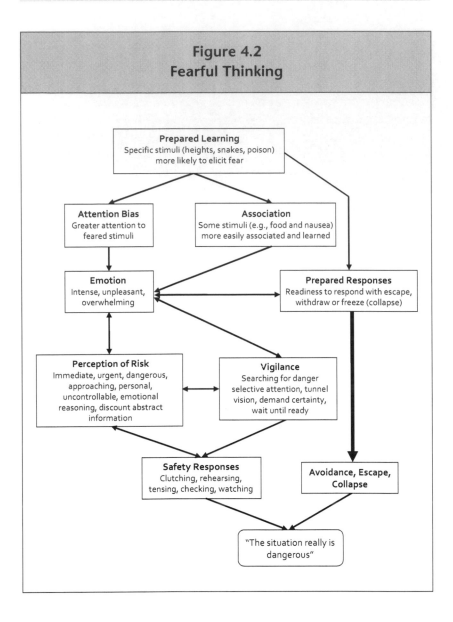

Figure 4.2
Fearful Thinking

OVERCOMING SPECIFIC PHOBIA

If you can do what needs to be done to overcome your fears, there's good news. There are simple and powerful techniques that can be used. Behavioral treatment for specific phobia has proven remarkably effective: most fears can be successfully treated in several sessions, without the use of medication. Intensive or prolonged practice, especially with guidance from a qualified cognitive-behavioral therapist, tends to produce even more significant progress. In the remainder of this chapter we will set out some simple guidelines that have proven effective and discuss how you can apply them. Our plan will include the following steps:

1. Identify your fears.
2. Identify your safety/avoidance behaviors.
3. Build your motivation to change.
4. Construct a fear hierarchy.
5. Evaluate the rationality of your fear.
6. Image-test your fear.
7. Practice "real-life" exposure.
8. Commit to a long-term strategy.

Let's go through these steps one by one.

1. Identify Your Fears

We define specific phobia as fear of a particular danger in the external world. We will not include here fears of a psychological nature or fears connected with one's self-image. For example, one might fear being in a crowded store or public bathroom or speaking in front of assemblies. This sort of fear has more to do with how we think others will perceive and evaluate us; it is a feature of social anxiety disorder, which we'll discuss in a separate chapter. Or you may fear having a panic attack—another kind of anxiety disorder to be discussed later. Here we'll limit ourselves to fears of a particular thing or situation that seems dangerous *in itself*, not for the way it makes us feel: something that raises the prospect of direct physical harm. A plane will crash, the elevator will fall, the dog or snake will bite you. Specific phobia generally produces a sense of immediate peril, with accompanying physical responses such as increased heart rate or adrenaline flow. It is immediate and visceral, not dependent (as other anxieties may be) on convoluted reflections, analyses, self-doubts, or imaginings of the future. It is an instant response of the nervous system to something in the environment.

This doesn't mean that your specific phobia isn't connected in your mind with events from the past. You may well have had a "learning experience" that reinforced or exacerbated a primal fear. Fear of injury or dismemberment is natural and biological—but if you have been in a car accident, or even witnessed one, you may have developed far more intense fears around driving. Perhaps you were once stuck in an elevator and went into a state of panic. You were always nervous in elevators, but now you are a confirmed lift-o-phobe. Or you may be haunted by a bad experience with a vicious dog. Experience *can* have an effect on your fear—but specific phobia is generally related to something you were already *predisposed* to fear. People without your phobia can undergo the same experience without any particular sense of trauma. Just another unfortunate experience.

Measure Your Specific Fear

The first step is to identify which situations or things you fear. Look at Table 4.2 and complete the form, identifying the level of fear that you experience in each of the situations listed.

Table 4.2 Fear Evaluation		
Choose a number from the scale below to show how much you fear each of the situations listed below and write that number next to the fears. 0_____25_____50_____75_____100 None Somewhat Moderate Very Extreme		
1. Flying	11. Meeting strangers ✓	21. Traveling in a bus, train, or subway
2. Elevators	12. Speaking in public ✓	22. Walking alone
3. Heights	13. Using a public bathroom	23. Being alone at home
4. Insects ✓	14. Eating in public ✓	24. Dirt or soiled things
5. Snakes	15. People seeing I'm nervous ✓	25. Lightning or thunder
6. Animals	16. Crowded stores ✓	26. Darkness or night
7. Blood or injections	17. Malls ✓	27. Standing in line waiting ✓
8. Rats and mice	18. Restaurants, churches, or movies ✓	28. Exercise
9. Water	19. Closed spaces	29. Increasing my heart rate
10. Hospitals	20. Open spaces ✓	30. People criticizing me

Now that you have completed this form, you can look back at the different things that make you afraid. For example, some fears might be of natural phenomena—such as thunder and lightning, darkness or night—but other fears may be of rats, mice, (other) animals, insects, or snakes. Certain fears involve your concern that people might be watching you and evaluating you negatively—such as fears of using a public bathroom or eating or speaking in public. These fears that involve evaluation by other people are part of social anxiety disorder—something that we will discuss in a separate chapter. Also, you may have checked off fears in crowded stores, malls, or restaurants. Here we are interested in what you are afraid will happen. For example, are you afraid that you will get so anxious that other people will think that you are losing control or looking foolish? If you are worried about being evaluated negatively then you may have social anxiety disorder. Or, you might worry that you will have a panic attack—and that you will become so anxious that you will collapse, lose control, get sick, pass out, or go insane. This is a different kind of anxiety disorder—namely, panic disorder. We will describe that later.

But if your fear is that **the situation is dangerous** and that something bad will happen to you *because of the situation*, then you probably have specific phobia. For example, you may fear you will get bitten by a snake, dog, or spider—or you may fear that the plane will crash, the elevator will fall, or you will drown. These are specific phobias because you fear the specific situation.

2. Identify Your Safety/Avoidance Behaviors

We've already touched on the way certain irrational behaviors make us feel safer when we encounter our fears. This comes from our deeply programmed instinct to *control* the situation—even if we really can't. For example, a person who fears elevators might feel safer by clutching the walls of the elevator, tensing their body, or holding their breath. Someone on a plane might hug a pillow or repeat a song in her head over and over. After a while these little rituals become associated with non-catastrophe. Eventually your instinctive mind comes to believe that they actually do keep you safe—that you survived *because* of them. This is your superstitious belief about fear and about seeking safety. It's important to be aware of these behaviors. See if your own response to phobic situations falls into any of these common categories:

- Tensing or clutching
- Scanning the environment
- Asking for reassurance
- Praying
- Repeating rote phrases
- Singing to oneself

- Altering your breathing
- Remaining motionless

Table 4.3 Safety Behaviors		
My specific fear is:		
Categories of Safety Behaviors	**Specific Behavior**	**Yes/No**
Tensing-clutching		
Scanning the environment		
Asking for reassurance		
Praying, repeating phrases		
Rehearsing distracting images or sounds (e.g., singing to myself)		
Breathing differently		
Moving in a different manner (slowly, quickly, rigidly, etc)		

Another factor to be aware of is the way in which you avoid your fears. Like your safety behaviors, your "avoidance behaviors," when continued over time, confirm your belief that you cannot handle a situation. In the case of elevators, you may use the stairs exclusively, avoid offices or apartments on high floors, or even contrive to live and work at ground level only. If planes are your phobia, you probably go on a lot of long car trips or perhaps use any less-than-perfect weather forecast as an excuse to cancel a flight. The more accustomed you are to these behaviors, the more you rely on them and the more you're at the mercy of your phobia. Part of your strategy, as we'll see, will be to wean yourself from them. You'll learn to do without them just as you learned to depend on them.

Table 4.4 Avoidance Behaviors		
My specific fear is:		
Examples of Avoidance Behaviors	Costs to Me of Avoiding	Benefits to Me of Avoiding

3. Build Your Motivation to Change

Many people with specific fears rearrange their lives around their fears—they avoid taking airplanes, walking up stairs, or interacting with animals. In order to overcome any of your fears and anxieties you should weigh the costs and benefits of overcoming your problem. For example, the costs could include doing things that are uncomfortable—or even frightening—spending time and money for treatment, or risking failure to get over your fear. The benefits could be that you no longer have to avoid situations or things that frighten you, you can travel more easily, you will be less worried about encountering your feared situation, and you will feel more in control of your own life. Use the form below to assess your trade-offs for overcoming your specific fear.

Table 4.5 Costs and Benefits of Overcoming Your Fear		
My specific fear is:		
Costs	Benefits	What I will be able to do if I overcome this fear

As you examine your responses, keep in mind that almost all the costs of overcoming a fear are when you first start facing that fear. Almost all of these costs will disappear when you overcome the fear. Are you willing to face some discomfort over the short-term to obtain long-term gains? Sometimes you have to be uncomfortable now to be free of fear later. Are you willing to do this?

In addition to weighing the costs and benefits of overcoming your fear, you should also consider the following: if you give in to your fears, they may spread to new situations. This is what we call generalization. For example, if you fear elevators—and you continue to avoid them—then you may also begin avoiding other things that make you uncomfortable. We will see that the generalization of fear and anxiety is a major problem with all of the anxiety disorders. Giving in to one fear makes other fears more likely. This is another good reason to confront your fears now— before they spread.

Would it be worth it? You probably know the answer to that. The ultimate question is, are you willing to do it? It's your decision.

4. Construct a Fear Hierarchy

Fear hierarchies can be used in the treatment of every anxiety disorder. They're called fear hierarchies because they depend on ranking the intensity of your different fears. You construct one by listing all the situations you can think of that are connected to your fear, in order from least frightening to most frightening. For example, say your fear is connected with elevators. This is a large and abstract concept, but you can break it down into smaller ones. The least threatening situation might be standing at the entrance to a building that has an elevator. Next would be walking down the hall toward the elevator. Next would be pushing the button and seeing the doors open. Subsequent steps might be getting in the elevator, seeing the doors close, riding up or down, having the elevator stop at different floors. Finally you might arrive at the idea of the elevator getting stuck or even falling—the worst thing of all (though of the course, the most wildly improbable).

This is a good place to start working because imagining something is generally less frightening than actually doing it. As you picture each step in the process, assess your degree of fear quantitatively. This will be subjective, of course, but you can still attach a number to it. Psychologists use the concept of Subjective Units of Distress, or SUDS; this simply means rating your fear on a scale from 0 to 10. The number 0 represents the complete absence of fear, while 10 represents total panic. 5 means a moderate amount of fear, one that's barely tolerable. For example if flying were the problem, you might start with assigning a 1 or 2 to sitting at home worrying about the flight. Usually (though not always) the numbers increase as you come closer in time to the thing most dreaded. Thus you might see your SUDS level rise at each stage of your trip: arranging a ride to the airport, driving there, checking in, waiting by the gate, boarding the plane, the engines starting up, taking off, encountering turbulence . . . all the way up to a plane crash. Don't be afraid of carrying the exercise to this point: it's just your fear, it's not reality. It's important to reassure yourself that no harm can come to you from the assessment itself. It will prove useful as you learn to confront your fear.

You'll end up with a list of situations, each of which has a number attached representing the fear level connected to it. You can add any non-numerical data that seems relevant. For example, any specific ways your fear expresses itself at each point: sweating, upset stomach, nausea, etc. If you're on a plane, does it matter whether you have a window or aisle seat? Is the elevator more frightening when it's noisy or silent? Note whether or not it affects your comfort level to have someone with you (for some, being alone in an elevator ranks high as a terror). Include any of your safety or avoidance behaviors that come into play at a particular stage: changes in body tension or breathing, the impulse to move around or hold still, an urge to start (or avoid) conversation. The more complete the picture presented, the more useful your fear hierarchy will be to you. You'll have a chance to refine all these perceptions later on, when you use your fear hierarchy in a simulation process, and then finally apply it to the real thing.

Table 4.6 Fear Hierarchy	
Please list your feared situations in order from least distressing to most distressing. In the last column write how upset each one makes you from zero (no distress) to ten (maximum distress).	
Situation	**Subjective Units of Distress (0–10)**
1. (Least Distressing)	
2.	
3.	
4.	

5.	
6.	
7.	
8.	
9.	
10. (Most Distressing)	

5. Evaluate the Rationality of Your Fear

As with any problem that you may have—overcoming fears, anxieties, being overweight, or procrastination—you should examine how motivated you are to change. The first thing to do is to ask yourself if you think your fear is rational or extreme. For example, you may have a fear of flying, but you may also believe that your fear is rational and that air flight is dangerous. Or you may have a fear of dogs and may believe that dogs are dangerous animals. Let's take the fear of flying. Certainly it is true that some airplanes crash and people get killed. And it is also true that airplanes have been the target of terrorists. But what is the probability of getting killed in an airplane? In order to assess this, we can examine the data that have been collected for air travel. And we can also look at elevators and dog bites.

For the year 2001, the likelihood (odds) in the United States of being killed by specific causes is the following:

- Homicide: 18,000 to 1
- Motor vehicle: 6,700 to 1
- Lightning: 3,000,000 to 1
- Commercial airplane: 3,100,000 to 1
- Dog bite: 19,000,000 to 1
- Snake, lizard, spider: 56,000,000 to 1
- Elevator (per trip): 398,000,000 to 1

Now, elevators are remarkably safe. Consider the fact that there are about 600,000 elevators in the United States, *each* carrying about 225,000 passengers per year—for a total of 120 billion passenger trips. In New York City—with 59,000 elevators—there were 13 fatalities over a three-year period, primarily due to kids using elevators as joyrides or due to carelessness by mechanics fixing the elevator. Looking at the actual odds—or probabilities—can help you test out the idea that your fears may be irrational.

One way of asking about how irrational your fear is is whether you would place a bet on it happening. With odds of 3.1 million to 1 I am betting I won't be killed in an airplane. Where would you put your money?

For example, as the elevator starts to go down, I have a sudden image of it crashing. What's really going on? I'm predicting the future and assuming it will be catastrophic. I know that in reality the chances of the elevator falling and killing me are almost 400 million to one—somewhat less than the chance of being struck by lightning in my yard, which I *don't* worry about. Moreover, I've made these kinds of predictions before and they have never come true. This *could* be the first time—but then anything whatsoever that I do *could* prove disastrous. I'm insisting on feeling completely comfortable before undertaking any risk, even though I know this is a recipe for paralysis.

Such reflections are not, by themselves, going to relieve you of your anxiety. But they can provide a mood or context for you to work within as you confront your fears. They help establish an atmosphere of safety, a belief that the underlying reality of the universe is that you are not really in danger, that the fears you harbor are merely distorted projections of your mind. You may still have to battle your inner demons, but you will at least know that reality is on your side.

6. Image-Test Your Fear

There are different ways of gaining exposure to your fear. The easiest is to *observe* someone doing the thing that you are afraid of. For example, if you have a fear of the elevator, you can observe people getting on and off the elevator. What do you see? Well, you probably see people arriving safely. Similarly, if you fear air travel, you can go to the airport and watch planes take off and land. This also provides you with direct information—literally, a picture of safety. Your therapist can also help you with this. For example, she can get on an elevator in front of you—showing you that she feels it is safe. Observing people facing the things that you are afraid of is helpful—but not enough.

The second step is to practice *imagining* the different situations that you fear—as listed in your fear hierarchy. For example, Ed was afraid of flying. His fear hierarchy started with imagining himself sitting at home a day before the flight, next—driving to the airport, next—walking down the ramp to board the plane, and, after several intermediate steps—imagining himself sitting on the plane during a storm with incredible turbulence. We will go through imaginal exposure in a few minutes.

The third step is *actual exposure*—actually going into the situations listed in your hierarchy. When you do the actual exposure, keep in mind that you need to feel some anxiety for this to work. You will start with the least frightening and gradually engage in exposure to each step along the way—until you reach the most feared situation. As you do this, you should notice any safety behaviors that you use—and eliminate each one of them. We will go through these steps in a moment.

You can now take your fear hierarchy, together with all its data, and use it to imagine an encounter with your fear. I call this kind of simulation imaginal exposure. It's a sort of practice exposure—a rehearsal for the real thing that allows you to see what is going on in a more detached, controllable way.

Here's how it works. Go through the steps in your fear hierarchy, from least frightening to most, at each stage calling up an image of that step in your mind. At each step of the way, note your SUDS—your fear level—and record it. Perhaps it's a 2 to begin with, as you simply contemplate the idea of riding in an elevator. The next image might be actually approaching the elevator, then getting in, and so on. Hold each image for a while—I usually recommend ten minutes—noting your SUDS at two-minute intervals. See if the number falls as you hold the image. If it does, keep holding it till the drop levels off and holds steady. Then move up the hierarchy to the next most frightening image and do the same thing. When your SUDS falls off at this level as well, just keep moving up. If not—if your fear level remains high even when you hold the image for ten minutes or so—you can either move back down the hierarchy to something less challenging, or you can discontinue the exercise for the day. You can always pick up tomorrow where you left off.

The drop in your SUDS level at each stage is the result of what we call habituation. It means that the longer you're exposed to an image, the less responsive you are to it. In effect, you get used to the feared image: less aroused, less concerned, and more indifferent. The point of the process is to habituate yourself to the various situations that cause your fears. You can go through the entire process on many different occasions. Your fear levels should decline over the long term as well, so that an image that was terrifying the first time you pictured it will be more tolerable after days or weeks of practice. Keep your records over time, noting how the numbers change, either in absolute terms or in relation to each other.

While going through this process, it's important to make your images as vivid as possible. Include as many details as you can think of. Don't rush through them or gloss over the subtler points. For example, if you imagine the elevator door opening, also imagine what the interior of the elevator looks like: how big is it, what are the lights like, what kind of paneling is on the walls, where are the buttons, does it have a railing, is anyone else inside? All these details make your picture more realistic and thus a better simulation for practice purposes. (Later, when you practice the real thing, you can use your fear hierarchy to re-evaluate your anxiety levels.)

A few other things to note: 1) Are you finding it hard to hold the image? 2) Are you saying or thinking things to yourself to distract or reassure yourself? 3) Do you have the impulse to engage in any safety behaviors: clutching, holding on, modifying your breathing, etc.? When practicing real-life exposure you'll want to catch these behaviors and consciously let go of them. Throughout the exercise, try to record as much data as you can, including overall length of time spent focusing on each image, the intervals between them, the levels themselves, and any accompanying thoughts, feelings, or reactions. All this is useful information, and it will help you gain insight into the workings of your anxious mind.

Table 4.7
Your Imaginary Exposure Record

In the table, list the date and time for each exposure exercise, describe the image that you are using, and then list your anxiety ratings—in sequence—every two minutes. For example, your anxiety ratings for the initial exposure might be 2, 4, 7, 3, 1. Also, note any safety behaviors that you use during the imaginal exposure—clutching, breathing differently, scanning the environment, reassurance seeking, etc.

Date/Time	Situation That I Imagine	Two-Minute Ratings of Anxiety	Safety Behaviors

Sometimes during imaginal exposure the fear level actually subsides to the point where the exercise becomes boring—so boring that the image starts to fade from the mind. This is encouraging—boredom is an improvement over terror—but it's important not to let your mind wander. Keep paying attention and you'll get the most from your exposure. If you do notice your attention wandering, bring it gently back to the image. If you're telling yourself, *I know this is just an image, it's not the real thing,* try to ignore that thought and just experience the image as though it were real. The more real it feels, the more effective the exposure will be. (In fact, as you'll come to see, the image in your mind during the simulation will be quite similar to the image in your mind during the real thing. Your fear is constructed out of these images, not out of the real situation.)

Some psychologists recommend relatively short-term exposures—as little as ten minutes at a time. They don't want the patient to feel too anxious or under pressure. It's important that these initial exercises be voluntary—that you feel you can stop anytime the discomfort gets too great (you can always resume later). However, there's evidence that longer, or what is called massed exposure, is more effective, and will help you get over your fears more rapidly. You might spend as much as an hour imagining a terrifying situation. It might leave you exhausted or emotionally drained. But it also might produce more dramatic results. There's no right or wrong way; some people make excellent progress with short-term exposures done frequently—perhaps several times a day. Consultation with a therapist can help you decide what method works best for you.

7. Practice Real-Life Exposure

When you've gone through imaginal exposure—enough so that it begins to make a difference in your fear level—you're ready for the next step: real-life (psychologists sometimes call it "in vivo") exposure. This works in a similar fashion, except that it's no longer a simulation. The idea is to actually place yourself in a fear-inducing situation and then go through the same steps in your fear hierarchy. Begin at the bottom (the least threatening), and practice the action involved over and over in ten minute sessions. At each stage, record your SUDS level at two-minute intervals, plus any accompanying safety behaviors, physical reactions, or other thoughts and responses worth noting.

Your plan might work like this. Say fear of flying was the problem. You might start with something mildly threatening: watching planes take off and land. To allow yourself enough time for the exercise, you'd drive to the airport a couple of hours earlier than usual (the driving in itself could be anxiety-producing, but you probably wouldn't want to make the trip more than once). Park yourself by a window and watch planes take off for a half hour or so. Pay attention to your fear level as the planes come and go, and record it every two minutes. You'll probably notice your SUDS level decreasing gradually as your mind acclimates to the experience. Then move up the hierarchy: perhaps you walk up to the counter and check in, then buy a magazine at the newsstand, then walk over to the departure gate. Note and record your SUDS level at each of these stages, spending enough time with each to allow the level to decline. Record your impressions as well. You may have someone with you or not, but your response to your companion (or lack of one) will be part of your notes.

Finally, boarding time approaches—the moment of reckoning. As you walk along the ramp to the plane, you note your SUDS level getting up close to ten. *This is not bad.* In fact, it's excellent—since you need to activate your fear in order to modify it. You now have a chance to learn something of vital importance: that you can *feel* anxious about something and still *do* it. The primitive, instinctual part of your brain is telling you that what you're doing is dangerous. It's as though you were a primitive hunter-gatherer climbing a tree or crossing a chasm. But there's no tree or chasm. The plane is, in fact, safe; otherwise all these other people wouldn't be calmly boarding it. Your increased anxiety amounts to no more than a *false alarm.* The alarm is saying, "Get out of here, this is dangerous!" You continue to hear the sound of the alarm, yet you choose to ignore it; instead you keep moving forward. The interesting thing is that the longer you ignore the alarm, *the quieter it will be.* The more you actually experience your fear in a context of safety, the more you'll actually learn—at a visceral level—that you have nothing to fear.

Throughout the plane ride you continue to observe and record your fear level. This includes the plane taking off, climbing to a high altitude, and perhaps encountering turbulence along the way. You simply note your fear level at each point. Maintaining awareness of your fear helps keep it under control; it simply becomes an event taking place in your mind, in which you have something like a scientific interest. It's no longer a barked command you need to obey.

What Do You Predict Will Happen?
As you look through your fear hierarchy and identify each situation that you fear, you can also identify exactly what you predict will happen. For example, when on the airplane, do you predict that the airplane will crash? Do you predict the dog will bite you? Do you predict that when you drive across the bridge that you will lose control and crash over the

side? As you go through your planned exposure to each of the situations in your hierarchy, you should write down exactly what you are predicting will happen; your level of anxiety before, during, and after the exposure; and the actual outcome. For example, if you fear getting on the elevator, your anxiety level before getting on the elevator might be a 7, while on the elevator it might be a 9, and when you get off the elevator it might be a 2. Your prediction before getting on the elevator is that it will crash. The outcome is that nothing happens.

Table 4.8 Predictions and Outcomes				
Indicate exactly what you predict will happen, indicate what actually happened, and before and after the exposure indicate your anxiety or fear from 0 to 10, where 0 represents the absence of fear, 10 represents the greatest fear imaginable, and the middle points represent various degrees of fear.				
Situation that I fear:				
My Prediction	Actual Outcome*	Anxiety Before	Anxiety During	Anxiety After

*Actual outcome: Describe what happened. Did you avoid, engage in the behavior, or seek safety? What sensations and thoughts did you have, etc.? For example, "I took the elevator, I thought I was going to panic, but I got up and down safely."

Look at Things Rationally

After you have listed your predictions of what is going to happen in the situation, you can begin to challenge these negative thoughts by looking at the evidence that proves that they are wrong. As with any fear or anxiety, there are numerous negative and extreme things that you are saying to yourself. We call these automatic thoughts—because they come to you spontaneously, they seem true at the time, and they add to your anxiety. We can categorize these thoughts as different distortions in thinking. Examples of automatic thought distortions for riding an elevator—and rational arguments against each of these—are shown in Table 4.9 below. A complete list of automatic thoughts can be found in Appendix H.

Table 4.9 Rational and Irrational Thoughts		
List any negative thoughts that you have and identify the kinds of distortions in thinking that you are using. Then give the best useful responses that you can give. You can go back over this form at later times and add to your rational responses.		
Automatic Thought	What Kind of Distortion is This?	Rational Response
The elevator will crash.	Fortune-telling Catastrophic thinking	The chances of the elevator falling and killing me are 398,000,000 to 1. I have made these predictions before and they have never come true.
Yeah—but this time it could happen. There is no guarantee.	Discounting the positive Perfectionism Demand for certainty	Of course anything could happen—but life has to be lived with what is probable—not with what my fantasy says.
I shouldn't get on until I feel comfortable.	Demand for certainty The need to be ready	The only way to make progress is to do things when you are not ready—like exercise and facing your fears. In fact, I will need to feel the fear to get over it.

Many people find it very helpful to go through these forms and develop coping statements that they can use before and during exposure. For example, if you fear elevators, then you can develop coping statements to read before you get onto the elevator that challenge and defeat your negative thoughts. Keep in mind that with many anxious thoughts you may believe that you need absolute certainty. Since there is no certainty in an uncertain world, you would never be able to function. The fact is that every day you do things about which you are not certain and do not have a guarantee. You rely on *probabilities*. What is the probability of the elevator crashing and killing you? It's 398 million to one.

What about your safety behaviors? They might include clutching the seat, breathing hard, checking for noises, singing to yourself, praying, or asking the flight attendant for periodic weather checks. Note and record the impulse to perform these behaviors whenever they arise—but if at all possible, *do not* indulge them. Safety behaviors maintain your fear; they keep you from experiencing it fully, and thus from developing a sense of security around it. One way to eliminate safety behaviors is to consciously do the opposite of what your impulse is telling you. If you have the urge to clutch your seat, let your arms hang as loosely as possible. If your attention is riveted to the sound of the plane's engines, put on earphones and listen to music. If you find yourself scanning the plane for exits, pick up a book instead.

A safety behavior that's especially important to avoid is the use of alcohol or tranquilizers. It's one that people commonly resort to, but it's really not helpful here. You might think, *Wouldn't this all be easier with a Valium or a couple of martinis under my belt?* You may have tried this in the past and felt that it helped "take the edge off" your anxiety, but it also reinforced your anxiety. Being in an alcoholic or drug-induced haze means that you are not experiencing the full effect of your fear—which you must do in order to eliminate it. When you dull your fear with alcohol or drugs, your mind associates safety with numbness—whereas in fact being numb has no connection to your safety. Chemical support is one of the safety behaviors you most need to eliminate; if you do, you will certainly not regret it.

Table 4.10
Your Direct Exposure Record

In the table, list the date and time for each exposure exercise, describe the situation you put yourself in, and then list your anxiety ratings—in sequence—every two minutes. For example, your anxiety ratings for the initial exposure might be 2, 4, 7, 3, 1. Also, note any safety behaviors that you use during the direct exposure—clutching, breathing differently, scanning the environment, reassurance seeking, etc.

Date/Time	Directly Experienced Situation	Two-Minute Ratings of Anxiety	Safety Behaviors

If you do engage in short-term exposure, you should plan to do it regularly—perhaps several times each day—every day.

I recall my own experience with an unplanned long-term exposure. I was hiking with my wife outside of Zermatt, Switzerland—and I insisted (in typical male fashion) that I was correct about the direction of the hiking trail. I had a fear of heights, and I was soon to be submitted to an unexpected massed practice. We ended up on a ledge overlooking cliffs on both sides. Needless to say, this was an exposure I did not plan. After an hour walking on this ledge—which I do not recommend—we finally came to a steep goat trail leading down the mountain. Much to my surprise, I had no fear walking down this trail, although prior to this, I would have been terrified.

The next morning we told the concierge at the hotel about our misdirected trail hiking. Appropriately, it seemed to me, she said, "Oh—you were in the Lost Valley. What a beautiful spot." Lost Valley? It didn't seem like Shangri-la to me when I was terrified. The concierge then said, "You might want to consider some parasailing off the mountain," apparently overestimating how effective this exposure was.

Parasailing off the Alps is a sport that looks exciting—and one that I will leave to my imagination. You use a large "sail" that you attach to your back and then, as you run, it takes you into the air over the cliffs and chasms of the Alps. I was very happy to make progress on my fear of heights at the Lost Valley, but I draw the line with jumping off cliffs.

This Is Hard to Do!

Finally, you may have certain beliefs that get in the way of doing exposure. Examples of these beliefs are the following:

1. I can't stand being anxious.

2. If I become anxious, it will get worse and worse and overwhelm me.

3. I must be a coward because I am afraid of doing this.

4. My problems must be related to deep-rooted issues from my childhood.

5. This exposure won't work.

Again, doubts about exposure—and self-critical thoughts about anxiety—are common. However, you can counter these negative thoughts with the following:

1. You can stand being anxious—as indicated by the fact that you have an anxiety disorder. The only consequence of being anxious is feeling uncomfortable. Feeling anxious is part of getting better with exposure.

2. With prolonged exposure your anxiety is likely to decrease because the thing you fear will not happen.

3. You are not a coward. In fact, your fears were probably adaptive to your ancestors. If anything, you are well adapted to a different and more dangerous environment. It is the right fear at the wrong time.

4. Your fears are not related to deep-rooted issues. There has never been any scientific evidence linking a specific phobia to such things. In fact, overcoming a specific phobia is quite simple.

5. Your doubts about exposure are understandable since we are asking you to do the very thing you are afraid of doing. However, hundreds of studies demonstrate that exposure does work, so it is likely to work for you. Of course, there is no guarantee, but you do things every day for which you do not have a guarantee.

8. Commit to a Long-Term Strategy

The techniques we've been discussing have proven highly effective for millions of anxiety sufferers. However, overcoming your fears is not a one-time effort, but a lifelong project. The instincts that produced your anxiety are deep ones, nurtured by millions of years of evolutionary history. It doesn't make sense that a few simple exercises performed once on a plane or in an elevator will make them disappear forever. People who use the techniques described here often experience dramatic changes. But they not infrequently experience relapses, especially in circumstances of stress or fatigue. It's best to anticipate such relapses; they're quite normal and in no way a sign of failure. Being prepared for them is an important part of learning to control anxiety.

What should you do when relapses occur? First of all, keep looking for opportunities to practice what you've learned. If you've overcome your fear of getting into an elevator, but then haven't come in contact with an elevator in months, you may well experience your fear all over again. Welcome it as an opportunity to practice. We're talking about long-term maintenance, just like physical exercise—you stay in shape by practicing dealing with your fears on a regular basis. Continue to look for situations that trigger your fear, and confront them as soon as possible. When the fears arise, use imaginal exposure right away, and real-life exposure at the earliest opportunity. Each time you do this, you strengthen your mastery over fear. Have patience—as long as you keep at it, you're making progress regardless of the short-term ups and downs.

Above all, don't become alarmed over a relapse. What worked before will work again. Go back to the exposure exercises, and do them over again as many times as you need to. In fact, what we call overpractice—continuing the exercises well past the point of relief—may help you solidify your gains. Avoid projections of how well or badly you are doing; stick to your practice in the moment and have faith in its efficacy. It's like a meditation. Staying present with discomfort is the best way to guarantee freedom from it in the future.

REWRITE YOUR PHOBIA RULE BOOK

Now that you have gone through the techniques for overcoming your fear, you can begin to rewrite your phobia rule book. Let's look at Table 4.11 and see what a Phobia-Free Rule Book would look like.

Table 4.11
The Phobia-Free Rule Book

Rules That Make You Afraid	Rules That Overcome Your Fears
If you are afraid, then it must be dangerous.	Your fear tells you nothing about real danger; emotions are not reality.
The danger is approaching rapidly.	The danger may be only in your head; it may not be approaching at all, or it may be approaching slowly.
Don't rely on probabilities—you could be "the one" who gets hurt.	Probabilities are reality. You could always be the one, but that's no way to live.
You must have absolute certainty, or it is dangerous.	There is no certainty. Uncertainty is neutral, not dangerous.
It will be catastrophic; it could kill you.	You probably have no evidence that it is going to be catastrophic. You've had these beliefs before, and you are still alive.
Focus on the threat; this will save you.	You should recognize that there is always some evidence of a threat, but there is also evidence of safety.
Look for clues that it is dangerous.	Use all the information, not just the signs of threat.
You will not be able to cope; you are potentially helpless.	You may be stronger than you think.
Ignore anyone who tells you it's safe. You could get overconfident.	Use the information other people have. After all, phobia is not evidence of danger, it's evidence of your emotion.
You must get out or avoid immediately.	You might be better off staying as long as possible to find out that it is really safe.
Use safety behaviors to tolerate the discomfort.	Safety behaviors maintain your fears. Eliminate them as soon as possible.
If you survive, it's because your safety behaviors helped you.	If you survive it has nothing to do with safety behaviors; it has more to do with the fact that it is safe.
Always avoid.	Try to do the things that you fear doing.

85

CONCLUSION

In this chapter we have reviewed the steps that you can take in overcoming specific phobia or fear. Even though you may have had a fear for years, you can be reassured that there is a good likelihood of overcoming this fear with the right interventions. Indeed, the model for overcoming fears outlined here is the foundation for overcoming all of the other anxiety disorders—although you will see that there are specific issues for the treatment of the other anxiety disorders. Look at Table 4.12 to review the main steps in overcoming a specific phobia, and use these steps for any new phobias that may arise or return.

Table 4.12 Rules for Overcoming Specific Phobia
1. Measure your specific fear.
2. How would evolution lead you to have this fear?
3. Build your motivation to change.
4. Is your fear rational?
5. Costs/benefits of eliminating fear
6. Avoid the spread of fear.
7. Identify your safety behaviors.
8. Identify your avoidance behaviors.
9. Construct your fear hierarchy.
10. Plan exposure.
11. Record Subjective Units of Distress (SUDS).
12. What do you predict will happen?
13. Look at things rationally.
14. Use imaginal exposure.
15. Use direct exposure.
16. Eliminate safety behaviors.
17. Anticipate relapse.

CHAPTER 5

"I'm Losing Control"
Panic Disorder and Agoraphobia

WHAT IS PANIC DISORDER?

When Paul first came to see me, his life had more or less fallen apart. About a year earlier, without warning, he had begun to experience symptoms of anxiety so severe that life as he knew it had come to a virtual standstill. He had stopped working and was on disability. He'd given up almost all his normal social and recreational activities; most of the time he was too terrified to even go outside. His family life had become a nightmare of stress. He spent almost all his time compulsively scrutinizing himself for the physical symptoms generated by his anxiety: dizziness, shortness of breath, increased heart rate, disorientation. When the symptoms came on—and almost any activity could bring them on—he was pretty much incapacitated. As a result of all this, he had sunk into a deep depression; he felt hopeless about his future and was coming to me as a last resort.

It all started one day when he was working out on the treadmill at the health club. The air-conditioning was broken and he was sweating profusely, but he kept up his workout. When he stopped he felt a bit short of breath, as though he were suffocating. He began breathing more rapidly in an effort to take in enough air but couldn't; moreover, the effort made him dizzy. As he sat down on the treadmill, he became aware that his heart was pounding. *Am I having a heart attack?* he wondered. Frightened, he asked someone to take him to the hospital. While he was there waiting for the doctor to see him, his breathing returned to normal. The doctor examined him and told him there was nothing wrong with him. He went home.

But something had begun happening, something quite unsettling. He began getting short of breath frequently. Every time he did, he worried he would get dizzy or pass out. This anxiety caused his heart rate to rise, which would alarm him all the more. He stopped going to the health club, since exercise seemed to bring on this condition. He stopped running and swimming, but his symptoms persisted at lower and lower levels of activity, until merely walking brought them on. After a while he discovered that he was experiencing the same symptoms from getting into an elevator or driving—anything the least bit stressful. His office was on a high floor, so he stopped using the elevator, but of course climbing the stairs was out of the question as well. That's when he stopped going to work. Eventually he became anxious on any trip outside the house, so he started staying home. His life became more and more limited. His doctors still could find nothing wrong with him physically, but he was finding it harder and harder to do the things he had always done, to lead any kind of normal life. It was at this point that he began to sink into depression. The day I first saw him, he was in a pretty terrible state.

What was happening to Paul may seem strange, but it is not at all unusual. Many people experience the same sorts of symptoms; they are those of a typical panic attack. A panic attack is an onset of anxiety about what is going on in your own body; it can be defined as a fear of one's own sensations. People experiencing a panic attack may feel shortness of breath, a pounding heart or heart palpitations, tingling sensations, ringing in the ears, trembling, dizziness, chills or hot flashes, choking, gasping, sweating, loss of bladder control, nausea, chest pain, and—frequently accompanying these—a sense of impending doom. Often sufferers believe they are having a heart attack or seizure or that they are going insane.

Of course, it's possible to have such symptoms for purely physiological reasons. That's why I always recommend that people with any of these physical responses have a medical examination to rule out the possibility of a serious health condition. The latter can include hyperthyroidism, mitral valve prolapse, hypoglycemia (low blood sugar), or a number of other ailments. Such symptoms could also be traceable to something as simple as caffeine, alcohol, or other drug addiction. But if all these can be eliminated as causes, yet the symptoms persist, it's likely the patient is suffering from a classic pattern of panic attack.

The onset of an attack is often linked to fears about encountering certain situations in the real world. These fears are often referred to collectively as *agoraphobia,* a Greek word meaning "fear of the marketplace." Some typical triggers for agoraphobia are vigorous exertion, being out alone, driving across bridges or through tunnels, crowds, heights, deep water, trains, planes, open fields, or elevators. All these situations involve the kind of stress associated with danger—or what would have been danger in a primitive environment. Therefore they're clearly linked to our evolutionary programming. But the added factor is that agoraphobia usually involves, not just fear of certain dangers (as in specific phobia, treated in the previous chapter), but fear that the mind and body's *reactions* to these dangers will spin out of control: that one will experience a heart attack, collapse, loss of sanity, or some other form of breakdown, up to and including death. The central indicator is *fear of one's own sensations and emotions*. (Some people have panic disorder but do not have fears of specific situations—that is, they do not have "agoraphobia.")

If one has these symptoms of agoraphobia regularly—particularly if the situations lead consistently to panic attacks—it's possible that one has developed what we call panic disorder. This is a disorder in which the fear of a panic attack becomes more or less constant. The criterion is not necessarily whether or how often you have panic attacks, but whether or not you've developed an abiding *fear* of such attacks. A simplified diagnostic test for panic disorder consists of these questions:

- Do you experience recurrent, unexpected panic attacks?

- If so, has at least one of these attacks been followed by a month or more of either a) persistent concern over having additional attacks; b) worry about the implications or consequences of the attack (heart attack, insanity, etc.); or c) significant changes in behavior related to the attacks?

Panic disorder and agoraphobia are often linked, and in this chapter we will treat them as parts of the same phenomenon. Agoraphobic fears can strike almost any place and time, though they seem to be more common under certain conditions. About 60 percent of panic attacks are due to hyperventilation. When we hyperventilate (breathe rapidly) we take in much more oxygen than we need and we do not exhale (or throw off) enough carbon dioxide. Thus, the blood has too much oxygen (hypocapnia). This leads our arteries and blood vessels to constrict, blocking the flow of oxygen to the brain. That leads to feelings of dizziness and a sense that you are suffocating.

Panic attacks have a higher incidence in summer, possibly because heat and dehydration tend to affect things like pulse rate and dizziness. People are also more likely to be outside in summer, where threatening situations are more often encountered. Attacks frequently occur in the middle of the night, possibly because of sleep apnea or carbon dioxide changes. These nocturnal panic attacks often jolt the sleeper awake in a confused and agitated state. Most people are able to go back to sleep once they realize what's happened. However those who suffer from panic disorder may be too terrified to sleep; they feel these nocturnal attacks are a sign of imminent catastrophe. Many patients believe their panicky symptoms are signs of a heart attack; each night they go to sleep not sure if they will wake up in the morning.

Sometimes the situations triggering panic attacks can be quite unusual. I once had a patient whose panic was triggered by any sudden cloudiness in the sky. As the sun darkened, he would experience an overwhelming sense of foreboding; he was afraid to go outside on a sunny day lest cloud cover appear. This had actually led to an earlier misdiagnosis: a Freudian psychiatrist he'd been seeing for over fifteen years had determined that he was mildly psychotic. He wasn't. He merely had panic disorder with agoraphobia. Once he understood this, we were able to work out a suitable and quite effective treatment.

YOUR FIRST PANIC ATTACK

Although there is no one pattern that can predict the onset of the first panic attack, there is evidence that it is more likely to happen if you have experienced a recent loss or threat in a relationship, illness (often undiagnosed; for example, a low-level fever that weakens you), increased responsibilities, hangover or drug withdrawal, fatigue, or losses in other areas in your life. But in many cases, it's impossible to identify a cause of the panic attack. This adds to your anxiety since you believe that panic can come out of nowhere, with no warning, and that it will debilitate you.

As I said, the first panic attack seems to come out of the blue and leads to the first *catastrophic* interpretation. This leads to increased *hypervigilance,* that is, continual focus on any signs of arousal or sensation. As you focus more and more on arousal, there is misinterpretation of what this arousal really is—*I'm having a heart attack* or *I'm going crazy.* This results in a panic attack.

For example, Janet was walking down the street and began to focus on the fact that her heart seemed to be beating quite rapidly. She began to notice that her mind was getting disoriented. The more she focused on her internal sensations, the more afraid she became that she was losing control. She then began to think, *Oh my God! I'm going to have a panic attack. I'm going to lose control and collapse right here on the sidewalk!*

This escalated her fear and her physical arousal even more, and she had a panic attack.

The agoraphobia, the fear of places or situations that will trigger a panic attack, begins to occur for many people. You anticipate anxiety in certain situations—*If I go to the movie, I'll feel closed in and have a panic attack* or *If I go to the mall, I won't be able to find the exits and I'll have a panic attack.*

As you anticipate more anxiety, you may begin to use safety behaviors to protect and prepare for problems. These include relying on other people or behaviors that you think will decrease danger, for example, needing to be accompanied, seeking reassurance, trying to decrease the impact of a stimulus, decreasing your behavior (e.g., exercise) so that you feel little arousal. This feeds into the belief that without these safety behaviors something really terrible will happen. For example, *If I don't hold on to the side of the building, I will collapse.*

Janet would hold on to the side of a building whenever she felt dizzy. She also began to notice that when she was outside she felt more disoriented if there was bright sunlight. So she began to wear sunglasses. After a few months, she realized that she felt safer if she had someone with her, so she would try to plan as much as she could with other people. She thought, *If I do get dizzy and feel that I'm going to collapse, my friend can hold me up. Or get me to a doctor in time, just in case I have a medical emergency.*

WHERE DOES PANIC DISORDER COME FROM?

The first thing we can say about panic disorder is that, like all other anxiety disorders, it has its roots in our evolutionary history. The fears it is built upon were at some point adaptive. To see why, we have only to look at a list of typical situations that trigger panic attacks. It includes strolling in public, entering a crowded store or theater, crossing an open space, sitting in an airplane, driving across a bridge or through a tunnel, standing at the edge of a balcony, looking up at (or down from) the top of a skyscraper, riding in an elevator, and so on. A diverse list indeed. What links all these fears? Why would these various situations all elicit the same sort of panic in individuals?

The obvious answer is that all of them represent the sort of danger that our prehistoric ancestors would have been exposed to. For example, being crushed in a crowd or stuck in a tunnel evokes the threat of suffocation; many who panic in these situations are given to hyperventilating, feeling that they are running out of air even when such is not the case. Others get a feeling of being trapped, as though they might be vulnerable to attack by hostile forces. Those who fear closed spaces will typically scan their environment for escape opportunities; they may prefer to sit in an aisle seat or near a fire exit. On the other hand, panic can be triggered by walking across an open field, suggesting a fear of predators. Our ancestors must have felt this fear on the Serengeti Plain; we observe today that a mouse will hug the bushes at the edge of a clearing rather than cross it directly. Looking down from a skyscraper evokes our natural dizziness from heights, while looking up at it from the sidewalk mimics that sensation closely. Virtually all the situations that trigger panic attacks have a similar link to primitive dangers.

But while these situations may have clear origins, it's not so clear why some people develop panic disorder. A panic attack is characterized not only by typical primal fears, but by a feeling that one's *reaction* to them will be catastrophic—something to be feared *in itself*. The panicker tends to focus on internal sensations—not so much *Something bad is going to happen to me,* but rather *I must be going crazy* or *I think I'm about to have a heart attack*—a trait that we call anxiety sensitivity. This amounts to a catastrophic fear of anxiety itself, arising from a distorted interpretation of the normal physical responses to danger. Shortness of breath means one is about to suffocate. An elevated pulse or heart rate—even from normal exertion—foretells a heart attack. This is why prolonged cycles of panic disorder can be initiated suddenly by a single panic attack that appears to come out of nowhere, yet replicates itself over a period of time.

Why are certain individuals more susceptible to this cycle of fear? No one knows exactly, but it seems to be a combination of innate predisposition and early childhood experience. There's some evidence of genetic determination, in that panic disorder often runs in families. (My own mother suffered from panic disorder, and I, too, had several panic attacks when I was younger. Fortunately I was studying cognitive therapy at the time, so I had a pretty good understanding of what was happening to me and was able to deal with it.) Panic disorder sufferers often seem to have higher anxiety sensitivity—i.e., they are more aware of their inner sensations and feelings. This sensitivity often predates the first onset of panic disorder, manifesting simply as a tendency to focus inward. However when fear is stirred up, this inner awareness becomes problematic. The sufferer begins to find evidence of disaster in every fleeting thought or sensation.

There are also some experiential factors. People who develop panic disorder are more likely to have experienced family disruption, or the threat of it. A significant percentage of agoraphobic adults report having gone through (or worried about) the loss of a parent or stable home environment. Some had difficulty going away to school or camp even at an early age. In most cases it's probably not accurate to call agoraphobia simply the continuation of an earlier separation anxiety; often the onset isn't until early adulthood and can be triggered by the loss of a relationship, home, or community. Many initial attacks seem unrelated to life's stresses; they just come out of the blue. Yet it's probably true that people with panic disorder are—for whatever reasons—the sort who tend to "bottle up" their feelings. Such persons may be reluctant to use problem-solving techniques in dealing with their emotions. They rely on themselves to keep their feelings under control—a scary assignment for anyone.

WHAT ARE THE STEPS IN BECOMING AGORAPHOBIC?

Like all anxiety rule books, the rules for having panic disorder and agoraphobia involve four main components:

1. Detect Danger. (You focus on your sensations as a sign of danger.)

2. Catastrophize Danger. (You interpret sensations as life-threatening.)

3. Control the Situation. (You try to control your breathing or you use safety behaviors.)

4. Avoid or Escape. (You avoid situations that make you anxious—or you escape.)

Either you avoid situations that make you anxious (and develop full-blown agoraphobia) or you use safety behaviors to help you through the situation. Your common safety behaviors might include getting someone to accompany you, trying to catch your breath, tensing yourself so you won't fall, or wearing sunglasses so the light doesn't bother you. But as long as you use safety behaviors you will think that the situation is still dangerous.

Your panic disorder and agoraphobia are not some mystery that comes out of nowhere—it simply reflects the rule book that you are following. Take a look at Table 5.1 below and the schematic following the table in Figure 5.1. ("How You Develop Panic Disorder and Agoraphobia") and you will see how your agoraphobia makes sense. It follows a set of rules.

Later in this chapter we will see how you can rewrite your rule book so you won't have agoraphobia or panic attacks.

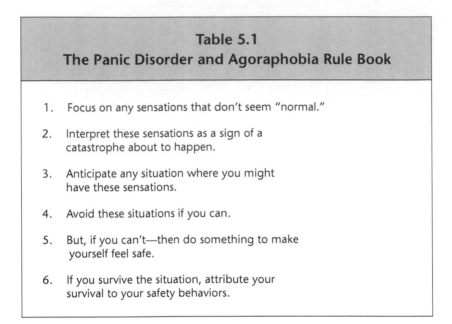

Table 5.1

The Panic Disorder and Agoraphobia Rule Book

1. Focus on any sensations that don't seem "normal."

2. Interpret these sensations as a sign of a catastrophe about to happen.

3. Anticipate any situation where you might have these sensations.

4. Avoid these situations if you can.

5. But, if you can't—then do something to make yourself feel safe.

6. If you survive the situation, attribute your survival to your safety behaviors.

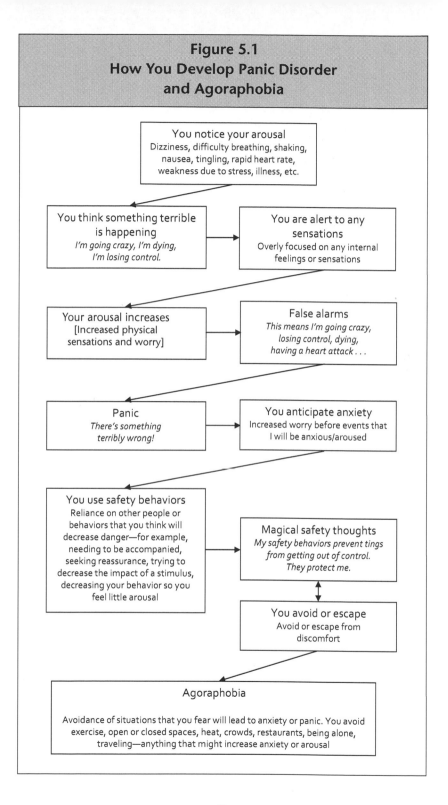

**Figure 5.1
How You Develop Panic Disorder
and Agoraphobia**

You notice your arousal
Dizziness, difficulty breathing, shaking,
nausea, tingling, rapid heart rate,
weakness due to stress, illness, etc.

**You think something terrible
is happening**
*I'm going crazy, I'm dying,
I'm losing control.*

**You are alert to any
sensations**
Overly focused on any internal
feelings or sensations

Your arousal increases
[Increased physical
sensations and worry]

False alarms
*This means I'm going crazy,
losing control, dying,
having a heart attack . . .*

Panic
*There's something
terribly wrong!*

You anticipate anxiety
Increased worry before events that
I will be anxious/aroused

You use safety behaviors
Reliance on other people or
behaviors that you think will
decrease danger—for example,
needing to be accompanied,
seeking reassurance, trying to
decrease the impact of a stimulus,
decreasing your behavior so you
feel little arousal

Magical safety thoughts
*My safety behaviors prevent tings
from getting out of control.
They protect me.*

You avoid or escape
Avoid or escape from
discomfort

Agoraphobia

Avoidance of situations that you fear will lead to anxiety or panic. You avoid
exercise, open or closed spaces, heat, crowds, restaurants, being alone,
traveling—anything that might increase anxiety or arousal

OVERCOMING PANIC DISORDER

Like all anxiety disorders left untreated, panic disorder and agoraphobia can result in a debilitating combination of anxiety and depression. It's not uncommon for the problem to persist for years, even decades. Some people—like Paul, whom we met at the beginning of the chapter—become so disabled that they can no longer work. Others are unable to socialize or travel—in extreme cases they may even become housebound. Sometimes the fear of physical ailments becomes a self-fulfilling prophecy: people with panic disorder are far more likely to develop cardiovascular disease, aneurysms, congestive heart failure, pulmonary embolism, or stroke. They are also more apt to be depressed and to attempt suicide. Left to run its course, panic disorder can be a devastating condition.

Yet despite all this, the condition is in fact highly treatable. There's a good likelihood (about 85 percent according to studies) that if you suffer from panic disorder you can improve substantially within a couple of months, using highly structured cognitive-behavioral therapy. Paul, whom we'll revisit later, is one example. Most patients treated in this way maintain their improvement a year later, even without medication. Most show a significant decrease in both anxiety and depression. Practicing certain recommended exercises (such as the ones offered later in this chapter), can continue this improvement indefinitely.

The steps taken in treating panic disorder are much the same as the ones we used in the last chapter to address specific phobia. I use them with a number of anxiety disorders. They are:

1. Identify your fears.
2. Identify your safety/avoidance behaviors.
3. Build your motivation to change.
4. Construct a fear hierarchy.
5. Evaluate the rationality of your fear.
6. Image-test your fear.
7. Practice real-life exposure.
8. Commit to a long-term strategy.

Once again we'll go through these steps.

1. Identify Your Fears

We have probably said enough about panic disorder for you to determine whether or not you are a sufferer. Again, the criterion is not whether or not you become afraid in certain situations, but whether your fear is of your own mental and physical reactions more than of the situation itself. If you are in any doubt, there is a diagnostic test called the Agoraphobic Cognitions Questionnaire, which you'll find in Appendix G.

Once you've made the diagnosis (which you might want to check out with a cognitive therapist), the next step is to identify the particular characteristics of your disorder. You can do so by making two lists. The first is a rather straightforward list of circumstances likely to trigger your anxiety: closed or open spaces, heights, exertion, nocturnal starts, planes, elevators—whatever it happens to be. No great mystery there. The second list goes a little deeper. It should be a list of the typical thoughts that pass through your mind when you are nervous or frightened. Here are some of the typical thoughts that patients report having when in the throes of panic disorder:

- I'm going to throw up.
- I'm about to pass out.
- I must have a brain tumor.
- I'm about to have a heart attack.
- I'm going to have a stroke.
- I'm about to choke to death.
- I'm going blind.
- I'm losing control of myself.
- I'm acting foolish.
- I may hurt someone.
- I may hurt myself.
- I'm going to scream.
- I'm too scared to move.
- I'm going crazy.

You can add to this list any other thoughts that come to mind regularly. Often it helps to simply see them written down on a piece of paper. This gives you a sense of how removed from reality such thoughts can be. You also become familiar with them, so that you can identify them more quickly when they arise.

2. Identify Your Safety/Avoidance Behaviors

As we saw in the last chapter, people with anxieties often employ safety behaviors to make them feel momentarily safer in the presence of danger—even when such behaviors do nothing to actually increase safety. This is particularly common among agoraphobics, who generally distrust their own ability to handle discomfort of any kind. Threats can come from anywhere at any time. When venturing out into the world they may have a whole array of safety behaviors they resort to: walking close to buildings, clinging to chairs or railings for support, getting others to accompany them on trips, hyperventilating, holding themselves rigid, wearing sunglasses at all times. Such strategies are usually either futile or counterproductive. The trouble with the illusion of safety is that it depends on magical thinking. It convinces you you're successfully protecting yourself. This only reinforces your belief that the situation is in fact dangerous.

One patient liked to walk with his eyes half shut in case a bright light triggered a panic attack. It didn't really work, but he did it anyway. Such behavior may make you feel safer, but it rarely prevents the attack you fear. In fact it may help bring it on. I knew a young medical student who was terrified of having a heart attack, even though his heart was perfectly sound. He would check his pulse every twenty minutes to make sure it wasn't going out of control. The result? Each time his pulse rose the slightest bit, he became alarmed—which caused his pulse rate to *really* jump, further convincing him he was about to have a heart attack. He was helping keep in place the condition he wished to escape.

We've already touched on examples of avoidance behavior. Indeed, agoraphobia is a condition pretty much defined by avoidance. Paul was a case in point: he ended up avoiding just about everything that involved the slightest stress or exertion. Since the thing most feared is one's own response, any situation has the potential to trigger that response. In advanced cases, what is to be avoided is no less than life itself. Still, making a list of the specifics can be helpful. It shows you in a clear, concrete way how much you're putting up with in the attempt to soothe your anxiety. This list will prove useful later on, when you start working to shed these avoidance behaviors.

3. Build Your Motivation to Change

As with any anxiety disorder, you should assess your willingness to tolerate the discomfort of facing your fears. In short, how motivated are you? Of all the major forms of anxiety, panic disorder probably involves the broadest range of threatening circumstances. You may be avoiding exercise, travel, walking down the street, malls, theaters, movies, walking up stairs, flying on airplanes, taking public transportation, and many other activities. What would it mean to you not to have to do this anymore? Would it allow you to exercise for health without obsessing about your heart rate or breathing? What's it worth to you to be able to do things independently, without someone along to provide support? To no longer rely on anti-anxiety medications or alcohol? To no longer have to fight to stave off depression? Even beyond eliminating these negatives from your life, there's the pride, confidence, and deep satisfaction that go with being master of your own fate. It's hard to appreciate what a difference such feelings make until you've experienced them.

On the other hand, to reach this goal you will need to do things that will make you uncomfortable. You don't have to take on the discomfort all at once; you can do it gradually, in a structured, supervised way. But you do need to be willing to play your edge, to push the boundaries of what's tolerable. It's best to be honest with yourself at the beginning. Then if you make a commitment to change, you're more likely to stick to it.

Table 5.2 Costs and Benefits of Overcoming Panic Disorder and Agoraphobia	
Costs	Benefits

99

4. Construct a Fear Hierarchy

In the previous chapter, we learned how to construct a fear hierarchy, which is a list of all the situations you can imagine in connection with your anxiety disorder, from least to most fearful (see page 71). You assign each situation a number between 0 and 10 according to how frightening it seems, 0 representing total absence of fear and 10 representing maximum terror. (This rating is sometimes called Subjective Units of Distress, or SUDS.) The list will be used in future exercises that will help you overcome your fears. However there are some special considerations in the case of panic disorder. Earlier (under "Identify Your Fears") we mentioned two different kinds of fear lists you might make. One was of things or circumstances that tend to trigger your fear, such as elevators, exercise, or crowds. The other was a list of reactions you might have to these situations. In the case of panic disorder, it's the latter we're interested in; panic disorder essentially *is* fear of one's own reactions.

Thus in constructing a fear hierarchy for panic disorder, you need to record two distinct elements. One is the specific situation you think might trigger a panic attack: being trapped in an elevator, riding on an express subway, entering a crowded store, and so on. You can rank these in the hierarchy according to how much distress you think you'd experience from each of them. But you should also record *how you think your distress would manifest itself*: fainting, suffocating, collapse, heart attack, becoming ill, throwing up, screaming, wetting one's pants, losing control in general, doing something publicly embarrassing, or going insane. It's important to identify exactly what you predict will happen in each situation. For example, you may be afraid to drive across a bridge. But *why* are you afraid of that? If you have panic disorder, you probably fear that the very experience of driving across the bridge will trigger a panic attack, which might cause you to lose control of the car. One patient of mine was terrified to sit in a crowded theater. He was afraid his anxiety might cause him to start screaming—which would be horrendously embarrassing in front of all those other people. In other words, it was his own reaction that he worried about. He didn't trust himself to remain in control.

These fears are based on predictions—on how you think you're going to respond to anxiety. You fear the situation because you believe that when it arises you'll respond by hyperventilating, fainting, becoming disoriented, collapsing, going insane, or in some way losing control of the situation. It's important to identify these predictions, because your self-help techniques will involve testing and challenging them. You'll learn to unhook from your fears by demonstrating to yourself that your predictions simply aren't accurate. Your fear hierarchy will be your guide in that process.

Table 5.3 Fear Hierarchy		
Please list your feared situations in order from least distressing to most distressing. In the middle column write how upset each one makes you from zero (no distress) to ten (maximum distress). And in the last column, write what you think will happen to you in each of your feared situations. Typical predictions include physical illness, collapse, heart attach, suffocation, going insane, other fears (specify).		
Situation	Subjective Units of Distress (0–10)	What Do You Fear Will Happen?
1. (Least Distressing)		
2.		
3.		
4.		
5.		
6.		
7.		
8.		
9.		
10. (Most Distressing)		

5. Evaluate the Rationality of Your Fear

In the case of specific phobia, we saw that being rational or irrational has mainly to do with being able (or not able) to predict what's likely to happen to us. Whether or not the plane is going to crash, the elevator is going to get stuck, the dog will bite. These are concrete, external facts that we can see and evaluate. In the case of panic disorder, it's somewhat different. The issue of what's going to happen out there in the world is secondary to what's going to happen inside us: the heart attack, collapse, or fit of hysteria we picture ourselves having. And yet these inner phenomena, too, have a certain objective reality: after all, they are either going to happen or they are not. What we can do now is see if they *do* happen the way we imagine. In short, we can treat them exactly as we treated external catastrophes. Then we can look back to see if our predictions of an inner meltdown were accurate or not. This will put our fears into a more reality-based perspective.

Here, for example, is a list of physical sensations commonly associated with a panic attack. Each is followed by 1) the panicky thought that often accompanies the sensation and 2) what a more rational response might look like.

Rapid heartbeat, shortness of breath

- *Panicky thought:* I am having a heart attack.

- *Rational response:* I've just seen a doctor who's told me my heart is fine. I've had these sensations before and been none the worse. My brain is sending me a false alarm, telling me I'm in danger when I'm not. My reaction is simply the body's normal physical response to an alarm.

Dizziness, weakness, disorientation

- *Panicky thought:* I'm about to collapse or pass out.

- *Rational response:* This is a temporary phenomenon caused by the fact that my blood is circulating to different parts of my body away from my brain. If I sit quietly and breathe normally, I'll return to a state of calm.

Racing mind, tension, shaking

- *Panicky thought:* I'm going to start screaming and lose control.

- *Rational response:* There's nothing to scream about. I have no clear idea of what "losing control" means. I can allow my mind to race without any danger; I can simply watch my thoughts and see where they go.

Rise in intensity of physical symptoms.

- *Panicky thought:* My panic is going through the roof. If it doesn't stop, I'll go insane.

- *Rational response:* Panic attacks are self-limiting. They eventually subside on their own. They are simply the result of arousal and pose no danger to me.

You can write out your fears in this way. Take such a list with you to remind yourself about how things can be seen realistically. Look at your rational thoughts every day.

In each case, the panicky thought is stimulated by a false belief about the nature of panic attacks and their symptoms. The fact is that arousal—which is what the physical and emotional changes associated with panic attack really are—is not dangerous. A rapid heartbeat has nothing to do with a heart attack; it's just something that happens when we're excited. It's natural for someone in a scary situation to feel dizzy or short of breath. These are normal reactions; people don't go crazy because of them. The true signs of insanity are delusions or hallucinations—confusing imaginary things with real ones. Physical anxiety is merely the body's effort to protect itself from a dangerous situation. Other than the discomfort it causes, there isn't anything harmful about it—we merely *believe* there is.

All the anxieties connected with panic disorder rest on this same false belief that you need to avoid things that make you anxious. But do you? Does anxiety carry any truly threatening consequences? As unpleasant as it may be, anxiety is both temporary and nonlethal. Avoiding it may *feel* more comfortable for the moment, but it also reinforces your conviction that the world is a dangerous place. This makes you *dependent* on avoiding anxiety; you're convinced you can't survive in its presence. Letting go of this false belief frees you to start practicing exposure to fear—which is the only way you can conquer it.

If you feel the panic actually coming on, you should recognize that all panic attacks are self-limiting. Your anxiety goes up—and then it comes down. I have never, in over 25 years of seeing patients, had a patient come in with a panic attack. All panic attacks end—simply because your anxiety is exhausted. If panic attacks are self-limiting—sort of like a tension headache—then what is there to fear?

In our next few steps we'll begin to work with panic. It will take courage and determination to carry it through, but a firm belief in one's ability to make rational decisions—*in spite of* fear's presence—will be an indispensable part of the effort.

6. Image-Test Your Fear

The next step involves imagining each situation in your fear hierarchy and allowing yourself to feel the anxiety it arouses. Keep in mind that if you're suffering from panic disorder, the thing to focus on is not the triggering circumstance—though perhaps that's where you begin—but the panic attack you fear it will produce. Your fear hierarchy should reflect this. First imagine the situation, then imagine your panicked response to it. Begin with the least threatening situation and work your way upward, pausing to linger at each stage until your level of panic (measured by your SUDS number, somewhere between 0 and 10) subsides to a stable level. (If you've forgotten how this works, see the previous chapter, p. 74.)

Here's an example taken from my patient Paul, whom I mentioned at the beginning of the chapter. Paul, you'll recall, had his first panic attack on a treadmill at the gym. He began hyperventilating, trying to control his shortness of breath and accelerated heart rate. It didn't work, and things went quickly downhill. By the time he came to see me he was avoiding not only vigorous exercise but just about anything that might lead to an increase in his heart rate.

Paul and I constructed a list of exercise-related situations that ranged from least to most anxiety-provoking. These became the steps in his fear hierarchy. They read as follows:

- Walking around the room
- Leaving the apartment and walking around in the hall
- Walking on the sidewalk outside
- Jogging very slowly on the treadmill at the health club
- Running at his old pace on the treadmill

When Paul had gone through the steps of imagining each of these situations, recording his fear levels at two-minute intervals, and noting the associated safety behaviors, it looked something like this:

		Table 5.4	
	Paul's Imaginary Exposure Record		
Date/Time	Situation That I Imagine	Two-Minute Ratings of Anxiety	Safety Behaviors
June 1/ 1:00 P.M.	Walking across the room	2, 2, 2, 1, 0	None
June 1/ 1:30 P.M.	Opening door and walking out into the hall—walking around in the hall	3, 6, 6, 4, 3	Looking for door to escape; watching my breathing
June 2/ 2:00 P.M.	Walking outside of building on sidewalk	6, 8, 8, 6, 5, 3, 3	Trying to walk slowly, holding my breath, walking close to building in case I fall
June 4/ 7:00 P.M.	Running on treadmill at health club	6, 8, 8, 7, 5, 4, 2, 2	Holding side rails; trying to breathe normally, tensing my hands, trying to catch my breath—taking deep breaths

What this told us was that Paul had a significant tendency toward panic attack every time he exercised; that the panic was greater the more vigorous the exercise; that despite this he was able to "habituate" to his fear by imagining it over time; and that becoming conscious of his safety behaviors was helpful. Keep in mind that this was an imaginary exercise only. Later, when he applied it to "the real thing," he was able to achieve similar, even more satisfying results.

In the case of panic disorder, there's a kind of intermediary stage between just imagining your fear and actually placing yourself in a scary situation. We call it panic induction—a way of deliberately exposing yourself to your own sensations. We've already seen how panic disorder is built around an unfounded fear of one's own physical sensations such as rapid breathing or dizziness. There's a way to experience these sensations in a controlled way, to find out *experientially* that they are self-limiting rather than catastrophic.

I actually had the chance to guide Paul through such a process the first time I saw him. He'd already told me on the phone (and I'd seen from his records) that his doctor had checked him out and found nothing wrong with him physically. At the time of our first appointment he called me from the lobby (I was on the tenth floor) and told me he was too afraid to either take the elevator or climb the stairs. I met him in the lobby. He was a fit-looking man but in a state of some trepidation. We started up the stairs slowly. At the first landing he was breathing rapidly. I asked him what he thought was happening. He told me he couldn't catch his breath and was hyperventilating in an effort to keep himself from collapsing. I told him to relax, to breathe slowly, and to clench and relax his hands before starting up again. We did this for each flight up.

After a while we made it to the office. There Paul explained to me what was going through his mind. Climbing the stairs, like running on the treadmill (or like any vigorous exercise) had accelerated his breathing and heart rate, convincing him he was about to collapse and go into a coma. I told him I doubted that was going to happen. I had him stand in the middle of the floor and breathe rapidly until he began to feel dizzy. I then had him stop and breathe slowly into his cupped hands (this balanced the oxygen and CO_2 in his bloodstream). Within a few minutes his breathing had returned to normal. There was no collapse. He seemed surprised but relieved.

At the next session we tried another panic induction. This time I had him breathe rapidly until he began feeling dizzy and then start running in place. This would simulate an escape response that would also force him to utilize the extra oxygen and to stabilize his oxygen and CO_2. Within a couple of minutes, his panic subsided and he stopped running in place. This is because running restores the balance of carbon dioxide and oxygen and his brain would now get enough oxygen, which would reduce his dizziness. All of this demonstrated to Paul that he could have a panic attack *without anything really bad happening*. We then constructed a number of fear hierarchies for his various anxiety-provoking situations: riding in elevators, climbing stairs, going outside, exercising, etc. We would rehearse each of these situations in our sessions, with Paul gradually becoming more accustomed to the fear that arose. Sometimes I would play the role of "Paul's Panicky Thoughts," while Paul took on that of his rational response.

Bob: *(as a "Panicky Thought"):* If you breathe any faster, you could have a heart attack.

Paul: No, I won't. I've hyperventilated before and nothing happened.

Bob: Yes, but this time your heart rate is going up.

Paul: That's just arousal. My body can handle it.

Bob: What if you get dizzy and collapse?

Paul: I'm not getting dizzy, so I won't collapse.

Bob: But there's nothing to hold on to.

Paul: If I'm not collapsing, I don't need to hold on to anything.

And so on. Fortunately, Paul was really committed to challenging his panicky thinking, which gave us a lot to work with. At one point, as we were riding together in the elevator, he seemed anxious. I asked him what he was afraid of. He said he thought the elevator might get stuck. I asked him what would happen if it did. He said that we might run out of air and suffocate. I pointed to the fan switch on the elevator. "Where does this fan get its air from?" I asked him. "From outside, I guess," he said with a sheepish grin. He calmed down a bit. Again, the primitive part of his brain had sent him the message that he was in a closed, airless space and would suffocate. By bringing to light this buried thought, he was able to contact the more advanced part of the brain—the neocortex—and use its intelligence to override the emotional part.

You can use panic induction yourself to test your ability to withstand a panic attack. Choose a situation that seems slightly threatening, but which you can always back away from. It might be something that starts you hyperventilating or drives up your adrenaline: say, looking down from the window of a tall building or stepping momentarily outside—something you can retreat from if the intensity gets too great. You can then practice inducing the symptoms in mild form and riding them out. See how long you can stay in the situation, and note whether your anxiety level subsides more the longer you do. That way you maintain control of the situation, while still exposing yourself to the world beyond your control. It's helpful to have supervision from a cognitive-behavioral therapist when doing this exercise, but you can also practice it on your own.

Table 5.5 Your Imaginary Exposure Record

In the table, list the date and time for each exposure exercise, describe the image that you are using, and then list your anxiety ratings—in sequence—every two minutes. For example, your anxiety ratings for the initial exposure might be 2, 4, 7, 3, 1. Also, note any safety behaviors that you use during the imaginal exposure—clutching, breathing differently, scanning the environment, reassurance seeking, etc.

Date/Time	Situation That I Imagine	Two-Minute Ratings of Anxiety	Safety Behaviors

7. Practice Real-Life Exposure

By now you'll have learned much about how panic disorder and agoraphobia work. You'll have identified your fears, along with your safety and avoidance behaviors, and built your motivation to change. You'll have constructed a fear hierarchy for each major anxiety and evaluated it for rationality. Your final preparation will have been practicing imaginal exposure and conscious panic induction. You're now ready for the big step: direct exposure to the situations that set off your panic disorder. This means venturing into the actual environment that's produced panic attacks in the past and seeing if you can deal with it any differently. Once again, the fear hierarchy you developed will be your guide. Use it also as a way to record your responses, as in the following table.

Table 5.6 Your Direct Exposure Record
In the table, list the date and time for each exposure exercise, describe the situation you put yourself in, and then list your anxiety ratings—in sequence—every two minutes. For example, your anxiety ratings for the initial exposure might be 2, 4, 7, 3, 1. Also, note any safety behaviors that you use during the direct exposure—clutching, breathing differently, scanning the environment, reassurance seeking, etc.

Date/Time	Directly Experienced Situation	Two-Minute Ratings of Anxiety	Safety Behaviors

Here's how it worked for Paul. One of his fears—very much in evidence when he first came to see me—was riding in elevators. It had already been the trigger for a number of panic attacks and loomed large in his consciousness. We tackled the issue together. Over a period of a few weeks, I had Paul spend some time with me riding up and down the elevator in my building (perhaps the building should have charged me a fee for the use of it in my practice). First in the fear hierarchy was standing outside the elevator. We'd do that for a while, with Paul noting the incipient symptoms of panic attack, but staying put until they subsided. Next he had to get on and off the elevator with the door held open. Next he had to close the doors while I remained with him, ride up one floor, and get off. Then he had to do the same thing alone. Eventually he got to where he had to ride up 40 floors unaccompanied. He did all this, growing more comfortable at each stage. After six weeks, Paul was able to return to work at his office on one of the top floors of a skyscraper. There was no more problem with elevators.

We still had one challenge left—the big one, the place where the whole thing had started: the treadmill at the health club. Paul's greatest fear was still that he would have a panic attack—with potentially fatal consequences— while exercising. He was sure his heart would give out any time he became short of breath. He hadn't been to the health club in almost a year.

Initially we practiced quick, shallow breathing in my office, to bring on just the kind of hyperventilation and dizziness he feared. We alternated this with having him run in place, to restore his oxygen/CO_2 balance. This quickly reduced the dizziness. We then had him practice running in place, slowly at first, then with increased speed, to see if the shortness of breath would return. It didn't. Paul was now ready to go back to the health club. He'd been so successful up to this point that he felt he could handle it without me. So he went alone.

Paul's plan was to get on the treadmill, run till he began to feel short of breath, and then employ the techniques he'd been practicing with me: keeping his awareness in the present, challenging his panicky thoughts, adjusting his running speed around the edge of his comfort level, and consciously refraining from any of his safety behaviors. He tried it, starting out slowly, keeping his arms and shoulders relaxed. He then worked up to a faster speed until he began experiencing shortness of breath—the normal sensation when exercising. Only now Paul was aware that it was normal. He refrained from tightening his hands and body. He was able to tell himself: *This sensation is not in itself grounds for a panic attack. It's simply my brain telling me I'm not getting enough oxygen to continue at this speed. If I slow down slightly and avoid quick, shallow gasps, I will recover my normal breathing.* Sure enough, he slowed down a bit, and within moments his breath had returned to normal. He found he could regulate his speed so that he stayed within a comfortable range. He also saw that range extend until he could stay mildly out of breath for long periods of time—as runners normally do. Paul's treatment program was now complete.

8. Commit to a Long-Term Strategy

From this time on, Paul's life returned to something close to normal. He was able to resume all his previous activities: work, social, recreational, and family life. It wasn't as though he'd become magically immune to fear: there were times when the old anxieties would loom, and he'd experience his fear of a panic attack. But when he did, things never got out of control. Sometimes he would just wait for the feelings to subside, knowing he was not in any real danger. At other times he was able to practice the techniques he'd learned for quieting his fears and regaining control. Each time he did this successfully, it increased his confidence. He went from being the victim of his fear to being its master.

This is not atypical. Sufferers from panic disorder who undertake the kind of treatment Paul did have enjoyed consistent success. The reduction of symptoms is often permanent, or if the symptoms do recur, they can be dealt with again just as effectively using the same techniques. This treatment allows you to develop your own self-help program, something you can keep with you for as long as you need it. It constantly retrains your thinking so that what was once fearful ceases to be so. The mind stops learning fear messages and begins to believe in its own safety. Once you've done this, you can use any recurring fear as an opportunity to practice; you can actually seek out panic-inducing situations (e.g., crowds, elevators, exercise) and work through your reactions to them. Eventually you'll arrive at a place of confidence and security.

It helps to have a few coping strategies to use when you feel a panic attack coming on. These are useful when the fear impulse arises unexpectedly. Even if you haven't had time to prepare, to devise a strategy, or construct a formal fear hierarchy, they can be there ready to employ at any moment. You may want to keep a list of them handy when you're out in the world:

- *Think about things differently.* Are you simply *mislabeling* your anxiety—calling it a catastrophe when it is merely a form of arousal? Why do you assume your panic attack is dangerous? No one dies or goes crazy from a panic attack. They last only a few minutes on average and subside on their own. Remember, this is merely what's happening *now*—it has nothing reliable to say about any future state.

- *Observe your sensations.* Note your bodily sensations in a detached way: heartbeat, tension in left leg, breath moving in and out, etc. Just experience these sensations in the moment as they arise—no commentary or predictions. Practice accepting your sensations without trying to control or judge them—they are simply what is happening. (If you practice meditation, this is an opportunity.)

- *Direct your attention elsewhere.* Rather than focusing on your sensations, try describing all the shapes and colors you see around you: a red book with a gray spine and a picture of a lake, a cylindrical blue coffee cup, a small black-and-white travel clock, etc. See how observant you can be; make a game out of it. Again, the key is to stay in the present.

- *Practice slow breathing.* Diaphragmatic breathing restores the natural balance of CO_2 in your bloodstream (hyperventilation blows off more oxygen than it takes in). Lie down on the floor or couch and place a book on your chest. If the book rises and falls it means you are breathing shallowly with your chest.

Now let the breath come from your abdomen, slowly rising and falling. Make sure the book is not moving. Make no effort to control your breath by making it either short and rapid or artificially deep. Let it be as it wishes, but keep your attention on it. This will have a calming effect.

- *Put time on your side.* All panic attacks are self-limiting. How will you feel after the panic has subsided and gone away? How will this panic feeling affect how you feel tomorrow? When you are anxious you feel that the whole world is happening to you right now. It's not. It's only a small slice of time. Put time on your side by imagining how you will feel in a few hours—or a few days. Or even a few minutes.

CONCLUSIONS

I have found that the most powerful interventions in treating panic disorder and agoraphobia are simply helping you understand the problem, practice exposure to panic symptoms, and eliminate your safety behaviors. Quite often, hearing about the evolutionary explanation of agoraphobia is the first time that your problem makes sense to you. These are situations—open areas, closed spaces, crossing bridges, swimming away from shore, walking away from home—that might have been quite dangerous in a primitive environment. Learning about false alarms—and how obeying these alarms increases your panic disorder—is quite helpful for many people with this problem.

Many people initially fear inducing the panic symptoms in the office. They fear that these sensations are dangerous and will go out of control. However, panic induction actually works and helps you realize that your fear of a panic attack is no longer important. After all, if you can tolerate panic attacks—and even terminate them on your own—then what is there to worry about?

I have outlined the different steps in overcoming panic disorder and agoraphobia in Table 5.7. The good news about this treatment is that once you improve you usually maintain your improvement for a long period of time. In fact, you may get even better after you complete this program, since your self-help—engaging in continual exposure to the situations that you feared—retrains your thinking to no longer fear what was once debilitating you.

Table 5.7 Overcoming Panic Disorder and Agoraphobia	
Intervention	**Example**
Learn about panic disorder and agoraphobia.	Fear of your sensations, false alarms, evolution of fear of open and closed spaces, learning to avoid or reduce anxiety, the role of safety behaviors, the importance of planning exposure to your fears
Identify your feared sensations.	Dizziness, shortness of breath, vertigo, disorientation, rapid heartbeat, sweating, tingling sensations
Construct your hierarchy of feared situations.	List situations from least to most anxiety-provoking, and identify your thoughts and feelings and sensations.
Identify your safety behaviors.	Are you using any behaviors to make you feel safer? Examples include clutching, tightening, breathing differently, praying, requiring someone to be with you, asking for reassurance, looking for exits, holding on to support.
Recognize that arousal does not lead to panic.	Challenge fear that any arousal will lead to a panic attack. What situations tend to trigger these fears that you will have a panic attack?
Realize that panic is not a catastrophe.	Challenge beliefs that panic leads to heart attack, collapse, losing control, or going crazy; challenging these beliefs
Practice an imagined panic attack.	Imagining what it would feel like and look like to have a panic attack, practicing talking back to your panic thoughts, breathing slowly, distracting yourself, observing and detaching
Practice having a panic attack.	Recognizing that sensations are arousal, not catastrophes, using slow breathing, breathing into a bag or your hands, running in place, riding out the arousal, challenging your negative thoughts about arousal and panic
Practice exposure to your feared situations.	Go through your fear hierarchy, identify your predictions of what will happen, go into the situations that you fear (e.g., malls, elevators, walking, crowds) and catch your panic. Recognize that your sensations are arousal, not the end of the world. Stay until the panic has gone away.

Table 5.8
Your New Rule Book for Your
Panic Disorder and Agoraphobia

Steps in Developing Panic Disorder and Agoraphobia	Rational Way of Looking at the Situation
Initial physiological arousal [Dizzy, difficulty breathing, shaking, nausea, tingling, rapid heart rate, weakness, illness, etc.]	*Arousal is not dangerous.* It's perfectly reasonable for anyone to have some unpleasant or unexpected experiences of feeling dizzy, short of breath, or a rapid heartbeat Almost everyone has these experiences at times, so the chances are good that this is normal.
Catastrophic interpretation [*I'm going crazy, I'm dying, I'm losing control.*]	*Nothing terrible is really happening.* People don't go crazy because they feel dizzy or because their heart is beating rapidly. Insanity is defined by hearing voices, seeing apparitions, or delusions that the world is plotting against you. Heart attacks are not the same thing as your heart beating rapidly. Your heart beats rapidly when you are excited, exercising, or having sex. Arousal is not the same thing as losing control.
Hypervigilance [You are overly focused on any internal feelings or sensations]	*I don't need to detect danger because there is no danger.* You may think that focusing on your heartbeat, breathing, and dizziness will help you catch things before they get out of hand. But it is really this over focus on your internal sensations that makes you more anxious. You can distract yourself from these sensations by directing your attention to the things outside you. For example, when you find yourself focusing on your heartbeat—redirect your attention to the objects in the room you are in. Describe the color and shape of all the things around you.

False alarms [*This means I'm going crazy, losing control, dying, having a heart attack...*]	*Nothing terrible is happening—once again!* Increased heart rate and rapid breathing may simply be signs of feeling anxious. How many times before have you misinterpreted these sensations? Why should it be dangerous now? Hasn't your doctor told you that you are okay? People don't go insane because they are anxious. Have you really lost control because you were breathing rapidly or because you were dizzy?
Anticipatory anxiety [Increased worry before events that I will be anxious/aroused]	*I don't need to worry since there is nothing dangerous about anxiety or arousal.* What if you are anxious in the future—so what? Anxiety is normal—everyone feels anxious some of the time. Haven't you done a lot of things even when you were anxious? Do you think that worrying about it will keep you from being anxious? You should plan on tolerating anxiety, so you can learn that there is nothing to be afraid of. Think of anxiety as increased arousal—very much like the arousal that you feel when you are exercising.
Avoidance [Avoid or escape from anything that makes me uncomfortable]	*I need to do the things that make me anxious.* Avoiding situations that make you anxious only adds to your future anxiety. Exactly what do you predict will happen if you confront these situations? Have these terrible things really happened? Have you really gone insane, had a heart attack, or lost complete control? Or did you simply feel anxious and afraid? As unpleasant as anxiety may be, it is temporary, normal, and nonlethal. It may feel momentarily more comfortable to avoid, but you are teaching yourself that the world is a dangerous place. You should make a list of places and experiences that you are avoiding and list them in your hierarchy of feared situations. Then you can practice the imaginary and direct exposure. You will find that facing your fears—and conquering them—will make you feel less anxious in the future.

| Safety behaviors

[Reliance on other people or behaviors that you think will decrease danger—for example, needing to be accompanied, seeking reassurance, trying to decrease the impact of a stimulus, decreasing your behavior, so you feel little arousal.] | *I don't need safety behaviors to control anything since there is nothing dangerous happening.*

These safety behaviors maintain your belief that the situation is really dangerous. You think, *The only way I got through this is because I relied on my safety behaviors.* You should make a list of every behavior that you engage in that makes you feel safer and then practice giving it up. What do you predict will happen? Do you think that you will not be able to survive the situation without the safety behavior? What will it mean if you actually get through the situation without any safety behaviors? Does this mean that the situation is actually safe? Giving up safety behaviors will help you get the most out of practicing your exposure to your fears. |

You should plan ahead for all of these negative thoughts that you have about your physical arousal and sensations. Plan ahead to confront the situations and feelings that you fear. And plan ahead to give up the safety behaviors. Getting over your panic disorder and agoraphobia can be liberating, but it will require some discomfort—especially your willingness to experience the anxiety that you fear. Getting over fear of fear will help you feel less depressed—and more empowered.

CHAPTER 6

"Never Enough"
Obsessive-Compulsive Disorder

WHAT IS OBSESSIVE-COMPULSIVE DISORDER?

Susan is terrified to touch the door handles of her own apartment. She pulls her sweater over her hand to turn the knob. She thinks the knobs might have been contaminated, and she's afraid of spreading germs to all the furniture. Whenever she touches something she thinks is unclean, she goes straight to the sink and washes in a thorough ritual, over and over, scrubbing between her fingers. Sometimes it takes only a few minutes; other times she doesn't feel clean until she's washed for a full half hour. Then she worries about touching the faucet to turn the water off. Her home isn't the only place she fears contamination. She doesn't like to touch money. She avoids public restrooms. Theaters, buses, parks, other people's homes—all are sources of paralyzing anxiety. For Susan, the risk of contamination is pretty much a constant presence.

In addition to physical contamination, Susan worries about "impure" thoughts. She was raised Catholic and, at one point in her childhood, took stories about the devil very seriously. Now she watches her thoughts anxiously for any appearance of that intimidating figure. She wonders if there's an evil part of her that's trying to tempt Satan. She looks for his number—three sixes—in everything from accounting figures to telephone listings. She tries desperately not to think about the devil, often saying a rush of "Hail Marys" to distract herself. She avoids movies—or even advertisements for movies—that might allude to him. She's reluctant to watch television because his image might pop up on the screen at any moment—even in something harmless as a soap commercial. At times she thinks she might be possessed.

Is Susan going insane? She's considered the possibility. *Maybe I'm schizophrenic,* she thinks. *Or maybe I'm having a nervous breakdown.* Her fears and compulsions have such a hold over her that it seems impossible to ever break free of them. The more she tries to get rid of her unwanted thoughts and obsessions, the stronger they seem to become. Her friends have no sense of what this is like; they find it all rather strange. It reinforces her feeling of being a kind of freak. She's struggled with this condition for a long time without success, and things have come to seem hopeless.

In fact, Susan isn't crazy at all. Nor is she having a breakdown. She merely has a common anxiety disorder known as obsessive-compulsive disorder (OCD). Like many with this problem, she is ashamed of it and hides most of her symptoms. The result is that she feels totally isolated; no one could possibly understand how she feels. As she sits in my office telling me about her worries and compulsions, I am touched with sympathy. I also see how much of what she says makes perfect sense to her—even though her thinking runs in channels that would seem strange to most people. The fact is, there's a consistent and logical thought process underlying cases of OCD that often escapes therapists unfamiliar with the syndrome. Once we understand how Susan's OCD works—how it really *does make sense to her*—we can offer her help. Her disorder, left untreated, can persist for years or a lifetime, but like other anxiety disorders, it is quite treatable. Her symptoms are real, and help is available for learning how to cope with them.

WHAT ARE OBSESSIONS AND COMPULSIONS?

The word *obsession* is often used in common speech to mean simply any concern or preoccupation that someone else finds extreme or exaggerated. That's a pretty broad, not to mention subjective, definition. In psychology, however, we define an obsession as a recurring intrusive thought or image that an individual finds unwanted or unpleasant and attempts to get rid of. The behavior by which he or she tries to get rid of it is known as a compulsion. The typical sequence that marks OCD is 1) the appearance of certain thoughts that seem to come from nowhere, 2) the feeling that such thoughts are distasteful, 3) an urge to suppress or expunge these thoughts from the mind, and 4) the simultaneous urge to placate these thoughts through certain compulsive behaviors. All this is a part of OCD and can exert a powerful influence over the way one thinks and acts.

Typical examples of obsessive thoughts are that you:

1. Are in danger of being contaminated
2. Have overlooked a mistake
3. Have unwittingly injured someone
4. Have left something undone
5. Need to arrange things in a specific order
6. Are about to do or say something inappropriate

With OCD, one experiences these unpleasant thoughts as beyond one's control. They are unwelcome intruders into the stream of consciousness. Obsessive patients are usually aware that there's something irrational about their thoughts (this distinguishes them from psychotics), but still the thoughts seem no less compelling. Often there's a strong urge to *do* something, to indulge in behaviors that will satisfy or neutralize the obsession. Your compulsions may include checking door locks constantly, repeated hand washing, avoiding any contact with dirt, extreme perfectionism over tasks, hoarding unneeded items, or constantly seeking reassurance from others. Or your compulsions can be mental rituals, such as silently repeating a thought, replacing an undesirable thought with an image, or silently repeating a neutralizing thought, such as a prayer or other self-talk. The underlying belief is that if these impulses are obeyed, if all the little rituals are performed, the unpleasant thoughts will vanish from the mind. Unfortunately this rarely happens, or if it does, the disappearance is quite temporary.

You experience your obsessions as *intrusive*. It's as if you feel bombarded by your mind, and you try *to escape from your mind* by neutralizing, avoiding situations that lead to obsessions, or even by yelling at yourself to stop thinking these disturbing, bizarre, and—you may think—dangerous thoughts. The usual reaction to obsessive thoughts is wanting to halt them. When Susan came to see me, her first question was, "Can you help me get rid of these thoughts?" To her, the thoughts were the problem—if she could just stop herself from having them, she'd be fine. She wouldn't need to resort to compulsive behavior to address them. I told her from the beginning that it wasn't my job to get rid of her obsessive thoughts. Her urge to get rid of them, I explained, was more the problem than the solution. Later in this chapter we'll see how learning to accept one's obsessive thoughts instead of battling against them is the key to freeing oneself from their tyranny.

HOW SERIOUS IS OCD?

About 2.5 percent of us have OCD at some time, with about four million Americans suffering from OCD at any one time. Approximately 80 percent of people with OCD become depressed. Anxiety disorders are also common with OCD—especially simple phobias and panic. Most people develop OCD during their late adolescence or early adulthood—although there are many children who have OCD. The course of the problem is often gradual—with increases and decreases in OCD occurring across the lifespan. However, about one in seven people with OCD will have progressive deterioration, becoming worse off over time.

The most common rituals are checking and cleaning (53 percent and 50 percent respectively)—36 percent of people with OCD have counting rituals, 31 percent need to confess, 28 percent have symmetry rituals, 18 percent hoard, and 19 percent are purely obsessional (pure thoughts). Multiple rituals are reported by 48 percent of people with OCD, while 60 percent report multiple obsessions.

For some people, mild obsessions are just a nuisance. One patient of mine was into little counting rituals: he would count his steps on the sidewalk, the number of cars passing by, the number of utensils on a table. Another needed to line up all the objects and furnishings in her home at right angles. Still another had a tendency to hoard large stores of food items. Such compulsions can be somewhat stressful to live with and occasionally annoying to others, but they are not necessarily incapacitating. However, I had one patient who was so overwhelmed by the need to count every angle he saw when he left his house that he couldn't get more than a few feet beyond the doorway. He became housebound and eventually had to be hospitalized. Another was so attached to certain eating rituals that from sheer embarrassment she could not eat in front of other people. Still another spent hours bathing and showering. All these created serious life issues. Not surprisingly, a good percentage of sufferers experience conflict with their intimate partners. Their obsessions and compulsions impinge on a couple's life together and produce stress and conflict.

WHERE DOES OCD COME FROM?

There is a significant genetic predisposition toward obsessive-compulsive disorder. Identical twins are four times more likely than fraternal twins to resemble each other in OCD, pointing to the genetic component. There is also an increased likelihood of birth abnormalities, head trauma, epilepsy, encephalitis, meningitis, and Syndenham's chorea (due to rheumatic fever), and a higher frequency of neurological "soft signs." Children with OCD have a higher rate of subcortical injury and higher levels of the thyroid-stimulating hormone (TSH).

Parents of obsessive-compulsive adolescents tend to be more perfectionistic than other parents are, often emphasizing responsibility issues. Moreover, OCD may be preceded by childhood experiences where the child either caused harm or believed that his or her thoughts preceded harm. This may contribute to the belief later that thoughts need to be controlled lest they cause negative consequences. The OCD symptoms may be increased by heightened stress.

As with other anxiety disorders, OCD has its source in evolutionary history—that is, it's linked to primitive adaptive behaviors. Even today, such behaviors may have some positive value: washing can reduce contamination; careful checking helps detect critical mistakes; hoarding instincts may be useful in planning for lean times. However in most OCD sufferers, these qualities are so *over*developed that their value is overshadowed by the inconvenience they cause. It's more useful to think of the disorder as simply an overdeveloped capacity to detect threats in the environment, rather than as a character flaw.

Animals will sometimes perform repetitive and apparently pointless rituals, but not out of any kind of mind state that we can associate with OCD. The reason for our uniqueness in this respect probably has to do with what I described in Chapter 2 as our theory of mind. Through language and conceptual thinking, we humans have developed the ability to picture what others are thinking. This also means we can reflect on our own thinking, evaluating it according to our standards of what is "normal." This can easily lead to a belief that there's something wrong with our thinking; that it's weird, neurotic, or messed up, with the accompanying urge to suppress or control it. Our theory of mind makes many things possible for us—including civilization—but it can end up convincing us (quite unreasonably) that we're going nuts. People with OCD often make these sorts of judgments about their own thinking. They see their thoughts as bad, shameful, or crazy. They think that there is a right way for their mind to operate—free of unwanted thoughts and urges. This is one of the core beliefs that must be challenged if we are to escape the tyranny that OCD imposes.

HOW DO OBSESSIVE-COMPULSIVES THINK?

People who suffer from OCD have certain characteristic ways of evaluating their own obsessive thoughts. These often take the form of false beliefs that not only distort reality, but strengthen the obsessions. Here are some of those false beliefs and how the mind typically defends them:

- *My thoughts are abnormal.* The things that go through my head are totally weird. Other people don't have thoughts like this. There must be something wrong with me.

- *My thoughts are dangerous.* Imagining a certain reality could make it come true. If I can't control or eliminate the images in my mind, there will be terrible consequences. The more I think about bad things happening, the more likely it is that they'll happen.

- *I can control my thoughts.* If I keep bad thoughts from entering my mind, they can't exert power over me. I can influence the kind of thoughts I have through effort and will power. Giving my thoughts free rein is too dangerous to be an option.

- *I need to be perfect.* It's not tolerable when things don't go exactly as I need them to. The slightest mistake can set off a chain reaction in which everything will unravel. I must maintain vigilance at all times.

- *I am totally responsible.* It's my fault that these thoughts have arisen; I need to take responsibility for them so that nothing bad will happen. That means doing everything I can to keep them from getting out of control.

- *I must have certainty.* I can't tolerate not knowing things for sure. Uncertainty means an inability to control. If I am to feel comfortable, all dangers must be identified and all risks eliminated.

Even though you are trying to suppress and neutralize your thoughts, you need to understand obsessive thoughts cannot be *stopped*. Your attempt to suppress or control them is driven by the belief that you cannot stand to think about anything that would be uncomfortable or terrifying in real life. You fear that your thoughts will lead to action (*I will lose control and act out*) or that your thoughts predict reality (*If I think I can be contaminated, I will be contaminated*)—what we call thought-action fusion. You're unable to see your thoughts as just thoughts. Although they pose no threat to you whatsoever, your mind confuses their presence with real danger. Thus your inability to control your thoughts seems terrifying. People use all sorts of techniques to try to eliminate unwanted thoughts: they distract themselves with other thoughts; they seek reassurance from others; they yell "Stop!" at themselves, they lacerate themselves with self-criticism; they abuse or restrain themselves physically (i.e., by slapping or pinching themselves); they try forcing themselves to be rational. None of these thought-control techniques work. Continuing to apply them, however—especially the constant trying and failing—merely strengthens the belief that one is being victimized by one's thoughts. Once bad thoughts appear, the ball game, so to speak, is over.

The great secret is that obsessive-compulsive individuals are no different from other people when it comes to the nature of their thoughts. We all have weird or crazy or disgusting thoughts and fantasies. In one study, 90 percent of people without OCD had weird thoughts. It is simply the way the mind works—just as our dreams come to us unbidden. Our minds are very imaginative. People with OCD, however, have a different view of the *significance* of their thoughts and fantasies. They tend to dwell on them, to treat them as ominous. They believe that having them can lead to moral depravity, loss of control, mistakes, or other dire consequences. They usually develop an inflated sense of responsibility for their thoughts, feeling the need to do everything possible to keep them from generating harm. In short, this anxiety disorder—like many of the others—is really anxiety over what goes on inside the mind; it is a fear of one's own thoughts and feelings. So-called normal people may have the same thoughts and feelings, but they treat them as mere background noise. In contrast, OCD sufferers believe that their thoughts and feelings have absolute power to destroy their well-being.

Furthermore, people with OCD are similar to many people with other anxiety disorders in that they fear their negative emotions—they believe these feelings will go out of control, overwhelm them, cause undue harm, and continue indefinitely. This fear of emotions—such as the fear that you will lose control of your anger and harm someone—leads you to notice them, dwell on them, and try to avoid them

Sam was a typical OCD patient of mine. He and his wife had some issues in their relationship that brought out tension between them. All these issues were pretty normal in the context of typical married life, and when they came up Sam and his wife would exchange words and become angry—also pretty normal. Each time this happened, Sam became terrified that his anger would go out of control. He was sure that if he didn't control the hostile thoughts in his mind he would become violent. He would think, *I'm so mad, I'd like to kill her*—and then be horrified by the thought. He had never been violent toward anyone in his life, but he couldn't shake the fear. It made him more anxious and self-critical; he would try and neutralize the feeling by reassuring himself that he was a good husband, by staunchly defending his own conduct, by scrupulously trying to eliminate the slightest hint of anger from his voice—just to prove to himself that he wasn't really angry. It didn't work. He just got more and more angry, which naturally made him more and more anxious. No matter how hard he tried to have only "good" thoughts, the unwanted hostile ones continued to invade his mind, keeping him in a more-or-less constant state of terror. If only he could stop these awful thoughts from arising, he felt, he'd be fine, and the issues in his marriage could work themselves out.

What Sam didn't understand until later was that any attempt at thought control actually *maintains the fear of your own thoughts*. When you tell yourself not to think about something, it generally produces the opposite result. If you tell yourself not to think of a white bear, what happens? Of course—you immediately think of a white bear. Similarly, when you demand of yourself that you *not* think a certain kind of thought—for example, a hostile fantasy or a sexual image that disturbs you—the very urgency you put into this demand virtually guarantees that it will pop up in your mind. That's the way our minds work—they're designed to make us think about anything important or urgent—especially anything threatening. So when the unwanted thought recurs—as it inevitably does—our failure to suppress it reinforces our feeling that we lack control. This in turn increases our anxiety, and in response to that, we redouble our effort to expunge the "bad" thought from our consciousness. This is the very essence of a vicious circle—a thought chasing its own tail endlessly, with no escape or relief.

Is there a way out of this dilemma? There is—through the *opposite* of thought control. There are techniques for learning to actually *release* control of your thoughts—even to invite unwelcome thoughts to flood your mind—that can change the whole dynamic of OCD. By exposing yourself gradually to the sources of your anxiety you can learn to embrace them with equanimity and dramatically lessen your fear around them.

We will explore some of these techniques a bit later in the chapter.

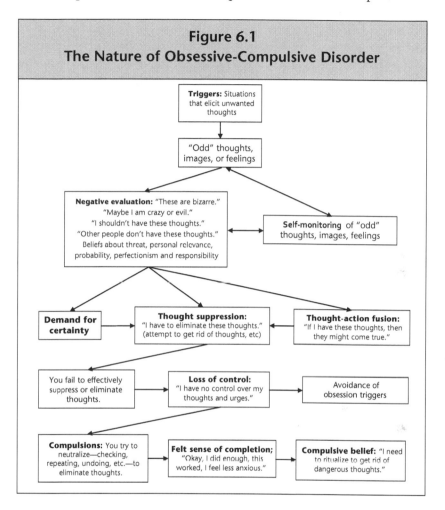

Figure 6.1
The Nature of Obsessive-Compulsive Disorder

Triggers: Situations that elicit unwanted thoughts

"Odd" thoughts, images, or feelings

Negative evaluation: "These are bizarre." "Maybe I am crazy or evil." "I shouldn't have these thoughts." "Other people don't have these thoughts." Beliefs about threat, personal relevance, probability, perfectionism and responsibility

Self-monitoring of "odd" thoughts, images, feelings

Demand for certainty

Thought suppression: "I have to eliminate these thoughts." (attempt to get rid of thoughts, etc)

Thought-action fusion: "If I have these thoughts, then they might come true."

You fail to effectively suppress or eliminate thoughts.

Loss of control: "I have no control over my thoughts and urges."

Avoidance of obsession triggers

Compulsions: You try to neutralize—checking, repeating, undoing, etc.—to eliminate thoughts.

Felt sense of completion; "Okay, I did enough, this worked, I feel less anxious."

Compulsive belief: "I need to ritualize to get rid of dangerous thoughts."

HOW DOES YOUR OCD MAKE SENSE?

How does obsessive-compulsive disorder develop and how is it maintained? Each step in this model represents something that you can change. Knowing the game can empower you in reversing this troubling problem.

THE OCD RULE BOOK

People with OCD follow a set of rules that guides them to monitor their thoughts, evaluate them in the most negative way possible, and use self-control techniques that increase their obsessive tendencies. Examine the rule book below and see if any of this fits your experience.

1. *Treat your thoughts and feelings as uniquely odd.* People with OCD have thoughts and images that seem odd or bizarre. Examples include thoughts that you might say or do something inappropriate (*I might start screaming at a party*), violent (*I could imagine strangling her*), or bizarre (*Maybe I am possessed by Satan*). The interesting thing is that 90 percent of the general public who do not have OCD also have the same kinds of thoughts and images. The difference is that the person with OCD believes that these are very odd and bizarre.

2. *Monitor your thoughts and feelings—make sure you catch every one of them.* Now that you notice that you have these odd and bizarre thoughts and images, you will search your mind for them. This self-consciousness about your thoughts and images—mind monitoring—is very common in all anxiety disorders, but especially so with OCD. If you have OCD, then you scan your mind and feelings for any sign of anything out of the ordinary. This makes you far more likely to pay attention to these thoughts and give them greater importance than they really deserve. When you notice them, you focus and dwell on them.

3. *Examine the content of your intrusive obsessions.* Your obsessions have important content for you—for example, fears of making a mistake, leaving things undone, or contaminating yourself. Write out the specific content of these obsessions. What predictions do your obsessions lead to? *I predict I will go crazy if I allow myself to have these thoughts,* or *I will get infected by deadly bacteria if I touch this paper.*

4. *Evaluate your thoughts as bizarre, evil, crazy, or dangerous.* For example, you can say to yourself, *These are bizarre, Maybe I am crazy or evil, I shouldn't have these thoughts,* and *Other people don't have these thoughts.* Because you feel ashamed

about your bizarre thoughts, you do not share these with your friends. You feel all alone: *No one else ever has strange thoughts or images.* Moreover, you may identify yourself—your personal worth—with having these thoughts and images: *If I weren't so evil I wouldn't have these thoughts.* One man had images of Christ having sex and thought this meant he was evil and would be punished by God. He realized that this was irrational, but he said he couldn't stand the fact that he had these thoughts.

5. **Assume your thoughts will lead to action or your thoughts are the same thing as reality.** This is called thought-action fusion. You can say, *If I have these thoughts, then they might come true.* Jack Rachman at the University of British Columbia has found that people with OCD often believe that their thoughts and images are predictive of reality—*If I have a violent thought then I will become violent.* As a result of this belief that thoughts become reality, you become desperately motivated to completely eliminate these thoughts.

6. **Try to suppress all unwanted thoughts.** You can say to yourself, *I have to eliminate these thoughts.* Given the belief that these bizarre thoughts are a sign of something defective and shameful, you try to get rid of them—sometimes telling yourself to *stop having these thoughts* or *try not to think of this.* Although this may momentarily bring some relief, the thoughts return—sometimes even more intensely.

7. **If you can't suppress or eliminate these thoughts then it's a bad sign for you.** When you fail to suppress the thoughts and images, you begin to notice them coming back, sometimes stronger, confirming your belief that these thoughts may be inescapable. Because you believe that you need to control your thoughts—rather than simply accept them—you think that failing to suppress means that things are worse than you anticipated.

8. **Assume that the return of these thoughts means you have lost all control.** You can say to yourself, *I have no control,* or, even better, *I am losing my mind.* You begin to feel more anxious and depressed and search for some way to eliminate these unwanted thoughts and images. This will, of course, fail.

9. *Keep trying to neutralize.* You can try to use checking, repeating, undoing, and praying to eliminate thoughts and unwanted images. As you engage in these neutralization rituals or behaviors, your anxiety may temporarily decrease. This is how your compulsions are reinforced.

10. *Keep neutralizing until you feel a sense of completion.* You may continue your compulsive behavior until a point where you feel, *Okay, I did enough, this worked, I feel less anxious.* This felt sense becomes the rule for how long compulsions will continue.

11. *Reinforce your compulsive belief that you need to ritualize to get rid of dangerous thoughts.* Since your compulsions have temporarily reduced your anxiety, you now have confirmed your belief that compulsions are the only thing that will work to neutralize your obsessions. This increases the likelihood that you will obsess and use compulsions in the future.

12. *Avoid any situations that trigger your obsessions.* Because certain situations or people may be associated with your obsessions, you may find yourself avoiding many experiences. For example, you may avoid doing your bills because you have checking rituals, or you may avoid washing because of elaborate bathing rituals, or you may avoid certain movies because they might elicit thoughts and images that disturb you.

We can now formalize your OCD Rule Book.

Table 6.1
The OCD Rule Book

1. My thoughts are odd.

2. They represent something awful or undesirable about me.

3. I shouldn't have these thoughts.

4. I need to pay attention to these thoughts—I should monitor them.

5. I have to obey my obsessions.

6. If I allow myself to have these thoughts, I could lose control.

7. I need to suppress these thoughts.

8. If I notice that I have these thoughts, I have a responsibility to do something about them.

9. If I can't completely suppress these thoughts, I am losing control.

10. I need to neutralize these thoughts—distract myself, do something.

11. I can stop neutralizing when I feel it's okay.

12. The only way to reduce my anxiety is to neutralize or ritualize.

13. I should avoid situations where I feel obsessive or have the urge to neutralize.

OVERCOMING OBSESSIVE-COMPULSIVE DISORDER

Though its symptoms often seem deeply ingrained in the personality of the sufferer, OCD is no less susceptible to treatment than any other anxiety disorder. The main steps in treatment are the ones we've already used in the last few chapters:

1. Identify your fears.
2. Identify your safety/avoidance behaviors.
3. Build your motivation to change.
4. Change your relationship to the obsession.
5. Construct a fear hierarchy.
6. Evaluate the rationality of your fear.

7. Image-test your fear.
8. Practice real-life exposure.
9. Commit to a long-term strategy.

Again, let's take these steps one at a time.

1. Identify Your Fears

People with OCD usually have little trouble identifying their fears. They are usually pretty insistent, intruding on the life of the sufferer with great impact. Any anxiety pattern that is a) built around unwanted thoughts appearing in your mind, which then b) demands some sort of strange or aberrant behavior to keep at bay (i.e., your obsessions and compulsions, respectively) is apt to be classified as OCD. If you have any doubt as to whether you belong in this category, you might want to fill out well-known Maudsley Obsessional-Compulsive Inventory test (see Appendix G).

It's useful to write down your own list of obsessions. Start with the basic fear (i.e., fear of contamination, making mistakes, lack of order, etc.), and then write out the predictions that underlie the obsessions. For example: *If I allow myself to have sexual fantasies, I'll get in trouble,* or *I'll be infected by deadly bacteria if I touch a newspaper someone else has read.* Look especially for thought-action fusion—the belief that an image in the mind is predictive of reality. *If I harbor violent thoughts, I'm going to do something violent.* Include any evaluations you make of your own thoughts: *I feel horribly ashamed, This is totally bizarre,* or *I'm hopelessly evil.* Finally, add a detailed rundown of your compulsions: what rituals you perform to get rid of dangerous thoughts, the things you avoid, any overwhelming urges you have that make life awkward for you. It's important to start with an accurate picture of what your OCD looks like and what place it occupies in your life. This will help you develop a realistic and effective treatment program.

2. Identify Your Safety/Avoidance Behaviors

This part isn't a great mystery. With OCD, your symptoms pretty much *are* your safety and avoidance behaviors. Compulsions—the things you do to keep your anxieties at bay—are basically safety behaviors. They're the things you think will protect you from your fears, like touching all the parking meters along the sidewalk or stacking everything in your drawers in neat rows. To another person, these safety and avoidance behaviors might look strange, but for the OCD sufferer, they are the only way to experience any sense of safety at all. Susan, whom I mentioned at the beginning of the chapter, would refuse physical contact with other people, objects outside her home, and even surfaces in her apartment that hadn't been recently scrubbed. Dan, another patient, had a fear he might become violent around a baby, so if a baby was present he would leave the room. Try to notice any people, places, or things that you avoid because of your OCD. For example, a patient who feared he might be possessed by the devil avoided horror movies, another man who feared radiation avoided watches, and someone else who feared contamination avoided traveling too far from home lest he need to use a public restroom. Other safety behaviors may be rigid ways that you feel you need to do things—for example, using paper towels to handle objects or washing in certain ways. You may think you need to continue a ritual until it feels right.

Add your specific safety and avoidance behaviors to your master list of fears. You can group them under general headings like "fear of contamination" or "fear of chaos." Be sure and note *how* you avoid things, as well as what you avoid (for example, do you contrive to get other people to do certain things for you?) The more detail you can give to these behaviors, the more fleshed-out and useful your master list will be in implementing your treatment plan.

Table 6.2 What I Avoid Because of My OCD
What I Avoid Because of My OCD:
1.
2.
3.
4.

3. Build your motivation to change

The key to overcoming your OCD will be exposure—both to the mental images you find disturbing and to the real-life situations that make you uncomfortable. Instead of continuing to avoid these images and situations, you'll expose yourself to them deliberately. You'll refrain from the neutralizing effect of acting out your compulsions and instead allow the world to engulf you in all its scary, disorderly, repellent variety. In the short run, this probably won't be pleasant. You'll undoubtedly feel more, rather than less anxious the first time you decide to confront your obsessions. You've built up a lifelong habit of obedience to the fear-driven messages in your own mind—worshiping, as it were, at the altar of fear. Changing that habit is bound to make you uncomfortable. It will touch you in your most anxious places. It will probably seem less like escaping prison than like walking straight into the mouth of the beast.

On the other hand, acknowledge the benefits as well as the costs. It will mean admitting the downside of what you've been doing up to now. I had a patient, Bill, who was reluctant to embark on the treatment I'd outlined until he drew up a list of the benefits to be gained and took a good, hard look at it. It looked like this:

Table 6.3 Costs and Benefits of Overcoming OCD by Using Exposure	
Costs	**Benefits**
I'll feel more anxious. I don't want to do it.	I might become less obsessive.
Maybe things will get worse.	I can use my apartment without having to sanitize it.
I'll feel disgusted and contaminated.	I won't feel out of control. I can socialize with people.

Bill was actually a little shocked to see all these things written down. He'd been kind of kidding himself that his OCD was manageable, that it wasn't a problem worth getting all worked up over. Fortunately he got some good input and a pledge of support from his wife. After talking it over with me, he decided the benefits of the treatment outweighed the costs and that he would go for it.

Table 6.4 Costs and Benefits of Overcoming OCD by Using Exposure	
Costs	**Benefits**

4. Change Your Relationship to Your Obsessions

Prove That Thought Suppression Does Not Work

As I mentioned earlier, any attempts to suppress your thoughts only give them more power. However, you may still believe that you cannot allow yourself to have these thoughts and that suppression will work. Carry out this experiment. Try not to think of any white bears over the next 15 minutes. If you think about a white bear, raise your hand. You will probably find that you cannot get the white bears out of your head. Thought suppression will not work. So, it may be time to give up doing this.

Prove That Thoughts Cannot Change Reality

As I have said before, a major part of OCD is thought-action fusion—the belief that if you have a thought it will change reality. For example, you might have the thought that something bad will happen to a loved one, so you try to suppress the thought or you try to neutralize it by praying. The fact is that thoughts do not change reality. There are a number of ways of showing that thought-action fusion is false. I will often demonstrate this with patients by saying over and over in the session, "I want to have a heart attack right now" or "I want Satan to possess me right now." I can ask you to use "the power of your thinking" to make a book rise in my office or to make the Yankees lose by twenty runs. Or I can ask you to repeat over and over, "I want to go insane" or "I want to be possessed by Satan." Once you realize that thoughts do not change reality, you are on your way to unraveling your OCD.

Allow Your Mind to Drift

You can try not to *monitor or control your thoughts*. You can practice allowing your mind to drift away from obsessions when they occur. For example, you can allow your mind to refocus on various objects in the room by counting and describing the different shapes and colors. As you demonstrate to yourself that you can ignore these thoughts, your fear of these obsessions will diminish.

Although thought drifting and distraction can be temporarily helpful—in fact, you may have been doing this already—we find that direct prolonged exposure to your feared obsessions is more powerful. This is because you will learn that you can tolerate these obsessions until they become boring.

Modify Your Image of Your Obsession

What would your obsession or urge *look like* if you made it into a visual image? Susan described her visual image as a large, menacing dark cloud that covered her and smothered her. I asked her to try to imagine it as a very small puddle on the floor. This felt much less threatening. Then I asked her to imagine the obsession or urge as a short, clown-like character who is sitting in the chair in my office, with his tiny legs hanging over the side. I suggested that he had a small, squeaky voice (which I imitated). This was a different way of experiencing the obsession. Rather than fearing her thought or her urge, she could laugh at it. Susan's homework assignment was to think of the clown when she had the urge to check. This made the urge to check seem a little silly.

Change Your Relationship to the Obsession

Your current relationship to your obsession is one of you as the victim and the obsession as your persecutor. You feel that you are battling with your obsession and that you have to get rid of him. This struggle only makes your obsession stronger and more frightening. But you do not have to get rid of the obsession. Think of the obsession as a visitor to your party—there are a lot of people there. He is one of them. You think he's a bit weird, but you realize that he has a right to be at the party. You have decided that you are not going to get into any arguments with him, but you will just let him be. He's there, but you are not angry with him, you are simply polite. He can accompany you as you go through the day, but you don't follow his orders.

Sing Your Obsession

When you have an obsession (e.g., *I am contaminated*) it feels frightening and overwhelming at times. To take away the power of your obsession you can practice having the obsession in a different way. For example, the obsession, *I am contaminated* can become words in a song. Jenny practiced singing softly, "I am contaminated," which helped take away the power of the obsession. It was hard to feel intimidated by a song.

Float Your Obsession

Rather than trying to control your obsession, you can stand back and observe it. Think of your obsession as a leaf floating along the water, while the water flows very slowly and the sun is reflected in the water. Your obsession is not something you need to control or judge; it simply *is*. And it passes by you and floats away. If you wait long enough another obsession will float by and float away. Obsessions come and go.

Take Care of Your Obsession

This is one of my favorite metaphors for dealing with obsessions. I ask you to imagine that an obsession is a lonely character with no friends. Everyone is yelling at him to stop—and that's the only attention he can get. Now that you are using your cognitive techniques your obsession is feeling he will be alone. Take a look at the story I wrote printed in the following box and think of your obsession as the character who shows up for an appointment—unannounced.

On My Mind

I was sitting in my office, worrying about my taxes, when I heard yelling coming from the waiting room. This surprised me because no one had an appointment. I opened the door and there was a very short man, with a wrinkled torn suit, his hair rising wildly in the air.

"I've got to see you. Right now. It's an emergency."

"But you don't have an appointment and . . . "

"I don't need an appointment, do I? If I'm here, why can't I see you right now?"

Filled with doubt and without any ready-made answers to this plausible question—and even more curious than I was disturbed—I said, "What's on your mind?"

"That's exactly it. Exactly. I knew you were the right person for me. I knew you'd understand."

"Understand what?"

"Something absolutely needs to be done—and done soon. I can't wait anymore."

"Done about what?"

"What's on my mind."

I thought, *Is one of my friends playing a joke on me? Is this "Who's on First?"*

"Who are you?" I gently and cautiously inquired.

"Why? Don't you recognize me? No—how could you? I'm in deep trouble."

"Have I met you before?"

"Perhaps yes, perhaps no. Maybe a thousand times or a thousand, thousand times."

"I don't recognize you."

"Ah. That's exactly the problem. Okay—I may as well tell you. I'm an intrusive thought. Yes, I know it sounds incredible. You're probably thinking, *I must be crazy to be talking with him.* But yes, I'm *real*. And I'm *here*!" For a moment he seemed happier but then looked down forlornly.

"You 'think' you're an intrusive thought. But you look like someone I might see walking outside."

"Think? Of course I think. I think, *therefore I am.*" He began laughing. And then he began to cough. Louder, gasping for air. "I don't have much time left."

"Look," he went on, wheezing. He sat down on the chair, his short legs dangling over the sides. "I used to be someone *important*. People would pay attention to me. They would analyze me. If I went off on a wild tirade, people would *interpret* me. Like I was the Sphinx. I loved it. 'What does it really *mean*?' Hours lying on the couch trying to understand me. Writing me down, tracing my history. 'Do you remember the first time you had this thought?' Ah, those were the days. Real class. Real sophistication. *Interpretations.* 'What does this remind you of?' I loved it."

"It sounds like those were wonderful times for you," I tried to empathize.

"Yes, people took me seriously. I was always busy. No one could get an appointment. I mean I could be *anywhere*—New York, Vienna, Beverly Hills—and I would pop up and people—I mean *educated people*—people with real medical degrees—would stand up and say, 'There he is! Again!'"

"Did it go to your head?" I gritted my teeth after saying this. So insensitive.

"What do you think?" he replied, somewhat contemptuously but sadly. Like he was lost in a reverie of a better time—one gone forever.

"I traveled in the best of circles. I didn't get any sleep—which, when you come to think about it, is the point. Yes, always on. Twenty-four seven."

"Then what happened?"

"Well, at first—back in the old days when I was cooking— at first someone thought, 'Let's get rid of him *completely.*' I loved that. What an *invitation.* To try to get rid of me completely." He began laughing and his cough got worse. There were tears in his eyes as he recalled those days. "Get rid of me. Hah! They began shouting at me. Stop. *Stop thinking!* It never worked—so they shouted more. All day shouting at me. It's the most attention I ever got."

"Then what happened?"

"Well, after a long time people began realizing that the shouting was making things worse. After all, you had to pay attention to me—and take me seriously—to shout at me. I never went away. I kept popping up. Then one day someone approached me—totally cool, level-headed—and said, 'Why should I take you seriously?' This guy with a bowtie—he took out a pad of paper and said, 'Let's test you out.' All day—every day—it seemed I was being tested. They barraged me with logic, asking me, 'What's the evidence?' They told me to go out and test out my predictions. It was exhausting."

"Then what happened?"

"Well, it was like being humiliated every day. None of my predictions held up. And, can you imagine, telling me, an intrusive thought, 'You're not really rational.' Well, you can imagine how the *other thoughts* felt about me."

"How did they feel?"

He looked down, a bit ashamed. "They wouldn't have anything to do with me."

And he looked at me, almost looking for reassurance that I wouldn't judge him. "That's when I began drinking."

"I imagine this must have been hard for you. At one time people were interpreting you, writing books about your *secret message*. And now you are feeling humiliated. How terrible."

"Oh, it get's worse."

"How?"

"Well, one day someone just said. 'Okay. Let him hang out. But we'll get on anyway.' That's the day I saw this psychologist *just walk past me.* He said, 'If you want to go along, that's cool. But I'm getting on with things with or without you.'"

"I can't imagine anything more humiliating for you."

"Oh no. It gets even worse. Then one guy said, 'So you think you're so powerful. Let's see you do this. Stand in front of the mirror and just keep repeating yourself.'"

"What happened when you did that?"

"I began to disappear. I was simply an empty voice. I finally checked myself into a rehab center for intrusive thoughts."

"Wow. What an experience."

"But can you help me?"

I wasn't sure what he wanted. In fact the longer I spent with him the more I doubted that this was real. But I thought, *It's a nice sunny day in New York. He's a tourist—I don't know how long he's going to be in town.* "Let's take a cab to the Empire State Building," I replied.

He brightened up. His feet began kicking. "I've never seen it. Okay."

We went downstairs and caught a cab downtown. He began fidgeting. "Watch the traffic. It's dangerous. I'm scared." A smile came over his face when he saw I was getting nervous, clutching the door in the cab. When we got to the Empire State Building, I took him inside and paid the fee to go to the observation tower, and we got in the elevator. There was a family from Pittsburgh in the elevator. He looked at them and said loudly, "Are you sure this elevator is safe?" His energy was growing. This is what he needed. We got to the roof, and I walked out to the deck with him.

We were standing there, and I looked at him and said, "Close your eyes." He closed them. I could see this made him nervous. Must be his lack of control. I looked out over the sky over Manhattan. The clouds were drifting in the sunlight. "Open your eyes." I pointed toward the western sky. "Isn't this magnificent?" I said.

I heard him groan, and then he gave a deep sigh that grew fainter. He coughed. "I can't take it any . . . longer." His voice became softer. I looked around, but the deck was empty. I thought I saw a shadow, very small, creeping away. In the smallest voice, below even a whisper, I heard him sadly say, "Thanks for everything."

He was gone. I felt sad. He was simply a prankster, and no one cared anymore. I looked over the buildings and saw the clouds reflected in the windows. I felt lost in the sky and the reflections, and for a moment, I was at peace.

Written by Robert L. Leahy © Association for Advancement of Behavior Therapy 2005

As the vignette illustrates, you can develop an entirely different way of relating to an obsessive thought—thinking of it as a silly character who craves attention. I have used this vignette with many of my OCD patients and they love it. They now think of the intrusive thought as a character who accompanies them on their walks, when they are jogging, and when they are working. They can say "hello" to the thought, rather than get upset and try to suppress it. Accepting the unwelcome visitor makes you a Zen warrior with your thoughts.

Practice the Thought Rather Than Suppress It

If you are afraid of the thought *I could go crazy,* practice saying this thought 30 minutes each day. It's important that you do this slowly, concentrating on what you are saying. Don't allow yourself to get distracted—it's going to be hard to stay with your feared thought. Initially, your anxiety will go up and then it will gradually go down. You will find that you will not go crazy—in fact, you will get bored. This should prove to you that having a thought is not dangerous. Thought flooding makes your obsession boring. Initially, you will feel more anxious, but eventually you will get tired of it.

5. Construct a Fear Hierarchy

Working from your master list, rank your fearful thoughts, images, and impulses in order from least to most distressing. Assign to each a number from 0 to 10 that represents your subjective level of distress, or SUDS. In the last chapter on panic disorder, the ranking assigned to a fear depended not just on the situation itself, but on the panic or mental breakdown one anticipated in reaction to it. With OCD, the actual situation resumes center stage. The OCD sufferer's fear is stimulated by a particular set of real-world (albeit imagined) circumstances: contamination, scarcity, disorder, and so on. In some cases there may be a fear of one's own reactions to a situation (as in the case of Sam, who feared getting violent with his own wife), but the fear in this case is not of one's anxiety per se, but rather of the destructive *consequences* of one's reactions. (*If I become violent, I will hurt someone I love.*) Tune in to what lies at the heart of your OCD. What can't you bear to tolerate in the world? What situation is so threatening that you must go to compulsive extremes to avoid it? Have the answer firmly in mind before you assign a number to your specific fear.

Table 6.5 Hierarchy of Obsession	
Please list your feared thoughts, images, and impulses in order from least distressing to most distressing. In the last column write how upset each one makes you from zero (no distress) to ten (maximum distress).	
Thought/Image/Impulse/Fear	**Subjective Units of Distress (0–10)**
1. (Least Distressing)	
2.	
3.	
4.	
5.	
6.	
7.	
8.	
9.	
10. (Most Distressing)	

Table 6.6 Hierarchy of Anxiety-Provoking Situations		
Please rank the order of anxiety-provoking in order from least distressing to most distressing. Assign each a SUDS number, and in the last column, write "yes" if you normally avoid that situation and "no" if your actions are not influenced by your fears.		
Situation	Subjective Units of Distress (0–10)	Avoided (Y/N)
1. (Least Distressing)		
2.		
3.		
4.		
5.		
6.		
7.		
8.		
9.		
10. (Most Distressing)		

6. Evaluate the Rationality of Your Fear

Even though you may not be able to wipe out powerful obsessions or compulsions with reasoning, it's still helpful to conduct a calm and rational examination of your fears. You can do this as though you were someone else entirely. You can ask yourself, *How would a rational person— someone other than me—look at the situation?* Knowing the answer may give you the courage to push on a bit.

For example, would it make a difference if you knew that virtually 100 percent of people have thoughts like yours? Does it really seem *likely* that you are evil or insane? That out of all the many people in the world there is something uniquely wrong with *you?* Does it make sense to demand perfection of yourself when it cannot be asked of anyone else? I often have conversations on such topics with my OCD patients; in many cases it's useful for them just to hear another perspective, different from the one they have been wielding. For example, I discussed with Susan her belief that she would be contaminated if she touched something another person had touched. She realized it made no sense in the light of everything we know about how diseases are transmitted. Similarly, she understood that her fear of being possessed by Satan was irrational. The knowledge by itself didn't take away her fear, but it affected her willingness to try a course of treatment. And that treatment eventually put her in touch with a more rational outlook.

The question perhaps most important of all to consider rationally is this one: what would happen if you simply *accepted* your intrusive thoughts—like the therapist in the vignette above? What if you no longer tried to get rid of them by neutralizing them through compulsive behavior? What do you predict would actually happen? Most OCD sufferers have never seriously considered this question. Since they haven't, they have no reason to make any assumption about what would happen—even though the assumptions they in fact make (assumptions of ensuing disaster) are responsible for massive amounts of anxiety. Maybe it isn't necessary to make assumptions of ensuing disaster. Maybe such assumptions aren't really *true*. In fact, since other people have similar thoughts *without* developing OCD, and *without* disaster, it stands to reason that there may be a different way of treating those thoughts, another way of holding them in the mind that makes more sense. Just to be open to this possibility is an important first step on the path.

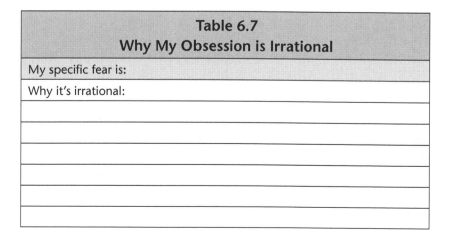

Table 6.7 Why My Obsession is Irrational
My specific fear is:
Why it's irrational:

7. Image-Test Your Fear

Just as in previous chapters, you can use your fear hierarchy to begin practicing imaginal exposure to your fear. I usually have patients start with something commonplace, something close to the bottom of the anxiety scale. For example, if your compulsiveness includes repeatedly checking the locks on your door, you could begin with the image of simply locking the door once and walking away. (It could just as easily be washing your hands just once or leaving some work detail undone.) Hold the image for ten minutes and see what happens. In all likelihood there will be an initial spike in your SUDS level (the number between 0 and 10 that you assign to your fear), followed by a gradual decrease as you become habituated to the fearful image. Eventually the image will probably fade into boredom—which is just what you want. This will begin to prove to the primitive part of your brain that the mere thought of an unlocked door is not dangerous. Another wrinkle you can add is, before you start, to record your prediction of what will happen over the course of the exercise. You might think, *I won't be able to tolerate it* or *My anxiety will shoot off the charts*. It will be interesting to see if that actually happens. If it doesn't, you'll have begun to dismantle your belief in the power of anxiety.

It always works best to move gradually toward images that are more and more distressing. For example, you may be obsessed by the notion that you will blurt out something inappropriate in front of other people (this is a commonplace obsession). Begin with the image of sitting home alone and blurting out something with no one around. That's not very scary. Move on to blurting out something in front of your spouse—that might be a little worse. Then in front of some close family or friends. Then a group of strangers at a party, and so on. Work your way up the hierarchy, practicing at each level. You might finally arrive at the worst thing you can contemplate—the thought of blurting out terrible profanities in church. See what *that* feels like. The remarkable thing is, you will probably be able to habituate to that image just as readily as you did to all the others.

Practice imaginal exposure sufficiently so that you're getting consistent results—that is, each time you do it, your anxiety drops off over a period of time. You can use either long-term or short-term periods of exposure. Generally the longer a successful exposure, the more effective it will be: 45 minutes of contemplating a frightening thought is not extreme. You can practice repeating the feared thought very, very slowly, as described earlier. It will very likely become very boring. On the other hand, more frequent short exposures—say ten minutes at a time—can also work. The idea is not necessarily to tax yourself, but to stick with it long enough for your anxiety level to subside during each exposure (say roughly to at least a 2 on the SUDS scale). When you've gotten to where this is routine, you're ready for the major challenge—applying the same technique to real-life situations.

8. Practice Real-Life Exposure

This is where you put your methods to the test—actually experiencing the situations that set off your obsessions, and responding differently. To a large extent, these exposures can be planned, so that they'll come at a pace you can handle. For example, when I was treating Susan for her fear of contamination, we began with the imaginal exposure of handling a dirty dollar bill. We then moved to direct exposure: Susan handled a real dollar bill for 30 minutes in my office, even getting so far as to rub it on her arms and face. At each stage we recorded her fear level and watched it gradually subside. In the next session she practiced rubbing her hands on the carpet in my office. Next she moved up the hierarchy by reaching into the wastebasket, sifting the trash there, and then not washing her hands for four hours. In between sessions she continued similar exercises at home. Before too long her anxiety level had decreased and her compulsions became far less insistent.

Ron was a compulsive cleaner, too, but he ran into a problem: he became convinced that using Windex would poison him. He realized this was unlikely, but couldn't shake off his fear. I brought some Windex to one of our sessions and, in front of Ron, sprayed it on my hands and rubbed it on my arms (it felt like after-shave lotion). He was startled but intrigued. A few minutes later I had him spray a small amount on his hand and leave it there. As he did, his anxiety level shot up. I asked him to leave the Windex on his hand while we talked about his other obsessions. By the end of the hour he had almost forgotten about the Windex, and it no longer seemed threatening. (I had checked out Windex pretty carefully beforehand to make sure it was nonlethal; in general, I don't recommend contact with cleaning products other than soap.) Let's say that your obsession is that you are going to say or do something inappropriate. Your hierarchy might begin with thinking, *I might say something inappropriate*. But your greatest fear is that if you are in church that you might say something inappropriate. So we would begin with your sitting at home alone thinking that you might say something inappropriate—and then move up the hierarchy over the next few weeks until you are in church, sitting and thinking that you might blurt out something inappropriate. You can practice repeating silently for 15 minutes the very thought you fear.

You can set up any number of real-life exposures on your own. The more planned sessions you put yourself through, the more prepared you'll be for the inevitable moments when your obsessions will break in uninvited. It's easy to set up a controlled situation: touching something you feel is dirty and then not washing or turning in a report *before* checking it thirty times over. But a controlled situation shouldn't be *too* easy. It has to be something that initially rouses your anxiety; the exposure has to feel like a real threat in order to do its work. Try to do some of these exposures every day, working them into your schedule whenever you can.

Opportunities for exposure also come up spontaneously, and it's good to respond to as many as possible. For example, the opportunity to confront contamination is almost constant: touching door handles, shaking hands, exchanging money, touching railings, and so on. Your planned exposure should include these spontaneous situations. Above all, don't wait till you feel ready. You'll never be altogether ready—which is exactly the point. You need to do the thing when you're feeling anxious about it—which means when you're *not* ready. Sooner or later you have to go through your anxiety to get past it.

This doesn't mean you can't be flexible. For example, if you find it too hard to ignore a compulsion altogether, then practice simply delaying it. If you can't stand the way the furniture in a room isn't quite lined up, try waiting 20 minutes before adjusting it—maybe even trying a little meditation during that interval. That should weaken the compulsion. When the 20 minutes have passed, see if you can go another 20 minutes. Consider that your compulsions are often quite rigid. The key to breaking them down may be through modifying them bit by bit, rather than trying to overcome them all at once. For example, if you're having a washing compulsion, interrupt the repeated washings by briefly doing something different—for instance making yourself a snack. Or try a different method of washing. Many people repeat their compulsions until they achieve a sense of completion. Therefore, try ending the compulsive ritual a bit before you feel this sense of completion. Getting used to imperfection can be an important step toward liberation.

Table 6.8 Exposure Record	
Date:	
What I exposed myself to:	
Duration: 20 Minutes	**Discomfort (0–10)**
Minutes: 1–2	
Minutes: 3–4	
Minutes: 5–6	
Minutes: 7–8	
Minutes: 9–10	
Minutes: 11–12	
Minutes: 13–14	
Minutes: 15–16	
Minutes: 17–18	
Minutes: 19–20	
Note: List your discomfort level in subjective units of distress (SUDS) where 0 represents no discomfort and 10 represents the greatest discomfort you can imagine.	

9. Commit to a Long-Term Strategy

Most people with OCD will probably never be entirely without obsessive thoughts or compulsions. That doesn't mean they can't be free from their power. The important thing is that your intrusive thoughts no longer severely prevent you from having a meaningful life. The key lies in acceptance—allowing the thoughts and compulsions to be there without attaching undue significance to them. As with all anxiety disorders, mastering OCD involves rewriting the rules that evolution and conditioning have instilled. From detect, catastrophize, control, and avoid, we move toward a new set of rules that actually works: evaluate, normalize, let go, and embrace. As long as these serve as guiding principles, the reappearance of obsessive-compulsive thoughts is not a problem; it merely signals that it's time for some periodic maintenance.

In short, you need to anticipate some relapse. Except that relapse isn't even the proper way to describe it. You simply have a tendency toward

OCD. Be aware of that tendency, and be prepared to deal with it when it emerges. You're more likely to experience OCD symptoms if you're under stress or depressed—but they may also arise for no apparent reason at all. Don't worry about the reasons. What matters is what you can do about it. All the exercises you've learned from this book can be dusted off and performed as often as needed. Exposure to, acceptance of, and detachment from one's compulsive urges—these should be your continual guides.

SUMMING UP YOUR NEW APPROACH TO OCD

We are ready now to sum up the various steps in dealing with your OCD. You will have to find for yourself which of these many techniques work best for you—and stick with your program because OCD will keep coming back at you. The exciting thing is that you can really make significant progress—but also keep in mind it won't be perfect progress.

Ask yourself, *Do most people believe these obsessions? Why not? What is the evidence for and against my obsession? What would I tell someone with a similar obsession?* Argue back at the obsession until you feel relatively confident that these thoughts are irrational. I have outlined in Table 6.9 the various thoughts and feelings that you might have if you have OCD and the interventions and techniques that you might use to help yourself. It will be valuable to do this under the supervision of an experienced cognitive-behavioral therapist. Keep in mind that reversing your current OCD does not mean you will never have these problems again—you might. However, if these techniques worked in reversing OCD, then they will very likely work again.

Table 6.9 How to Handle OCD	
Problem	**What to Do or Think**
You have "odd" thoughts and images.	Everyone has odd thoughts and images. This is normal. It means nothing about you.
Motivation to change	Examine the costs of having OCD—feeling anxious, worried, out of control, ashamed, impaired in work and relationships. Are you willing to tolerate some discomfort to change this? How will your life be better if you do change this?
You have negative evaluations of thoughts and images: • They are threatening. • They represent something awful about you. • You believe that there is a high probability of something bad happening. • You believe that you need perfect solutions.	These "odd" thoughts and images don't mean anything about you or the future. They are not threatening. People do not go crazy from these images or thoughts. They do not represent anything about you as evil or out of control. Look at all the evidence about how decent you are. Ironically, people who think that their obsessions indicate lack of control or lack of decency are overly conscientious. Thoughts do not predict that something bad will happen. Reality is not determined by your thoughts. There are no perfect solutions. You can aim for "good enough" or "just as good as."
You believe that you are responsible for eliminating any threat.	Inflated beliefs about responsibility place a burden on you. You are not responsible for eliminating any possibility of a negative—you are only responsible for acting as a reasonable person would act. How would a reasonable—non-OCD—person act?

You think you need to suppress all thoughts and images.	Suppression never works—the thoughts come back. You can actually practice repeating your worst obsessions—for example, "It's possible that I can become contaminated" or "It's possible that I could overlook something." Repeat this for 20 minutes each day—until you are bored.
You believe that you have no control.	You are basing this belief on the fact that you do not have total control over your thoughts and images. It's impossible—and unnecessary—to control thoughts and images. List all the behaviors and outcomes that you have control of each day. You will probably find out that you have a lot more control than you think.
Engaging in compulsions	Each time you practice a compulsion you reinforce your belief that you have to eliminate obsessions and that compulsions are the only alternative for you. Rather than practice compulsions you can delay engaging in a compulsion and you can practice exposing yourself to the things that make you obsess—and completely refrain from the compulsion.
You continue with a compulsion until you have a felt sense of completion.	You have been engaging in your compulsion until you felt that things were either done "completely" or that you felt a sense that you had done "enough." If you do engage in a compulsion, try to terminate it prior to a sense of completion—do things imperfectly.

Table 6.10
Rewrite Your OCD Rule Book

1. **Build your motivation.** Recognize how you will be better off without OCD. Your OCD has had a significant impact at times on your life. It keeps you from doing things other people easily do. It can interfere in your work, relationships, leisure time, and many other things. But to modify it you will have to do some things that are uncomfortable.

2. **Examine why your obsessions are irrational or too extreme.** What would most people think—since most people have the same thoughts that you do. Why aren't they obsessive-compulsive? Perhaps they accept their thoughts and get on with their lives.

3. **Examine your negative beliefs about intrusive thoughts.** Ask yourself if you really have to pay attention to thoughts, if thoughts really make you responsible, if thoughts will overwhelm you or change reality, or if you really need to suppress thoughts.

4. **Change your relationship to the thought.** Invite your thought in, observe your thought floating as a leaf on water, and take care of your thought as if it were a lonely person.

5. **Avoid self-monitoring thoughts.** You can practice allowing your mind to drift away from obsessions when they occur. For example, you can allow your mind to refocus on various objects in the room—by counting and describing the different shapes and colors. This shows you that you don't have to pay attention to your thought.

6. **Practice the thought rather than suppress it.** If you are afraid of the thought *I could go crazy*, then practice saying this thought 15 minutes each day. You will find that you will not go crazy—in fact, you will get bored. This should prove to you that having a thought is not dangerous.

7. **Eliminate compulsions.** Identify a trigger for your obsessions and compulsions. For example, if you are a compulsive hand washer, then the trigger might be having dirty hands. Put your hands in some dirt—for example, rub them on the floor or pick up some garbage in your basket. Get your hands dirty. Now, don't wash them for an hour. Tolerate the anxiety. If you are afraid of making a mistake, then practice making mistakes on papers and bills. See what happens. This is called exposure with response prevention.

8. *Delay compulsions.* If it is difficult to eliminate the compulsion initially, practice delaying doing it. When you notice your obsession, try to wait 20 minutes before you engage in the compulsion. This will weaken the desire to do the compulsion.

9. *Modify the compulsion.* Your compulsions may be quite rigid. Breaking them down can involve making modifications in them. For example, if you feel you need to repeat something over and over, interrupt the repetition—do something different in the middle or your repetitions. If you have washing rituals, try a different way of washing. Many people repeat their compulsions until they achieve a felt sense of completion. Try modifying this by terminating the compulsion before you feel the felt sense of completion.

10. *Plan relapse.* OCD will come and go in intensity. Even if you successfully reverse your OCD there is a good chance that thoughts and urges will return. Don't be alarmed. It simply means that you should once again implement the techniques that you have just learned.

OCD can feel debilitating to you. In addition, you may also feel ashamed and self-critical of your problem. Try to keep in mind that OCD is an ability that has evolved to protect us—it is just overdeveloped. You are not trying to harm anyone with OCD, and there is nothing immoral about it. Even though you may have suffered a long time, you can improve with the right kind of help.

Many of the exercises that I describe here may feel difficult to you— even impossible. That is part of OCD—the belief that giving up rituals or neutralization is impossible and that your anxiety will escalate and overwhelm you. You can practice your self-help gradually, always keeping in mind that you are not trying to eliminate obsessions, you are simply trying to reduce the impact that they have in controlling your life. Keep trying—because practicing a new way of relating to your obsessions can have a significant positive effect. And give yourself plenty of time.

CHAPTER 7

"Yeah, But What If . . . ?" Generalized Anxiety Disorder

WHAT IS GENERALIZED ANXIETY DISORDER?

Linda seems to worry all the time. She worries that her daughter Diane is having problems in school. Not that Diane isn't generally doing well, but she's been struggling recently with her math skills, and once or twice she has come home in tears after being teased by other kids. When Diane is late getting home, Linda begins to wonder if the school bus has had an accident. Linda's been divorced for four years, and Sam, her ex, is sometimes late with his support payments. She worries that he'll stop making payments and she won't be able to afford to stay in the house. She also worries about work: if she screws up she could get fired, and probably never find another job. Every time she gets sick she worries her health insurance won't cover the costs. The list of things to worry about seems endless. Nothing about her life seems safe or secure.

All this worrying is having an impact on Linda's health and well-being. When she goes to bed she has trouble falling asleep. She tosses and turns, or lies there tensely, listening to her heart beating. She tries her best to relax, but nothing works. She is sure the lack of sleep will make her unable to function at work the next day. Linda also has developed physical symptoms, including indigestion and frequent headaches. At times she feels short of breath or dizzy. The doctor finds nothing wrong with her. "It's mainly just tension," he says and offers her a prescription for tranquilizers or sleeping pills—but Linda doesn't want to start down that road. She feels she should be able to deal with her problems without medication. So far she hasn't figured out how.

When Linda thinks about her life, she realizes that nothing bad has really happened. Diane is a healthy, competent, cheerful child and does have friends at school. Linda knows she's much better off divorced from

Sam—and has no shortage of men friends. Her boss keeps praising her work, and recently offered her a new position with a raise. She has no real *reason* to worry so much. In fact, that's what her friends keep telling her. "You have a great life," they say. "Think positive." Or, "Just take your mind off it." Of course none of this helps; in fact, it can be rather annoying. *Don't they realize I'm* trying *to stop worrying?* she thinks. *Do they imagine I* want *to be like this?* One friend, much given to amateur psychologizing, has told her, "I think you're just trying to punish yourself for the failure of your marriage." This makes Linda furious—it implies she's *choosing* to worry out of guilt or self-pity. And yet a part of her has the nagging thought that maybe it's at least partly true. *Is there something I'm doing that I'm not aware of?* she thinks. *Could I be creating all this anxiety myself?*

The answer is yes and no. Linda is actually undergoing a fairly common though challenging problem known as generalized anxiety disorder, or GAD. Roughly 7 percent of us will experience it at some point, with females twice as likely as males to suffer from GAD. People with GAD worry about lots of things—or everything—not just one or two specific problems. They often exhibit related physical symptoms: indigestion, fatigue, aches and pains, muscle tension, frequent dizziness and disorientation. One study shows that 93 percent of those with GAD suffer simultaneously from other forms of psychological problems including the other anxiety disorders described in this book. Your chronic worry can result in nausea, irritable bowel syndrome, fatigue, aches and pains, difficulty concentrating, indecisiveness, and feelings of hopelessness. In fact, 25 percent of people who see a physician for symptoms related to a psychological problem have GAD. Your anxiety and your worry may lead you to smoke more, drink excessively, misuse drugs, binge eat, or lose sleep. Most worriers avoid doing the things that they really need to do—so, if you are a worrier, you should ask yourself what you are avoiding. You could be avoiding initiating contact with people, getting your work done, making important phone calls, asserting yourself, pursuing new opportunities at work or in your personal life, or in gaining new skills and education. Your worry keeps you frozen—since you are afraid of the future, you will underperform, underachieve, and undersocialize.

Because their tension and worry has worn them down over the years, they usually first seek out help for their *medical complaints*—often problems such as nausea, muscle aches, insomnia, and fatigue. In about three-fourths of the cases of GAD, their worry has preceded their depression—and their depression is often a chronic, low-level depression marked by pessimism, lack of confidence, and difficulty in enjoying things. GAD persists—if untreated. One year after being diagnosed (but not treated) 85 percent of people with GAD are still having significant problems.

Not infrequently GAD begins with worrying about one specific thing (in Linda's case it was her marriage) and then expands to take in a range of concerns. When the problem persists long enough, things can start to look pretty bleak. Depression can creep up so gradually an individual may not recognize its presence for a long time. But it's not hard to see how a worrying mind state that focuses on the negative—on what has gone and will go wrong—can be linked to depression, even though it's often hard to say which condition is the cause of the other.

People with GAD tend to wait a long time before seeking help. They dismiss their condition as mere everyday, run-of-the-mill fretting, the kind everyone does. Many people who finally seek treatment realize they have been suffering from GAD for decades. For many years GAD sufferers had little hope of effective treatment. Occasionally medication would be helpful, and in a small proportion of cases (around 20 percent), traditional psychotherapy would produce results. However with newer forms of cognitive-behavioral therapy, we now have a better understanding of how the worry syndrome works, and how patients can work to reverse its symptoms. The good news is that 75 percent of people with GAD can be significantly helped with newer forms of cognitive-behavioral therapy.

Linda was a good example of this. She'd gone through years of fruitless agonizing, either writing off her symptoms as an inevitable part of life, or blaming herself for their existence. Once she began treatment, we were able to identify her syndrome and begin to confront it. Although Linda's GAD was clearly a recognizable affliction rather than any kind of self-destructive urge, I was able to help her see that there were choices she could make that would lead her out of her dilemma. In particular, she was able to identify some of the irrational beliefs supporting her constant worrying. Once she did that, she could begin to surrender those beliefs and live a more normal life.

Whether or not you actually suffer from GAD depends on how much you worry and how severely it impacts your life. It's probably true that everybody worries some of the time—it's part of the human condition. In fact, when they "loosen" the diagnosis for GAD (including people with a shorter duration of worry), 24 percent of people have GAD. But when does it become a disorder? In general, if your worrying is truly chronic, something you can't turn off, something so constant that it keeps you from enjoying the good moments, chances are you fit the pattern. Another key is how much your worrying is impinging on your other activities. When it's keeping you from functioning at work or damaging your relationships with others, you probably have reason to consider yourself a GAD sufferer. In Appendix G, you'll find two diagnostic tools that may be of use. One is the Leahy Anxiety Checklist, and the other is the Penn State Worry Questionnaire. Completing these (and continuing to use them every week) may give you some sense of how your worrying syndrome measures up to the average, indicate whether it's something that could benefit from treatment, and provide a measure of your progress as you go along.

WHERE DOES GAD COME FROM?

I think back to a conversation I once had with a patient of mine, Dan, who'd been a worrier all his life. His worries hounded him day and night, and clearly made him miserable. At the same time, he put so much energy into worrying that I couldn't help but wonder what was driving it. So I asked him a few questions.

Here is the puzzle: "You are making thousands of predictions that don't come true. And now you are making the same prediction again? Why?"

Let's consider the following exchange between Dan and me—Dan is telling me that he has been a worrier all his life:

Bob: You are telling me that you've always been a worrier. What sort of things are you worrying about now?

Dan: A better question might be, "What don't I worry about?" I worry about offending people because I might have been rude. I worry about whether my work is up to par. I worry that I might lose my job, and I worry about whether I'll find the right woman to settle down with.

Bob: It sounds like a lot of things are on your mind. Let's take your worry about offending people. What makes you think that you might offend someone?

Dan: I don't know. Sometimes I get wrapped up in myself. I worry that I might not listen carefully enough to someone and come across as conceited.

Bob: Does this worry bother you?

Dan: Yeah. I think that I'm worrying all the time. I can't seem to get any control over it. I can be sitting at my desk at work and worry about whether I'll get a project done. Or I can be lying in bed and worry that I will never get to sleep.

Bob: Do you think that—perhaps on some level—you might think there is some advantage to all this worrying?

Dan: I know it sounds irrational, but I think it might help me avoid being surprised by something bad. Maybe if I worry, I'll catch it before it gets out of hand. Maybe I'll motivate myself to get things done.

Dan had put his finger on something basic to the psychology of worrying. To understand it, let's once again go back to the world of our distant ancestors living in the jungle or on the savanna. Danger was everywhere, often appearing suddenly—a predator leaping out from the undergrowth, an illness, a slip when climbing a tree or crossing a stream. As we have seen, many of our deepest fears are evolution's built-in responses to such dangers. But there were other kinds of dangers—more long-range, future-oriented ones. Food shortages in certain seasons. The possibility of animal attacks, not "now" but hours or days from now. As humanity evolved, detecting and responding to these kinds of danger became more and more important. It was useful to study patterns of animal movement, both to protect against predators and to ensure a supply of game. It was important to know what kinds of weather to expect in certain seasons, in order to gather plant food effectively. Storing fuel or food supplies, constructing shelters, making tools or clothing for future use—all these things required planning, which in turn involved thinking about the future. And that's exactly what people with GAD tend to do in excess. They're always thinking ahead, trying to anticipate what might go wrong, what might be a threat. That instinct undoubtedly kept many of our ancestors alive and enabled the human race to survive.

If it weren't for the capacity for worry it's unlikely that our primitive ancestors would have been able to do any farming. Imagine if you were to grow your crops—and not plan ahead, not save seed, not plow a field, not irrigate the land, if you could irrigate. Or imagine if our ancestors never saved anything—so they only lived from hand to mouth. It's precisely the capacity to worry—to plan, to think ahead, and to take steps before something terrible happened—that allowed our ancestors to advance at all. Civilization is built, partly, on the capacity to worry. That's why I often think of worriers as conscientious people.

In this context, of course, worry makes perfect sense. The worrier, however ineffectively, is simply trying to anticipate and avoid danger. But in this case the danger isn't falling out of a tree or being surprised

157

by a hungry crocodile—it's more about the future: How you will provide for a famine. What the social consequences of making a mistake will be. What you'll need to take with you if you're migrating. All these skills and abilities have to do with being able to use your imagination. Even more important, they require you to *pay attention* to what's in your imagination. For certain types of people, imagining a problem means that there *is* a problem, one that needs to be addressed. To worry is simply to prepare for the worst; it's the only way to avoid all the terrible things that could happen. This is a perfect description of the underlying attitude Dan had acknowledged to me—his belief in the *efficacy* of worrying. Worry was a tool and a strategy to avoid catastrophe.

Of course we know that in our own lives today, this mind state is *not* generally effective, but rather the reverse—it's paralyzing. That's because it's a poor and unrealistic way of dealing with risk management. Worry, after all, is really about risk—it's a tool for detecting and managing it. But if your ability to assess risks accurately is impaired, your cautious instincts won't do you much good. You'll overestimate some risks and probably miss others completely. If you treat all risks as equal, you'll probably end up locking yourself in the basement and wearing a rubber suit to protect against radiation. Or—a less extreme version—you'll end up like Linda, worrying all the time about practically everything. You'll be on risk overload, unable to deal with anything effectively.

From the perspective of evolutionary psychology, then, a worrying mindset makes sense—even if the context has changed significantly since hunter-gatherer days. But why do some people worry more than others? Why do some of us have a harder time evaluating risks accurately? We don't know all the answers. But we do know that there is a certain genetic predisposition to the disorder—according to one study, as much as a 38 percent causality. This doesn't mean you're doomed to be a chronic worrier. There are ways of altering your perspective so that your worry doesn't exert control over your life. But if you have a deep-seated tendency to worry—particularly if you've always been more or less that way—chances are you were born with a certain predisposition. It's good to recognize that, because the more clearly you see and accept it about yourself, the better you'll be able to deal with it.

There are other factors too, family history being chief among them. If your parents were divorced when you were young, your chances of developing GAD are approximately 70 percent higher. This probably helps explain why many worriers tend to obsess about the possibility of a relationship falling apart, a home being lost, or sudden financial insecurity. If your parents were "overprotective," you're also more likely to develop GAD. One of my patients, Priscilla, talked about how when she was a kid her mother hounded her constantly with warnings: "Don't cross the street alone." "Don't talk to strangers." "You can't go out in the sun without a hat." Reasonable cautions in many cases, but with Priscilla's mom it was extreme and unabating. Her mother also tended to obsess over other people's possible disapproval, to talk openly about financial worries, and to air her anxieties over her job—all this in the presence of a small child who couldn't possibly understand any of it. So in addition to her genetics, Priscilla had taken on Mom as a role model. By the time she grew up she had developed a habit of seeing the world as a vast jungle of potential disasters.

Recent events in your life can also aggravate a tendency toward GAD. Dave was a fairly even-keeled fellow all through high school, college, and beyond. He held down a good job, had an active social life, and seemed to manage things pretty well. Then he and Vicky got married and had a couple of children. Suddenly he felt a lot of new responsibility. At the same time he got a promotion at work with lots more expected of him. He began to worry. *What if I mess up on the job? What if I get fired? What if I can't support my family? What if I become such a slave to my work that I don't have time for my kids?* Soon he was developing all the symptoms of GAD: insomnia, tension, irritability, and a stomach ailment. Any major stresses or disruptions in one's life—divorce, sudden illness, a falling out with a partner, and so on—can trigger these symptoms, even in people with no previous history of anxiety.

In most cases of GAD, there's probably some combination of these factors. You may have inherited a tendency to worry, but also had experiences that exacerbated it. You may have had parents who were overprotective, or who projected their own worries palpably within the family. You may have experienced one or several traumas as a child that increased your feelings of insecurity. As you matured and took on more responsibility, you may have seen conscientiousness cross the line into intense worry—a sense of responsibility carried to extremes. It's interesting that about half of chronic worriers began their pattern during childhood or adolescence, while the other half started worrying as adults.

THE WORRIED MIND

As we've already mentioned, the main premise of the worrier is that things are uniformly dangerous. No risks can be tolerated. It is here, in the mind of the worrier, that the four rules of anxiety come into play: detect danger, catastrophize danger, control all the circumstances, and avoid discomfort. Sticking to this set of rules greatly interferes with one's ability to assess risks in a balanced and rational way. It ignores the fact that *everything* we do (or don't do) has a risk attached. Entering into a relationship carries the risk of it falling apart; having money carries the risk of losing it; and going to a party risks getting rejected. The worried mind tries to guard against these possibilities by identifying risks as soon as possible and collecting as much information as it can about their terrible consequences. This makes us reluctant to commit to any course of action wholeheartedly. Furthermore, the process never stops: the mind continues to collect more and more worrisome information. As worriers know, this tendency to always see the dark side tends to blot out any balanced assessment of the "real" pros and cons of a situation. Ironically, the research actually shows that 85 percent of the things people worry about have a neutral or positive outcome.

As a worrier, you ask yourself the following questions—all focused on danger, risk, and personal control:

- What is the risk of something bad happening?
- What information can I gather to tell me what my risk is?
- Am I getting this information *in time* to take action?
- Am I missing the important information?
- Are there precautions I can take to reduce risk?
- Will I be able to avoid the problem—*before it occurs*?

What are the consequences of continuing to worry all the time? There are, of course, plenty: chronic anxiety and depression, a lack of joy, reduced effectiveness at work, a restricted social life, more difficult relationships, poor sleep, and any number of stress-related physical ailments. Instead of the death one hopes to avoid by worrying, one dies thousands of small deaths daily. In return for one's supposed safety from catastrophe (a dubious safety at best), one misses out on the opportunity to live one's life to the fullest. Worriers have a hard time just staying in the present moment—they are living in a future world that actually seldom turns out as bad as they think it will. And, in fact, worriers worry that they worry too much. They think that they need to worry to avoid surprise, but they think they need to stop worrying because it's driving them mad.

There's also an interesting relationship between worry and your emotions. Notice that when you worry it's almost always in the form of language. You make some kind of statement to yourself about the future: *I could lose my job*, or *I'm sure that lump will turn out to be malignant*. When you make such statements you are thinking in *abstract terms*—language is essentially an abstraction of reality. You seldom worry in visual images—which tend to be more emotionally evocative for you. And when you think in abstract terms you are temporarily departing from your emotions; you're focusing on thoughts rather than feelings. In short, worry, in addition to being a strategy to fend off disaster, is also a way of blocking your emotions. In physiological terms, it activates the cortical part of your brain (the "rational" part), and blocks the amygdala (the "emotional" part). When your emotions are causing you discomfort, the rational activity of worrying is a sure-fire way to shut them out. You are essentially anesthetizing your unpleasant feelings.

The anesthetic, of course, is only temporary. Researchers have found that when people worry, their physical and emotional responses are suspended for a short time—but then bounce back as free-floating anxiety. In a sense, your anxious arousal incubates—it goes underground—for a short period of time. The original stimulus to anxiety is lost, while the anxiety itself continues, producing restlessness, tension, arousal—and the urge to seek out yet more "dangers" to worry about. Underneath it all is the assumption that you can't stand ever being unhappy, anxious, scared, or uncomfortable, that those feelings must be avoided at all costs. By succeeding (temporarily) in banishing them, you reinforce two very powerful beliefs: 1) that you can get rid of discomfort by worrying, and 2) that negative emotions cannot be tolerated. In fact your relationship to worry is similar to that of an alcoholic to drink: you need it to dull the pain. Only here the drug is *thinking* itself: you try to think your way out of your discomfort. You are thinking, not feeling. You think you need to think—but, we will see, you really need to feel—and to come to terms with your emotions.

To neutralize the distress of difficult feelings, those feelings must be confronted—they must be *felt* first in order to be released. You have to go through your discomfort to get past it. That's why your treatment for GAD will involve contacting your underlying emotions. Only in that way can your agony dissipate.

161

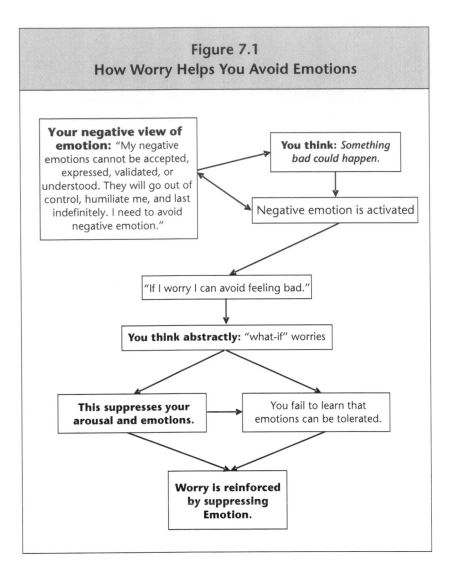

Figure 7.1
How Worry Helps You Avoid Emotions

Your negative view of emotion: "My negative emotions cannot be accepted, expressed, validated, or understood. They will go out of control, humiliate me, and last indefinitely. I need to avoid negative emotion."

You think: *Something bad could happen.*

Negative emotion is activated

"If I worry I can avoid feeling bad."

You think abstractly: "what-if" worries

This suppresses your arousal and emotions.

You fail to learn that emotions can be tolerated.

Worry is reinforced by suppressing Emotion.

The other important thing to understand about GAD—this will also be crucial in developing a treatment program—is that it carries with it a fundamental *inability to relax*. One constant in the lives of worriers is tension, both physical and mental. That's because they're in a constant state of readiness for danger—as though they were walking through hostile terrain on the lookout for predators or enemies. Normally a threatening stimulus produces this reaction for a short time only. If nothing bad actually materializes, a person tends to habituate to it and eventually relax. People with GAD, however, never get to that point. They remain hyperalert for danger, always seeing it as though for the first time. It's almost as if they are continually facing threat. Their symptoms are like the responses that physical threats normally produce: muscle tension, irritability, restlessness, sweating. It's as though something bad is really about to happen. When your brain sends out that message, all sorts of things are set off physiologically: more epinephrine is released, breathing and heart rate become more rapid, kidneys work harder, and so on. Since the body is not equipped to keep this up indefinitely, you eventually collapse from exhaustion. It's like the fight-or-flight response on a daily basis. Only in this case the dangers are largely in your head.

Note that with GAD, the mind is following the same basic rules that apply to all the other anxiety disorders: detect, catastrophize, control, and avoid. First, your mind scans for possible threats, trying to anticipate them as far ahead of time as possible. Next, you catastrophize the threat by assuming the worst-case scenario and making it the basis of your predictions (worrying seems to go with pessimism). Then you launch the control stage, checking out every bit of information, staying up to all hours, nagging others, trying to cover all the bases. And you direct your control toward your own mind by telling yourself to stop worrying. That doesn't work. At the same time, you actually avoid the situations that trigger your worry: an unpleasant task, a difficult conversation, a trip to the doctor. Once again, our work will be to replace these rules with a set of anxiety-free rules that make more sense.

THE WORRY RULE BOOK

It's time to write your Worry Rule Book. This is the rule book in your head that you refer to that keeps you up at night and keeps you worried all day.

Table 7.1
The Worry Rule Book

1. You need *absolute* certainty.

2. There is *danger* all around you.

3. You have to be ready to respond.

4. You have to be in control.

5. If a worry pops into your head then *you have to do something about it.*

6. You need to avoid *any emotional discomfort.*

7. You need the answer *right now.*

8. You can't live in *the present moment.*

9. You need to avoid doing things that make you anxious.

Let's look at each one of these worry rules.

1. ***You need absolute certainty.*** You keep saying to yourself, *I know that the odds are a million to one—but I could be that one!* You're right, you could be. Then you would be very unlucky. But it's unlikely to happen and demanding certainty will only make you worry more.

2. ***There is danger all around you.*** But there is a lot more safety and normalcy than you think. Almost all of your worries have proven false. And, after all, if things were so terrible and the world had ended, you wouldn't be reading a book right now.

3. ***You have to be ready to respond.*** You can't let your guard down. You have to be ready to respond to any threat that can happen at any time. Stay hyperalert. Keep your eyes and ears open. But the consequence of this is that you are always feeling anxious, tense, and irritable; and you just can't relax.

4. **You have to be in control.** Being in control at all times is a sign of how responsible you are. You feel it's the only way to avoid terrible things happening. So, try to control everything around you. The consequence is that you are a control freak, continually trying to control things that are not within your control. You equate not being in control with being in danger.

5. **If a worry pops into your head then you have to do something about it.** You think you need *to take control.* You don't. You could just sit back and say, *Well, there's another thought.* It's just a thought—nothing else.

6. **You need to avoid any emotional discomfort.** But the reality of life is that all of us suffer, fail, and are surprised by bad things that happen. Spending a life worrying only adds to your suffering.

7. **You need the answer right now.** You assume that if you don't have the answer immediately that things will unravel. It's as if you feel that something terrible is approaching rapidly—the relationship will fall apart, you will get rejected, your whole life will change. Why do you need the answer right now? Perhaps you won't get the answer until whatever happens has happened. And perhaps the answer is not so bad.

8. **You can't live in the present moment.** You live in a future that never happens. As a result, you miss what's going on around you that could be enjoyable and you can't live a life where you accept and enjoy the current experience. You are always living somewhere else—the future—which almost never turns out as badly as you expected.

9. **You need to avoid doing things that make you anxious.** You wait to feel *ready*—but days, weeks, even years go by and you still don't feel ready. You don't realize that you have to do things now—even if you are not ready to do them. It may be that the motivation to do something comes *after you start doing it.*

Okay. Let's put this all together in Figure 7.2. If you are a worrier you probably can see some of yourself in the schematic. Your parents may have been overprotective, continually pointing out danger, worrying in front of you, or not giving you any clear guidelines as to what will lead to punishment and what will lead to reward (thereby making life seem unpredictable to you). Your mother or father may have been cold and aloof, making you feel uncomfortable about your own emotions, or they may have confided in you about their own problems—so that you had to take care of them. You may have experienced a trauma as a kid and handled it by worrying about the next bad thing that could happen. You then developed a set of concerns—about what people thought, danger, responsibility, and being in control. You then activated worry as a way to avoid risk, anticipate danger, solve problems, motivate yourself, eliminate uncertainty, and eventually avoid difficult emotions.

Ironically, since bad things *are not happening,* you conclude that your worry is *working.* In the event that something bad does happen, you conclude that you need to worry even more. You haven't accepted the fact that bad things will happen anyway, even if you worry. *It is hopeless and you may be helpless.* But the best way to be ready for something bad happening is to be able to solve problems that really exist—and to be able to live a life worth living. Because you live in a world of danger and loss—which exists in your head—you have not fully grasped the wonderful things that are currently right in front of you. You have one foot out of reality.

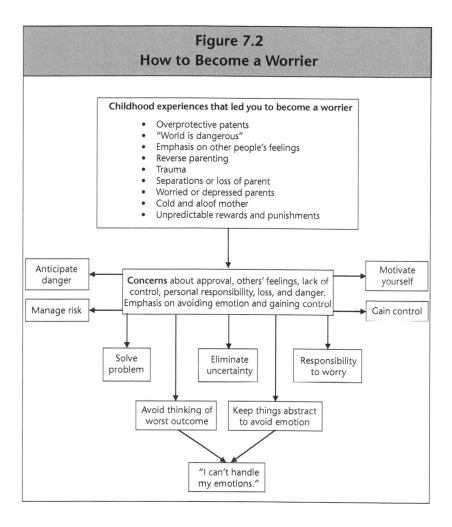

Figure 7.2
How to Become a Worrier

Childhood experiences that led you to become a worrier
- Overprotective patents
- "World is dangerous"
- Emphasis on other people's feelings
- Reverse parenting
- Trauma
- Separations or loss of parent
- Worried or depressed parents
- Cold and aloof mother
- Unpredictable rewards and punishments

Anticipate danger

Manage risk

Concerns about approval, others' feelings, lack of control, personal responsibility, loss, and danger. Emphasis on avoiding emotion and gaining control

Motivate yourself

Gain control

Solve problem

Eliminate uncertainty

Responsibility to worry

Avoid thinking of worst outcome

Keep things abstract to avoid emotion

"I can't handle my emotions."

OVERCOMING YOUR GAD

The good news is that there is a lot that you can do to overcome your anxiety and your worry. Notice how I mentioned both—anxiety and worry—because I will be talking about anxious arousal (rapid heart rate, tension, feeling jittery) and worry (the way you think). Keep in mind that when you are worrying you are thinking in abstract terms, trying to solve or avoid problems—and you are temporarily blocking your emotions. So we will review techniques that you can use to calm your anxious arousal and ways to calm your anxious mind.

Because GAD is so much less specific in its symptoms than most other anxiety disorders (that's why it's called *generalized* anxiety disorder), our procedure for overcoming it will be a little different from the one used in previous chapters. Worrying is a process that tends to go on all the time—not just when certain frightening situations pop up. It mingles with virtually every mental activity taking place in your mind. Thus it makes less sense to construct a fear hierarchy in which you expose yourself to specific situations in a controlled way. It's also hard to isolate specific safety or avoidance behaviors, since worrying really *is* your safety behavior. It's what you do to make yourself feel temporarily safe and avoid what you really fear most. You escape your anxiety by worrying.

Your habit of worrying is simply the way your mind has learned to think about everything. It's a kind of free-floating anxiety that attaches itself to whatever comes along. To overcome it, you need to teach your mind other ways of thinking (or not thinking) about things. There are a number of ways to do this that have proved effective for GAD sufferers. I've put them together into a list of 13 steps.

1. Build Your Motivation

You're probably more ambivalent than you think about getting rid of worry. On the one hand, it's wearing you down, ruining your daily enjoyment of life, interfering with your relationships, keeping you up at night, and making you depressed. But on the other hand, you may be harboring a very powerful secret belief—secret even from yourself—that your worry will protect you and help you solve problems. Starting out with a list of pros and cons may be useful. Write down as many of the advantages of worry as you can think of (such as *Worrying helps me figure things out,* or *If I didn't worry nothing would get done*). Seeing them on a page may change the way you feel about them. They may even look a little silly—which is good. Then write down a list of the stresses and burdens that worrying brings to your life. You shouldn't have much trouble thinking of these, if you're honest. When you look at the two lists, it should supply you with excellent motivation. Discussing your list with a friend or a therapist may be helpful also.

For example, Ellen thought that she needed to worry to be a good mother—to make sure that nothing terrible happens to her kids. She also thought that she needed to worry to be able to get her work done at the office—and to anticipate how things might go badly, so she could prevent things from unraveling. The question, though, is whether worrying about things was the best strategy.

A better strategy would be to make up a list of things that *she could do*. For example, she could make sure that someone was home when her kids got home, and make sure that they had her cell-phone number. But she could not be sure how other kids would react to them, so she had to choose between worrying about something that she could not control and letting go of control and certainty. We also developed a "to-do" list for work—including getting things done every day that were on her task list. Worrying about getting things done was a lot different than getting things done. If you get things done, you will have less to worry about.

I recall having the same experience recently. I had agreed to write an introductory article for a special issue of a journal. I found myself procrastinating—and then worrying about being late. I got a warning letter from the journal editor: "Bob, where is the article?" I worried about that. Then I decided to take my own medicine. *What is the to-do list today? What can I actually do* today? I decided to outline the article, I began feeling better and then I developed more of the motivation to write it. It's interesting, isn't it, that the motivation came after I took action? It wasn't the worry that motivated me, it was taking action.

Keep this in mind: action is different than worry. *Act—don't worry.*

One reason the effort to give up worrying seems daunting may be that you're focusing on the wrong goal. Many people come to me saying, "Help me get rid of my worries." No wonder they're not feeling very optimistic. Getting rid of worry altogether seems like an impossible task, the mere thought seems overwhelming. Well, that's because it *is* an impossible task. You'll probably never be able to eliminate worry from your life. But if you think you need to, you're barking up the wrong tree. The goal is not to get rid of your worries, but to function in spite of them. Worries come and go, they appear in the mind, pass through, and disappear again. The important thing is to learn not to identify with them, buy into them, or believe what they're telling you. Even if worries are active in your mind, they don't have to be a problem. You don't have to be bothered by them. And you don't have to obey your worries.

What you'll be doing, therefore, is stepping away from your worries. You won't have to exhaust yourself battling them. If you understand this from the start, it may give you some confidence that you can succeed. That's a powerful motivator.

2. Challenge Your Thinking

It's helpful to decide just how rational you think your worries are. Deciding that they're *irrational* won't stop them from happening. But it may lessen the urgency with which you respond. For example, a patient of mine, Ellen was consumed with worry about a report she was working on, convinced her boss wouldn't like it. She was so tied up in knots over it, she wasn't getting anything done. Meanwhile, the deadline was approaching. I gave her a list of questions that I frequently use in cognitive therapy. Here they are, together with Ellen's answers.

Table 7.2 Challenging Your Worried Thinking	
Worry: "I'll never get this done."	
Question	**Answer**
How much do I believe this?	75%
What is the evidence for this worry?	I haven't really started this. I feel nervous and afraid I won't have time.
What is the evidence against this worry?	I've done tasks like this before. I often feel nervous before something has to get done. I usually procrastinate and then I do it.
What action can I take today?	I can start to outline the steps to complete and assign them to myself. I can start collecting information.
What are the advantages and disadvantages of doing these things today?	Advantages: I can feel like I am making progress. I can get my mind off of worrying. I can find out it's not as hard as I thought it would be. Disadvantages: It feels difficult. I don't want to do it.
What's the advantage of doing what I don't want to do—but needs to be done?	If I do things that I am anxious about I will find out that I can tolerate these things and that I am not helpless. I can feel empowered.
What is the next step?	Outline the task.

Other questions that you can ask—or things that you can do—to challenge your worries include the following:

- Is worrying really going to help me?

- What advice would I give a friend?

- How could I handle it even if it did happen?

- What are some good reasons that I don't need this to work out?

- How many times have I been wrong in the past when I have worried?

- What did I worry about in the past that I no longer worry about?

It may help to write down this or a similar list of questions, together with your own answers. There's something about seeing your mind's nervous gyrations recorded in black and white (as opposed to echoing chaotically in your head) that makes them seem both less authoritative and more manageable. You may not feel like a very rational person when you're consumed by worry. But you can *pretend* to be one—at least for a while—and see what that looks like.

3. Set Aside Worry Time and Test Your Predictions

One of the most unusual techniques that we use for worry is to assign a specific time and place for you to worry. You have noticed that you seem to be worried all the time and that you feel you have no control over your worry. Worry time allows you to limit your worry to a specific time and place—and to put off your worries until later. It's a way of taking a break from the worry and learning to let go of worry for right now.

Assign a specific 20 minute period each day—certainly not before bedtime. Sit down in a chair and write down your specific worries. Keep your worry records—so that you can see that you seem to worry about the same thing over and over. You will think, *But what if I have a worry at a time other than the worry time?* Okay. Write down your worry on a piece of paper and put if off until worry time. You will find that you are able to do this and that when worry time comes around that you are not really worried about this anymore.

171

After the first week of worry time, use your worry time to write out your worries as predictions—for example, *I'll be late, I won't get this done on time, John will be angry, My kids aren't safe,* or *I'll never get any sleep.* These are your predictions. Each day—and at the end of each week—go back and write down the actual outcomes. Many of your predictions will prove to be false—for example, you will get things done and your kids will arrive safely. Some of your predictions may prove accurate—but if you are like most worriers, even the negative predictions (for example, *I won't get this done on time*) will not be a catastrophe.

Table 7.3 Worry Log		
In the first row, specify what you think will happen and when you think it will happen. In the middle row, rank your SUDS level associated with this prediction with zero indicating no distress and ten indicating maximum distress. In the last column, list exactly what actually happened, then compare your prediction to the actual outcome.		
Prediction	**Subjective Units of Distress (0–10)**	**Actual Outcome**

4. Validate Your Emotions

As we've seen, part of the strategy of worrying is to avoid painful emotions. Anytime you're worrying, you're off in the realm of thought, insulated from that of feeling. Worrying is essentially your *escape* from feeling. This is not a healthy relationship to have with your emotions. You may have developed the attitude that certain emotions—anxiety, anger, frustration, grief—will get out of control. You may assume a need to be rational all the time. You may even be ashamed of the way you feel. But everyone has feelings similar to yours. No one is rational all the time—nor should they be. Emotions provide an important function; they tell you about your needs. Your rational mind can help you figure out how to meet those needs—but without your emotions to guide it, it's a rudderless ship. In short, you need to validate your emotions. Not only do you have a right to them, your being able to feel them is absolutely crucial to overcoming your GAD.

One helpful technique is to keep a journal of your emotions. Any time you become aware of a feeling (sad, angry, anxious, confused, afraid, hopeless, happy, curious, excited) write it down, together with the situation that triggered it. Try not to comment on the feeling in any way—whether it's pleasant or unpleasant, why you're having it, whether it's justified, what it means psychologically—just the pure feeling itself. This last point is important because any of these distractions takes you out of the realm of feeling and back into that of thought. Either carry your journal around with you, or make a point of writing in it every day for ten minutes or so at a time—if possible, several times a day. At each interval, record the main feelings you remember. Keep this up for at least a month. As you look over this record later, you'll begin to see patterns; you'll begin to recognize your principal feelings and to see what triggers them. As you do so, your emotions will make more sense. Most important, you'll be less *afraid* of feeling them. The more you're able to feel them, the less your need to keep them at bay through worrying.

Helpful ideas to keep in mind about your emotions are the following: Your emotions mean that you are alive. Everyone has difficult feelings. Feelings are temporary and don't kill you. It makes sense to have mixed feelings, because life is complicated. Feelings are not facts and feelings don't hurt people. Only behavior can hurt someone. Your feelings go up and down in their intensity. Since they are temporary, they will pass and you will feel differently.

5. Accept Limited Control

One of the most powerful hidden beliefs behind worrying is that you have the power to control everything in your life. You may, for example, be stalled in traffic, and begin to worry that this will cause you to be late for work. You feel a strong, almost irresistible urge to do something about it—even though there's nothing to do. In effect, you're worrying about whether you ought to be doing something to correct the situation. This worry is being piled on top of your other worries, the ones about missing an important meeting, or whatever. We often don't realize how much our feeling of needing to do something personally, of being responsible for fixing a bad situation, adds to our level of tension. When we surrender that responsibility, a load is lifted. The question of whether or not you're going to be late for work has been taken out of your hands by a traffic jam. So you might as well let that one go.

The fact is, hardly anything in our lives goes as planned. Yet we continue to plan, and then to behave as though our lives depended on the plan going perfectly. We actually believe we have the power to make this happen. But reality is reality, whether we control it or not. If we can't control it, there is no point protesting, obsessing, complaining, seeking reassurance, or—our present subject—worrying about it. None of that will change what is. This is the point of the famous Serenity Prayer: "God grant me the serenity to accept the things I cannot change; the courage to change the things I can; and the wisdom to know the difference." One can easily imagine this prayer being recited by a congregation of worriers.

What are some limitations that you could accept? Could you accept not being in control, the possibility of disappointment, the fact that things may not go exactly as planned?

Consider accepting reality as a *given*—*it is what it is*.

If it's unpleasant, unfair, uncertain, and unknown—then you have to accept that it is what it is—even if you don't like it or know it—and even if you cannot control it. It is what it is and protesting, worrying, ruminating, or seeking reassurance won't change what it is.

You can protest against it, you can complain and you can push and stomp your feet. But reality is what it is. So take yourself out of it, give up the struggle for a moment, and accept that you cannot know or control everything—and let it go.

Breathe in, breathe out. Let go.

6. Accept Uncertainty

Most of us are keenly aware that nothing in the world is certain. Yet this is one of the hardest truths for GAD sufferers to accept. Anything in their future that's short of absolute certainty is the signal for worrying to begin. Since virtually everything *is* uncertain, this means that for the GAD sufferer, worry is pretty much a constant.

How do we gracefully accept the uncertainty of life? Linda, whom we met at the start of this chapter, was one of those for whom it was difficult. She worried, for example, that if a certain sequence of events took place—her daughter getting sick, having to stay home to take care of her, missing work, wearing out her boss's patience, getting fired, losing the house, being out on the street with no money—then she would end up as a homeless person. "Really," I said to her. "A homeless person. You actually worry that might happen?" "I know it's unlikely," she responded. "But it *could* happen. There's no guarantee it won't."

I had to admit that was true: there was no guarantee. Of course, Linda was ignoring other risks—such as the risk that worrying was aggravating her own health problems and thus increasing the chances of financial stress, not to mention undermining her daughter's sense of security. She was also ignoring the fact that just about any far-fetched scenario she could have come up with, any disaster from an auto accident to a comet crashing into the earth on her doorstep—*could* happen. She was fastening onto this particular worry because it was triggered by her emotions, mainly around her daughter and her job. It touched her deepest insecurities. But what Linda was demanding in order to feel secure was that *all* uncertainty, down to the last thousandth of a percent, be eliminated. When she saw this and realized the impossibility of it, she was able to detach somewhat from the imagined nightmare.

Linda could look at the probabilities and realize that it was very unlikely that her boss would get so angry that he would fire her. But she said, "I know it's unlikely—but I could be *the one.*" No matter how much you challenge the idea that "I could get fired," it's still possible. No matter how unlikely, it still could happen. No matter how much reassurance she gets, it still could happen. She could be the *unlucky one.*

But you are also the unlucky one if you have generalized anxiety disorder. The key here is learning to accept uncertainty as part of living a full life. Here are the seven steps in accepting—and practicing—uncertainty.

- Ask yourself, *What are the advantages and disadvantages in accepting uncertainty?* The advantages are that you will worry less and live more in the moment. The disadvantages are that you might—just might—overlook something that you could have done to prevent something bad from happening.

- In what areas of your life do you *currently* accept uncertainty? You accept uncertainty in driving a car, eating in a restaurant, going to a party, starting a new project, even starting a conversation. You've accepted a lot of uncertainty because it was necessary to live your life. Accepting the uncertainty that underlies your specific worry will just be more of the same thing.

- Are you equating uncertainty with a negative outcome? We know that 85 percent of the things that people worry about have a positive outcome. Uncertainty doesn't mean terrible outcomes. In fact, it's neutral.

- If you had to make a bet, how would you bet? If you think, *It's possible that this blemish is cancer,* how much would you bet it is? You might find that if you have to put your money where your mouth is, you might change your point of view.

- What would be the advantage of saying, *It's good enough for me to act on?* If you accept reasonable probabilities that reasonable people accept, then you can live a more worry-free life. If nothing is ever good enough, your life won't be good enough. You will be a chronic worrier.

- Practice *repeating* to yourself, *It's possible that something bad will happen.* Repeat this slowly, over and over—for twenty minutes each day. Repeat your specific worry: *It's possible this is cancer,* or *It's possible I could get fired.* You will find that it's hard to pay attention to your worry for 20 minutes. It becomes boring.

- Ask yourself, *Do I actually have a need for some uncertainty?* Yes—a need for uncertainty. Life would be boring otherwise. Would you watch the same television program if it were entirely predictable—or watch a sporting event if you always knew the final score before the game occurred—and you knew before the game exactly what would happen? I doubt it. Too boring.

7. Let Go of Your Urgency

Closely related to the demand for both control and certainty is the urge to figure things out *now.* You wake up in the middle of the night and think, *I wonder if that woman I met will go out with me?* or *I've got to get that job I applied for.* All of a sudden, you need to know the answer right away. You start thinking about it, weighing the auspicious signs against the discouraging ones, careening from hope to despair. You lie awake for hours, but instead of settling anything, your thoughts just generate more and more anxiety. By morning you're a wreck—but of course no closer to knowing the answer than you were when you first woke up.

Why are you doing this? You may know of no good reason why the matter must be settled right away—yet in your mind it must. Somehow a belief has lodged in your consciousness that you cannot rest until you know what the future holds. This urgency arises from your primitive brain's conviction that you are facing an emergency situation, like a wild animal attack. But it's not a real emergency. For one thing, there's no way to find out what's even going to happen except by waiting to see. Nor is there a way of knowing whether what happens will be good or bad. And even if you did know all that, there wouldn't be much you could do about it at 3 A.M. in bed.

8. Try to Go Crazy

Like many worriers, you worry that your worries will so overwhelm you that you will lose control and go insane. When you start worrying you try to stop, but that doesn't work, and then you fear you will lose control. In this exercise you intentionally try to worry so intensely that you will go insane. Intensify your worry, come up with the most extreme examples, and then try to go insane.

Bob: I want you to make your worries so extreme, so powerful that you will risk going insane. The only way to overcome your fear of losing control is to see what happens when you lose control.

Linda: I can't just simply lose control like that.

Bob: Why not? Just start your worries—about Diane, your ex-husband, your job, what your boss thinks of you, not getting your work done. Flood yourself with these worries until you lose total control.

Linda: Won't I go crazy?

Bob: I've never seen anyone go crazy from worrying like that. But what do you think?

Linda: It sounds far-fetched. But, okay, I'll try it.

Bob: Just flood yourself, repeating all your what-ifs.

Linda: (*getting a bit nervous*): Okay. What if Diane gets kidnapped? What if a car hits her? What if she gets sick and she gets . . . sicker? Let's see. What if my ex doesn't send a payment and then I can't pay the bills and then . . . I can't think of anything.

Bob: Let me help. What if he doesn't send a check, and you get evicted?

Linda: Okay. I get evicted. I am out on the street. I can't take
care of Diane. Wait . . .

Bob: What's happening?

Linda: (*smiling*) This all seems so far-fetched. I can't see this
happening. It's too extreme.

Bob: I notice that you are smiling. Have you gone crazy yet?

Linda: (*smiling back*) Not yet. But, who knows what could happen?

9. Practice Your Worst Fears

I've mentioned that your worry is a way to avoid the emotional
impact of what you are worried about. Rather than have an image of
ending up as a homeless person, you worry about all the ways that you
can get fired and the financial problems it might create. Linda had the
same kind of worry—that she would end up getting fired, her ex-husband
would stop support payments, and she might eventually end up on the
street. But she didn't let her mind go to the image of being homeless. This
was the worst outcome.

In order to test out the idea that you can't stand facing the worst
outcome, you can practice the image of the worst outcome. The important
thing here is to get a clear visual image of yourself in the situation. For
Linda, the image was a picture of Diane and her with their bags sitting on
the sidewalk. Now I asked Linda to think through this image and tell me
a detailed story of what would happen.

Linda: I see Diane and me sitting there, very upset, and I am
thinking, *Where am I going to go?* But . . . you know, I can't
really imagine this happening. I have savings and my family
would help us out . . .

Bob: So the worst image seems far-fetched? That's okay. Let's play
out the worst image. Keep telling the story.

Linda: Well, I am sitting there worrying. That's me. And then I
think, *We will have to go to a homeless shelter,* and so I call the
police to find out where there's a shelter. And I guess we go
there.

Bob: Then what happens?

Linda: I guess they let us in and give us some cots and some food.

As Linda played out the worst case scenario she began feeling less
anxious. It seemed so implausible, too improbable. There were so many

reasons why she would not end up homeless. And, in fact, though, even thinking about going to a shelter and getting a cot and some food was not the catastrophe she thought it was. Facing your worst fears and practicing them can help you overcome your worries. If you can face your worst fear you won't need to worry about it to avoid it.

10. Do What You Are Avoiding

Like many worriers, Linda avoided things that made her anxious. (All anxiety disorders involve avoidance of unpleasant emotions.) As I learned more about her work situation, I began to realize how many things she avoided out of anxiety. She would avoid outlining a task from start to finish, because it might seem overwhelming. She would avoid talking with co-workers about the work if she felt the least bit insecure about her own role. She would avoid getting clarification from her boss. And she would avoid starting the task, because it was so fraught with anxiety. Like many office workers, Linda used her computer as an escape. When she got to work she would check the news, Google a few topics of interest, and shop online. She finally admitted to me that she spent about two to three hours each day on these surfing safaris. When we sat down and added it all up, we realized she was wasting the equivalent of about 18 weeks of work a year—about three-eighths of her total work time!

We set up a structure in which Linda would do her work first and save any web surfing as a reward. Two hours of work, then ten minutes of goofing off—that was the rule. Linda tried it, and managed to stick to it. Almost immediately she began making more progress at work than ever before. The most important lesson Linda learned from this was to face her anxieties instead of avoiding them. Once she saw it was possible to be worried about a task and yet do it anyway, it freed her in a thousand ways. Best of all, her job-related worrying, both at work and at home, dropped off dramatically.

11. Practice Relaxation

Since it arises from primitive fears, worry always involves tension. This tension is in the body as well as the mind: when the mind perceives danger, the body prepares itself for combat or flight. When there's no real danger, there's no more need for the body to be tense; indeed what the body needs most in between crises is to relax. That's why relaxation techniques can be extremely helpful to people suffering from GAD.

Addressing tension in the body can have a powerful effect on tension in the mind, and vice versa; the two are invariably linked together in a circle of mutual influence. The most effective relaxation techniques address both body and mind together.

There's one technique I've found to be particularly effective in reducing physical tension and arousal. It's called Progressive Muscle Relaxation, and is described more fully in the Appendix A. It's quite easy to do. You start by sitting in a comfortable chair or lying down in a quiet, comfortable place. Slowly and gently proceed through the muscle groups in your body, first tensing and then releasing tension in each muscle. At the start, notice your breathing. Breathe in as you tense each muscle, hold the tension for about five seconds, then breathe out as you relax it. You can think *tense* to yourself as you breathe in, and *relax* as you breathe out. Wait 15 seconds between muscle groups. You will pass through your lower arms, then your upper arms, then your legs, in each case both left and right. Then your stomach, shoulders, back, chest, neck, face, eyebrows, mouth—anywhere you find a muscle to tense. Always go slowly, and remember to think *relax* as you release the tension. Do this twice each day for 20 minutes.

This technique can produce a very calming feeling. But its greatest effect won't be immediate; it will only be felt through continued practice. As you practice, be aware of any specific tension you may feel in a part of your body. Concentrate more on that area. For example, right now as I lean forward to type this on my computer, I notice a slight tension in my right shoulder. I lean back, then tense and relax that shoulder. It feels better. Tensing and relaxing. It's good practice in letting go.

12. Practice Mindfulness

One way to counter the debilitating effects of worry is to calm the mind. Perhaps the best way to do that is by practicing mindfulness. Mindfulness is not a form of thinking, nor is it an attempt to suppress thought. Rather it's a practice of stepping *out of* our thoughts and into the present moment, of observing what is going on in that moment without comment, judgment, or interpretation. It's an exercise that has particular relevance for worriers. When we worry, we construct anxious scenarios out of the past (bad things that have happened) and the future (bad things we imagine will happen). But past and future are constructions of the mind. We rely for the one on our distorted memories, and for the other on our fevered imaginations. What is real is the present; until we learn to live there we can know little peace. The agitation caused by our contemplation of past and future vanishes in the present moment. That's why practicing mindfulness can have a powerful impact: it interrupts the parade of past- and future-oriented thoughts that keep us in a constant state of inner panic.

Mindfulness is really the heart of all the many disciplines known collectively as meditation. The latter is a vast subject, far beyond our present scope. But the essential techniques used to cultivate mindfulness are simple, practical, and quite accessible to anyone. They're practical on many levels. If you set aside periods of time each day to meditate, you will find yourself experiencing a calmness that will spread outward through the rest of your day. If you practice mindfulness in moments of stress, you will probably find your ability to handle that stress increasing. And what you learn from these periods of practice will be quite useful in altering your perspective—which is what our approach to anxiety is all about. (For more information on this topic, see Appendix E, which includes some basic instructions and a list of resources you might care to explore.)

13. Observe Your Thoughts

A state of mindfulness is especially good for doing this. Worry is very much a habit. People who worry all the time are accustomed to regarding their thoughts as reflections of reality, a map of the dangers out there that one must avoid in order to feel safe. All our anxiety is built on that assumption. But if we are mindful of our thoughts, if we see them simply as events in the present, then those thoughts no longer have the same power. Their content ceases to matter. They're just events in the mind, rather than descriptions of real threats. The key to seeing them that way, stripped of their terrifying aspect, is to cease battling them and simply observe them. If we watch our thoughts mindfully, we gain a perspective on them that we do not otherwise have. We distance ourselves from them, rather than identifying with them. And as we have already seen throughout this book, gaining distance on our anxious thoughts is the key to mastering our anxiety.

This is one more thing you can do during your worry time. As you sit there consciously fretting about everything under the sun, make a list of all the anxious thoughts that pass through your mind. Usually there won't be that many at any one time; they'll tend to start repeating themselves. Then go over those thoughts one by one, letting each one just sink in rather than trying to fight it off. Use the time to study your experience of the thought: how it makes you react, what further anxieties it provokes, how it feels in your body (this is a good one to be aware of). Remain physically present. Try to watch each thought in the moment, without getting caught up in where it's going. After all, it's *just a thought*. If your thoughts were reality, you'd have been dead a long time ago. (Appendix E: Mindfulness, has some suggestions for observing your thoughts that may prove helpful.)

SUMMING UP YOUR NEW APPROACH
TO YOUR GENERALIZED ANXIETY DISORDER

We have reviewed a number of very effective techniques that, when used in combination, *consistently*, over a period of time, should have an impact on your generalized anxiety disorder. You will need to develop new habits for relaxation, acceptance, thinking, and dealing with your sense of urgency, uncertainty, control, and risk. This won't happen overnight and you are likely to have some bouts of worry. Don't worry about them—simply keep using these techniques.

Let's review some of the things that you will need to keep in mind— I've listed them in Table 7.4. You will need to do some of these things every day for weeks and weeks in order to make the kind of progress you will want. Don't expect perfection and don't expect to eliminate your worries right now. Make progress a little bit each day.

Table 7.4
Rewrite Your GAD Rule Book

1. Relax your mind and relax your body. Practice muscle relaxation and mindful breathing. Learn how to stay in the moment and let go of your thoughts and tension.

2. Examine the advantages of letting go of worry. Be honest with yourself about your mixed motives about worrying. Part of you wants to decrease worry, the other part feels a need to worry to be prepared. The key here is in knowing whether your worry will lead to productive action. If not, then it's useless mental energy.

3. Keep in mind that a thought is a thought—it's not reality. Keep your thoughts *in mind* and recognize that reality is not the same thing as your thoughts. As you become a mindful

---

observer of your breathing, you can practice simply *observing* your thoughts. You can stand back and say, "That's just another thought." And then you can practice saying, "Let it go."

4. Ask yourself if your worries are really rational. Practice the cognitive therapy techniques. Examine the evidence for and against it, ask yourself what advice you would give a friend, and review how many times you have been wrong in the past.

5. Set aside worry time, write out your predictions, and keep a worry log to test out what actually happened. You will find that your worries are almost always false predictions and you can set them aside for your worry time—which, I hope, will eventually bore you.

6. Validate your emotions. Keep a daily journal of your emotions—both positive and negative. Identify why your emotions make sense, why they are not dangerous, and why other people would have many of the same feelings. Validate yourself.

7. Accept your limitations. You can't control or know everything. It's not all up to you. You can learn to *accept uncertainty and accept limitations*. The more you accept what you cannot do, the greater your sense of being empowered in the real world.

8. Realize that it's not urgent. You don't need to know right now. Nothing will happen if you don't know. But you can focus on enjoying the present moment—and making the best of the moment in front of you.

9. Practice losing control. Rather than trying to stop or control your worry, flood yourself, surrender to the worry, repeat the worry, bore yourself with constant repetitions of exactly the same worried thought. You will get bored and less worried.

10. Try to go crazy. You can't go crazy from your worry. But you can learn that letting go of control allows you to overcome your fear of losing control.

11. Practice your worst fears. Imagine the worst outcome, and repeat it. You will find that with time your images and thoughts will become boring. Think about it—the "cure" is boredom.

12. Practice uncertainty. Flood yourself with your "what-ifs" until you are bored with yourself.

CHAPTER 8

"I'm So Embarrassed!"
Social Anxiety Disorder

WHAT IS SOCIAL ANXIETY DISORDER?

Ken, in his midtwenties, had been anxious around other people since he was a kid. He was short for his age, and recalls being teased and humiliated by bigger boys. All through high school and college he was too shy to ask girls out; he never really had a steady girlfriend. He had a few male friends in college, but on the whole it was a lonely period. He spent a lot of time in his room. He was awkward at parties or in social groups, so he avoided them. He rarely spoke up in class, even though he was a good student and knew the material; he was too self-conscious in front of the professor and the other students. When called on to speak he would panic and his heart would pound. He always felt, *I'll look dumb. What if my mind goes blank? I'll make a complete fool of myself.* To avoid this, he would sit far in the back, trying not to be noticed.

After college, things got worse. At least there he had felt comfortable with a few familiar faces in his dorm or dining hall. The working world proved a lot more intimidating. Interviewing for a job was torturous. The one he finally took involved little contact with other workers; most of the day he spent alone in a small cubicle. His life became a picture of isolation. He'd go to work in the morning, come home in the evening, and fix dinner or order in. He'd sit in his apartment and read, watch TV, or surf the web. He'd fantasize about sex, but never have a date. He wanted to meet women but didn't know how to go about it and lacked the willingness to find out. Life felt lonely and empty—with no end in sight of his misery. Ken did have a couple of friends in the city whom he knew from college. Occasionally they'd go out together on weekends and hit the bars. But these were anxious times for Ken. He knew his friends were going there to meet women, and the thought of it terrified him. He'd have a few drinks and sometimes smoke some marijuana, but even so, it was painfully difficult for him to join any kind of conversation, especially if women were involved. "How do you just start talking to a stranger?" he asked me when we first met. "It seems pushy to go up to a woman and introduce yourself. Won't she think you're just coming on to her and be offended? Besides," he continued, "I always feel I have nothing to say. Guys are supposed to be cool and self-confident, and I'm not. I think women can tell how insecure I am. That's why they're not really interested in me. I don't know why I even go along on these outings. I feel like such a dork in front of everyone. It's embarrassing."

It wasn't only women who produced this reaction in Ken. He had trouble being part of any social occasion. He hated being around most groups of guys, who were always kidding and laughing and talking about sports. He dreaded lunch in the cafeteria, having to sit down at a table with other workers. (He had an idea that he took too long to chew his food, and that others mocked him for it.) He would try to get through work meetings without having to say a word. He was hesitant to ask for information in stores or directions from strangers. He'd look like a fool. He was even nervous to use a public restroom—standing next to someone at a urinal often made him unable to urinate, which he found terribly embarrassing. Worst of all, whenever he felt uncomfortable with other people, his voice and hands would shake and he would start sweating. He felt his social awkwardness was on view for all to see.

When Ken first came to see me, he was depressed. He had taken to drinking and smoking marijuana alone. His job performance had fallen off. He believed nothing could help him. He told me he'd been sure I wouldn't want to work with him—he was too much of a "loser." He didn't even feel worthy of being my patient!

Fortunately, I managed to help Ken, and he was able to overcome his problems to a remarkable degree. But the fact remains that social anxiety disorder, or SAD, is not only one of the most common anxiety disorders, it is one of the most crippling. Though SAD sufferers often pass unnoticed in the general population—they're often seen as simply shy—the consequences of the disorder can be quite severe. People with SAD are less likely than others to be married or in a relationship. They earn less money and tend to be less successful in their careers. They're more likely to be unemployed. They have higher rates of alcohol and substance abuse, and are more apt to be depressed or attempt suicide. They are also more likely than the average person to suffer from one of the other anxiety disorders discussed in this book.

In a national study of 8,000 people ranging in age from 15 to 54, the prevalence of SAD was over 13 percent. SAD sufferers are somewhat more likely to be female, although males and females show up equally in clinical practice. It's unclear why males are more apt to seek help, but one possibility is that they believe their shyness is inconsistent with a "masculine" role, and so see the problem as more severe. The age of onset of SAD ranges considerably between childhood and late adolescence, although interestingly, the typical adult patient doesn't seek out treatment until around 30 years old. The delay may be partly due to the feelings of embarrassment and shame that go with the disorder. But SAD sufferers may also be slow to recognize their condition. In the culture at large, being "shy" is not necessarily considered an abnormality. One study indicated that around 40 percent of adults thought of themselves as shy, while 95 percent admitted to shyness at least some of the time. If shyness is the *norm*, people with SAD might be less likely to seek help. Also, because of the isolation factor, social anxiety is often less of a problem for other people than for the sufferer. Hence there's less pressure from others to seek help. The most common situations that people with SAD fear or avoid include public speaking or more formal interactions (70 percent), informal speaking (46 percent), asserting themselves (31 percent), and being observed by others (22 percent). Finally, because of the chronic nature of the problem, SAD sufferers may tend to believe they are beyond help—that their social anxiety is simply an inalterable part of their personality.

For all these reasons, it may be hard to determine whether or not your social anxiety rises to the level of a disorder, or is merely represents your normal human complement of shyness and reserve. Part of the answer, of course, will be subjective: are social anxieties making you miserable? Are they seriously restricting your life? Or are they something you can live with more or less comfortably? Only you can answer that question—but it may also help to have a more "objective" self-evaluation. The Liebowitz Social Anxiety Scale is a diagnostic test that will help you assess your social anxiety in a clinical context (you'll find it in Appendix G). This test may also allow you to identify symptoms you weren't quite aware of, and to connect them to one another.

WHERE DOES SAD COME FROM?

If you've read the previous chapters, you'll know where the answer begins: way back in our evolutionary history. In a primitive environment, there was clearly survival value in not being attacked by other humans. Antagonizing strangers, or even members of one's own tribe, could lead to sudden violence. Therefore, people developed submissive behaviors, the purpose of which was to assure others that one is not a threat. These behaviors are exhibited by many animals as well: for example, a dog, encountering another more dominant dog (one with more status within the pack), will lower its ears, crouch, look down, refrain from barking, and hide its teeth. The signal being sent is, "Don't worry, I'm not challenging you." Similarly, primitive humans who refrained from challenging more aggressive or dominant humans were probably more likely to survive. For example, common appeasement gestures when entering the territory of strangers is to offer gifts, bow, lower the head, salute, or even crouch on the ground in a position lower than the person one is greeting. The situations that make us feel socially anxious often involve potential challenges to others—such as meeting a stranger (especially outside of one's own home), standing up in front of a group, confronting someone in authority, or asserting oneself. The strategy proved effective: the tendency would be for more rash or aggressive types to kill one another off. Thus a certain amount of deferential behavior was built into the human character. No one kicks a sleeping dog—or a submissive dog.

This behavior is reflected in virtually every human culture. When entering the home of a stranger, or the presence of someone in authority, the almost universal custom is to bow, speak softly, and in general offer signs of deference. These are sometimes known as appeasement gestures. They acknowledge the dignity and status of the other person, while signaling a lack of hostile intention. In many cultures the protocol includes offering gifts as a token of respect. We see all of this in our own culture today. We bring house presents when visiting. We shake hands with strangers as an acknowledgment of friendly intentions. Even when confronting those we are not well-disposed toward, we feel the impulse to be courteous and polite (at least initially). There may be a variety of motives behind all this, but certainly a part of it is simply our innate urge to get along with others as a survival strategy.

SAD sufferers, of course, carry this behavior well beyond the point where it's effective. For one thing, they usually don't acquire any greater feeling of safety from behaving deferentially. Despite their submissive gestures, they continue to fear being criticized (i.e., attacked) by others. This may be because actually being afraid (as opposed to merely signaling respect) is more convincing in a primitive context. Or avoiding all social interaction may, for some, have been the simplest way to reduce the risk of confrontation. In any case, a lack of assertiveness, though it may involve sacrifice, certainly reduces the danger of retaliation. And SAD sufferers are nonassertive.

A predisposition toward SAD can sometimes be seen in infancy. Studies have shown that infants differ in their temperament, some displaying what's known as behavioral inhibition. This includes timidity, caution, wariness, and a dislike of novelty or change. Such infants are more easily alarmed or startled. Their temperament makes them more likely to develop SAD as either older children or adults.

On the other hand, the genetic determinant in actual cases of SAD is not thought to be that great—one study estimates the genetic causation to be only 17 percent. So clearly, other factors are important—one of them being your family history. Even if you have a predisposition, family dynamics probably influence whether or not you develop the disorder. SAD sufferers are more likely to come from families with a history of suppressed conflict—i.e., there were tensions in the home, but no one was encouraged to express any feelings. The disorder seems linked to parents, especially mothers, who were nervous, depressed, or less responsive to a child's distress. Often parents who are socially anxious themselves discourage their children from interacting with others, or venturing out into the world. It's almost like shyness training. Its effects can last a lifetime.

The parents of pathologically shy individuals tend to be more critical and controlling, less supportive of their children. They are likely themselves to feel embarrassed by their children's social problems. They tend to attribute a child's shyness to an abnormal personality, rather than a natural response to stressful situations ("Why are you such a nervous Nellie? You're scared to talk to anybody," rather than "Don't worry, everyone feels a little anxious in front of a group.") Children tend to internalize such explanations of their behavior, and, inevitably, to condemn themselves for it. Employing guilt or shame to "correct" shy behavior ("What's wrong with you?"), or focusing on the opinions of others ("What will people think if you act that way?") can push a child strongly in the direction of social paralysis.

It's possible, of course, that one's actual life circumstances during adulthood can contribute to developing SAD. But evidence suggests this is rarely a major factor. True cases of SAD (as opposed to mere shyness) tend to be severely life-altering. If you have SAD chances are you've had a long history of social anxiety, whether genetically or environmentally driven. Some people can fall into situations where social anxiety becomes more of a problem. Perhaps a job has transferred you from a secure, comfortable environment to one that's tense and unfriendly. Or you go through a divorce and suddenly find yourself living alone without a family or support network. This is more the exception, however. People with SAD tend to create their isolated circumstances. Their isolation reinforces the belief that they will be rejected.

WHAT IS SAD THINKING LIKE?

The essence of SAD is fear of being *evaluated negatively by others*. This fear is what makes almost any social encounter fraught with anxiety: public speaking, asking for information or directions, going out to dinner, approaching members of the opposite sex, making requests, using public restrooms or dressing rooms, speaking up in class, making phone calls, being introduced to new people, job interviews, meetings, presentations, parties. On any of these occasions you can imagine the possibility that you will stumble, misspeak, or look foolish, and that people will scorn or criticize you. As a result you may be subject to trembling, blushing, sweating, stammering, dry mouth, or nervous tics; when speaking you may fumble for words or go blank entirely. You fear that others will notice these signs of awkwardness and judge you for them, which only intensifies your anxiety. (SAD differs from panic disorder in that the latter is a fear of the effects of your panic on yourself, but with SAD the fear is of how others will evaluate you.) As a result of all this, you tend to avoid social encounters if possible. You may be lonely and miserable, but this seems somehow safer than interacting with other people. You become used to a life of isolation.

At the heart of this syndrome is a way of thinking we can describe as *excessive self-focus*. SAD sufferers tend to carry around a negative image of themselves, which becomes the most important part of their experience. This focusing on the self—as if you are standing back and watching yourself—increases self-critical thinking in general. In fact, in one study simply having anxious people sit in front of a mirror for long periods of time—or asking them to think about themselves and their feelings— increased self-critical thinking. If you suffer from SAD, when you arrive at a party, you're not really focused on the other people in the room; you're focused on how *you* look to *them*. You exaggerate the attention paid to you, thinking only of your own thoughts, feelings, and sensations, believing that other people can actually see them just as you can. You assume other people are always noticing you—your anxiety, your discomfort. Your image of yourself is based on the perspective of other people, but it's focused on you; it is the self as object. This imagined self that others are supposedly seeing is always being compared to an idealized "self," which is the person you think you should be. This person is invariably poised, self-assured, charming, confident, whereas you yourself are bumbling, foolish, and inept. The difference between the two is the source of the contempt you imagine others hold you in—as well as the source of your contempt for yourself.

Unfortunately, this self-absorbed way of looking at the situation contains some critical distortions. For one thing, it warps your perceptions of what is going on with other people. For example at the party, you may be so fixated on how people are seeing you that you actually fail to notice important social cues: how others are actually responding, what they are saying or doing. You're not learning anything about them, or expressing any real interest in them—despite the fact that successful social interaction is based largely on sympathy for others. You're neither feeling nor expressing sympathy for others; you're worried only about how *they* perceive *you*. In short, you're living in a self-centered world of your own.

Now it is possible that you might have the negative thought, *She didn't like me at the party,* but not care that much. For example, you might say to yourself, *I never knew her before, so what difference does it make?* Or you might say, *Well, maybe I wasn't at my best, but I have lots of other friends.* After all, *She doesn't really know me.* However, people with SAD do not view social evaluation that way. On the contrary, they often have the following underlying beliefs that serve as *rules.*

- If I am anxious, then people will see my anxiety.

- If people see you are anxious, then they will think you are a loser.

- I should always appear in control and confident.

- I have to get the approval of everyone.

- If I don't, it means I am defective or inferior.

- It's terrible not to have people's approval.

- There is a right way—a perfect way—to do things socially.

- I should always do things the perfect way when around other people.

People with SAD also believe that it is useful to worry about social interactions. They believe that their anticipation of social failure might help them avoid something bad from happening, but they also believe that their anxiety will incapacitate them. Examples of these beliefs about worry are the following:

- If I worry about this, I might be able to come up with a way to make sure I don't make a fool of myself.

- My worry will prepare me and protect me.

- If I worry, then I can plan ahead and practice what I will say.

- But if I worry too much when I am there—interacting—then I will get distracted and make a fool of myself.

There are also typical beliefs that make you use *safety behaviors* that you think will prevent you from looking foolish:

- If I hold a glass really tightly, then my hand won't tremble.

- If I talk really fast, people won't think I'm a loser and have nothing to say

- If I have a few drinks, I can function better.

Unfortunately, these safety behaviors actually make things worse. For example, holding a glass very tightly increases the likelihood of your hand shaking. Talking rapidly makes you lose your breath and become more anxious. It also makes other people think that you are dominating the conversation. Drinking before social engagements does not allow you to learn that you can interact without drinking. It also increases the likelihood that you might act inappropriately or even become an alcoholic.

Another distortion involves your ideas of how people are judging you. You don't really know how, but you make assumptions. One patient of mine went to a memorial service for someone he barely knew. While sitting in the church he realized he was the only adult male without a tie. He was so mortified he had to leave. The truth was, barely anyone even noticed, and if they had, they wouldn't have thought much about it; after all, he was neatly dressed in a jacket and dress shirt and looked quite presentable. Another patient had to give a talk at a conference. He didn't want to appear nervous, so he decided to hide it by writing out the talk and reading it word for word. He thought this would make him seem more self-assured; instead the talk came across as stilted and boring. One study of people with SAD showed that they tend to smile less often. People who don't smile in social situations don't generate very positive feelings in others. So even though all you care about is making a good impression, the result is the opposite. You tend to be blind as to how you come across.

Ken, whom we've already met, once had a lesson in this. There was a group of young men in college who never seemed to like him much. He was always uncomfortable around them. Later, after he'd made some progress with his SAD, he ran across one of these young men in the city and became friendly with him. The man acknowledged that in the old days at school, the group had considered Ken to be a good-looking, intelligent, well-mannered fellow—but rather conceited. Ken was stunned. "I couldn't believe it," he told me. "How could they have thought I was conceited? I felt totally inferior to every one of them." The fact was, Ken's preoccupation with his own "inferiority," reflected in his withdrawn behavior, had come across to the group as self-absorption and aloofness. It's not at all uncommon in social situations for shyness to be misinterpreted as conceit.

All this is part of a certain downward spiral endemic to SAD sufferers. The less confident they feel, the worse an impression they make; the worse the impression, the less positive response they get from others; the less positive the response, the further their confidence erodes. By isolating themselves, they cut themselves off from rewarding opportunities; this makes them feel even more lonely and isolates them all the more. Because they anticipate judgment, they avoid intimacy with others; as a result they don't allow others to get to know them. It all becomes a self-fulfilling cycle: your fear causes you to behave in ways that bring about exactly what you fear most.

Unfortunately, the agonies of SAD aren't necessarily confined to social occasions. Social anxiety can dominate your thinking even when alone. You're either brooding over your last social encounter (the "postmortem") or worrying about the next one. In the former instance, you go over what happened, reviewing your performance to see how you did (usually badly, in your estimation); you think about all the mistakes you made, and how stupid they made you look to others. When you think about the next encounter, you worry about how you'll come off, or plan how you're going to make the right impression. Perhaps you rehearse what you'll say to a woman you want to ask out, or your boss when you ask for a promotion. Unfortunately, your preparation tends to desert you when the time comes around. That's because it's the product of fear, and a fearful state of mind is not generally conducive to relaxed, confident, or effective communication.

SAD sufferers often resort to a number of safety behaviors, which they believe will shield them from embarrassment or criticism. Memorizing a speech, or writing it out in advance, for example, is a common strategy, though it rarely produces the desired effect of poise or self-assurance. Keeping your hands in your pockets so others can't see them shaking is another. Talking rapidly or loudly in order to seem confident (or artificially slowly to seem relaxed) is still another—though it's likely to suggest insecurity more than anything else. One patient of mine insisted on wearing a jacket even in the warmest weather, so that no one could see him sweating. It only made him look odd (and of course sweat all the more). Regardless of whatever short-term effectiveness they may have, these behaviors are of little help in the long run. They only reinforce the key belief that one can only be successful socially by masking every sign of one's insecurity. (We'll come back to this unhelpful belief later.)

One of the most self-destructive safety behaviors of all is the reliance on alcohol or drugs as a boost to confidence. Randy, a patient of mine, began by having a few beers at home before going out to a gathering. He believed this would not only take the edge off his anxiety, but make him more interesting to other people. Though there was little evidence that this was the case, he continued to rely on alcohol in this way, until he rarely met anyone socially without being more or less drunk. A few times he started to behave inappropriately, resulting in a breakup with a woman he was dating. Another patient, Jean, felt too scared to go to parties at other people's homes, so she tried hosting gatherings at her own house. To fortify herself, she would have a few drinks beforehand and a few more as the party went on. As often as not things would start to unravel: food would be burned, dishes spilled, and awkward topics introduced into the conversation. People stopped coming to the dinners. Most of us know stories like this, some of them not very pleasant. What begins as an attempt to mask the symptoms of SAD can end up as a serious case of alcoholism or drug abuse.

The thing most important to understand about SAD is that although it appears to be about what other people think of you, it's actually about something deeper: what you think of yourself. Yes, people with SAD are concerned about the opinions of others, but so are we all, and rightly so; it's a key to getting along in this world. The difference is that SAD sufferers believe themselves to be, in fact, inadequate, unworthy, inferior, incompetent, and boring. A constant barrage of self-judgment goes on in the mind, and it's this, more than anything, that triggers social anxiety. Who wouldn't be afraid of facing strangers, or half-strangers, if you knew for a fact that they would despise you—that you *deserved* to be despised? In the following pages I offer a range of techniques you can use to cope with your SAD. However they vary, they are all based ultimately on your ability to release self-judgment, to let go of the belief you have in your essential unworthiness.

Some of the typical distortions in your thinking are described in Table 8.1. You will recognize that you have worries before your interactions, self-focus during the interaction, and a self-critical postmortem after.

Table 8.1 Typical Social Anxiety Worries			
Typical Distortions in Thinking	Before Entering Interaction	During Interaction	After Interaction (The Postmortem)
Mind reading	People will see that I am a nervous wreck.	She can see that I am anxious. She sees my hands trembling.	Everyone saw that I was nervous and that I was losing my train of thought.
Fortune-telling	My mind will go blank.	I'll never get through this conversation.	I will continue to mess up anytime I meet new people.
Negative filter	My hand will tremble.	I just lost my train of thought.	I didn't tell the story the right way.
Discounting the positives	Even though some people like me, there are always people who won't like me.	Even though I am doing OK right now, I could always still mess it up.	Even though people seemed interested in my conversation, no one asked me out.

Catastrophizing	If I look anxious, it will be just awful.	If I keep getting more anxious here, I will be totally unable to speak.	I can't stand the fact that she didn't seem interested in me.
Personalizing	I'll bet no one else has these fears of speaking.	I can see that everyone is focusing on me and noticing what a nervous wreck I am.	I was probably the only person at the party who was so uninteresting.
Labeling	I'm inept.	I must be a loser.	I was a loser.
All or nothing thinking	I am continually messing up when I meet people.	My entire performance so far is a disaster.	I totally messed up—there was nothing positive in this.

AN OVERVIEW OF SOCIAL ANXIETY DISORDER

Let's try to take an overview of the process and experience of social anxiety disorder. In Figure 8.1 I present a detailed schematic that describes what we have already reviewed about SAD. Look over this figure and see if any of these processes are familiar to you. It may be that not everything here applies to you—but you may begin to make more sense of your social anxiety by putting it all together.

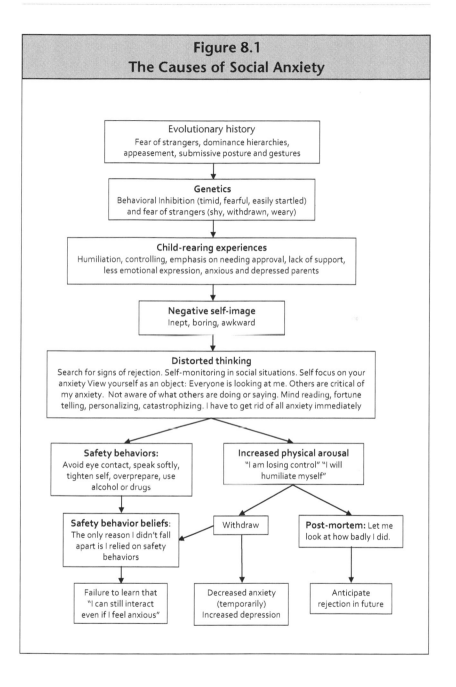

Figure 8.1
The Causes of Social Anxiety

Evolutionary history
Fear of strangers, dominance hierarchies, appeasement, submissive posture and gestures

Genetics
Behavioral Inhibition (timid, fearful, easily startled) and fear of strangers (shy, withdrawn, weary)

Child-rearing experiences
Humiliation, controlling, emphasis on needing approval, lack of support, less emotional expression, anxious and depressed parents

Negative self-image
Inept, boring, awkward

Distorted thinking
Search for signs of rejection. Self-monitoring in social situations. Self focus on your anxiety View yourself as an object: Everyone is looking at me. Others are critical of my anxiety. Not aware of what others are doing or saying. Mind reading, fortune telling, personalizing, catastrophizing. I have to get rid of all anxiety immediately

Safety behaviors:
Avoid eye contact, speak softly, tighten self, overprepare, use alcohol or drugs

Increased physical arousal
"I am losing control" "I will humiliate myself"

Safety behavior beliefs:
The only reason I didn't fall apart is I relied on safety behaviors

Withdraw

Post-mortem: Let me look at how badly I did.

Failure to learn that "I can still interact even if I feel anxious"

Decreased anxiety (temporarily) Increased depression

Anticipate rejection in future

In order to clarify your reading of the above schematic, I will go through these various steps.

1. *Causes of SAD.* This includes the evolutionary history of submission to dominance hierarchies and fear of strangers. There is moderate genetic determination of SAD. During infancy this inherited disposition is expressed early in behavioral inhibition and fear of strangers, as well as sensitivity toward rejection. In addition, people who develop SAD come from families that are overcontrolling, nonsupportive, and critical.

2. *Self-Image and Beliefs about Others.* People with SAD often have low self-esteem and believe others are rejecting and critical of weakness. As a result people with SAD will search for any signs of rejection, scanning other people for lack of interest in them. People with SAD will focus on any signs of their own ineptness and believe that everyone is focusing on this ineptness.

3. *Negative Distorted Thoughts.* People with SAD engage in mind reading (*You think I'm a loser*), personalizing (*The reason you are yawning is you think I'm boring*), and fortune-telling (*My mind will go blank*), and believe that any mistakes that they make in front of others are absolutely terrible (*It would be a catastrophe if I lost my train of thought and if people thought I was anxious*). Thus, the person giving a talk will think that everyone can see that she is anxious (mind reading); if someone in the audience is talking to someone else, it is a sign that the talk is going badly (personalizing); they will predict that they will lose their train of thought (fortune-telling) and they believe that it is absolutely terrible that people think that they are anxious (catastrophic thinking).

4. *Negative Beliefs about Anxiety.* People with SAD believe that any time that they are anxious their ability to think and perform will be dramatically impaired, and they believe that everyone can see their anxiety. They believe that they cannot talk or interact with people if they are anxious. They think that they have to feel comfortable, calm, or confident before they do anything. Consequently, they believe that they have to both eliminate their anxiety and hide it from others. Since their anxiety is not eliminated, they become more aroused and anxious and more

fearful of losing control and being humiliated. They are afraid of their own anxiety.

5. **Reliance on Safety Behaviors.** Anticipating rejection and anxiety, people with SAD use strategies to avoid appearing anxious. This includes overpreparing or reading a speech verbatim, avoiding eye contact, lowering the voice, or using alcohol or drugs. Reliance on these safety behaviors reinforces the belief that one can never appear anxious and maintains the belief that one will be rejected in the future unless one eliminates any signs of anxiety.

6. **Withdrawal and Avoidance.** People with SAD may become so anxious that they will leave the situation. If they feel that they are too awkward or uncomfortable, they will leave a party. In the future, they are likely to avoid situations that they think will elicit their anxiety.

7. **Postmortem.** After engaging in social interactions, people with SAD review their "terrible" performance, focusing on any signs of their awkwardness or possible rejection by others. This further supports their belief that they are inept and need to worry to prepare for the worst in the future.

THE SOCIAL ANXIETY RULE BOOK

Okay. Let's write out your Social Anxiety Rule Book—the rules that you follow that will guarantee that you will feel shy, self-conscious, and want to avoid any interactions with other people. So, follow these rules and you will be as anxious as you can be:

Table 8.2
Social Anxiety Rule Book

Before you interact with people:

1. Think about all the ways you can look foolish and anxious.

2. Rehearse in your mind how anxious you will feel.

3. Try to prepare all kinds of safety behaviors to hide your anxiety.

4. If possible, come up with an excuse to avoid people.

When you are around other people:

1. Assume that people can see every anxious feeling and thought that you have.

2. Focus your attention on how anxious you feel.

3. Try to hide your anxious feelings.

After you interact with people:

1. Review how awful it felt.

2. Assume that people are now talking about how awkward you looked.

3. Focus on any signs of imperfection in how you appeared.

4. Criticize yourself for being less than perfect.

A CLOSER LOOK AT YOUR SOCIAL ANXIETY RULE BOOK

Let's look at each of your socially anxious rules to make sure that you understand how you are making yourself feel worse than you need to feel.

Before You Interact with People

1. *Think about all the ways you can look foolish and anxious.* Before you go into any situation, you can review in your mind all the ways that you can look awkward, incompetent, or out of control. For example, you can anticipate that your mind will go blank, you will sweat profusely, your hands will shake, and you will mutter nonsense.

2. *Rehearse in your mind how anxious you will feel.* Now you can think that your anxiety will escalate out of control to catastrophic levels. You can anticipate you won't be able to stand it and will have to escape as soon as you can.

3. *Try to prepare all kinds of safety behaviors to hide your anxiety.* Since your general rule book tells you to be prepared for the worst, you can think of all the superstitious things that you can do to feel safe. For example, you can prepare word for word exactly what you will say, you can wear a jacket so your sweating won't show, you can hold the glass tightly so no one sees your hands shaking, and you can speak softly and slowly so no one can see you are anxious.

4. *If possible, come up with an excuse to avoid people.* It's always ideal, if you want to maintain your anxiety, to avoid people. Sit by yourself, don't speak unless spoken to, don't make eye contact, and—if possible—don't even go.

When You Are Around Other People

1. *Assume that people can see every anxious feeling and thought that you have.* Your expertise in mind reading will come in handy. And you can also assume that you are always the center of attention—and the worst kind of attention. Everything that you are feeling that makes you feel bad is immediately apparent to everyone around you. You don't even have to say anything. They can see every anxious thought, every anxious sensation, every feeling of psychic pain that you have. You are a walking transparency of anxiety.

2. *Focus your attention on how anxious you feel.* Rather than listen to what is being said—or looking around at what is really going on—it's always best (if you want to be a nervous wreck)—to focus on every anxious thought and sensation you have. Keep thinking, *Am I feeling really anxious?* or *Is my face blushing?* or *Am I sweating?*

3. *Try to hide your anxious feelings.* It's essential, in building your anxiety to new heights approaching panic, that you make sure that no one ever knows that you are uncomfortable and anxious. Hide every sensation and symptom that you have. Wear a jacket to hide your sweating, wipe your hands constantly so no one has to touch your sweaty palms, speak in a deep voice so no knows you are about ready to fall apart.

After You Interact with People

1. *Review how awful it felt.* Your postmortem is essential to remind you of how badly you have been doing. By doing a postmortem you might be able to learn how to avoid ever appearing anxious again. You need to be responsible for your anxiety. So think back about how you appeared like you were trembling or you said the wrong thing or there was a pause in the conversation because (you can assume) everyone was thinking about how anxious and boring you are. Keep reviewing your post-mortem to make sure you didn't leave anything out.

2. *Assume that people are now talking about how awkward you looked.* The great thing about meeting people is to be able to talk badly about them later, so you can assume that everyone you met is now sitting around laughing about you. They are sending e-mails to strangers ridiculing you. This is the entire purpose of their lives now.

3. *Focus on any signs of imperfection in how you appeared.* As you think back about how badly you did, don't let yourself off the hook by saying, *Everyone gets anxious,* or *I'm only human.* No you are not *just human*—you should always appear perfect and in control. Anything less than perfect means you are accepting yourself as a total loser. It's important to continue to think in all-or-nothing terms. Either perfect or a zero.

4. *Criticize yourself for being less than perfect.* Since it goes without saying that you were less than perfect you should spend as much time as you can criticizing yourself. Teach yourself a lesson you will never forget. Tell yourself that you were inferior, a loser, *always* screwing up, and that there isn't a single thing in your long life that you have ever done right.

You can at least take pride in the fact that you have mastered the rules and the many detailed skills of being a nervous wreck whenever you are around other people.

OVERCOMING YOUR SAD

Like generalized anxiety disorder (GAD), SAD has a broad range of symptoms. Since it's based on a fundamental, deep-seated anxiety around other people, SAD is a rather all-encompassing disorder. You'll be working to change not just specific behaviors but the whole way you see yourself in relationship to other people.

Our method will be the same as with any anxiety disorder: to challenge the thinking that supports it. There are many ways you can do this, from reflecting on some of your core beliefs to exercises you can actually perform that put these beliefs to the test. They don't need to be practiced in any particular order, but you should try to use as many of them as possible, since they reinforce and support one another. Together these steps constitute an effective body of treatment, especially if you're working with an experienced cognitive therapist. The good news is that over 75 percent of people with SAD can be significantly helped by appropriate treatment—often in twenty sessions—with the overwhelming majority of patients maintaining improvement long afterward.

Let's look at the steps one by one.

1. Build Your Motivation

People with SAD often feel that change is hopeless. Anxiety around social situations seems like a built-in part of their nature. Moreover, their strongest impulse is to avoid the stress of social interaction; the idea of subjecting oneself to any more of it than necessary seems unbearable. This is because they are unable to imagine anything but agony coming from such encounters. They fail to realize that it's possible to enter an anxiety-generating situation and *not* have it be painful.

It's true that in order to make this change, you'll have to experience moderate discomfort. You may have to push yourself into uneasy situations when your impulse is to run from them. You may be asked to confront thoughts and images that are unpleasant, and to abandon the security of isolation. If you've come to rely on drugs or alcohol to dull the pain, you may have some addiction work to do. On the other hand, the life benefits of freeing yourself from SAD are considerable. They include not only increased comfort in social situations, but the freedom to be more assertive, have greater effectiveness at work, improve relationships, and end loneliness. These benefits can extend into every area of your life. Getting over your social anxiety can help you get over your depression, substance abuse, and reliance on others, and it can dramatically improve your ability to have better relationships.

2. Stop Making Assumptions about What Others Think

This step could also be called "Don't be a mind reader." Your discomfort in the presence of others is often based on what *you* assume that *they* think about *you*. You may feel nervous talking at a meeting. You assume others can tell this from your shaking hands or trembling voice, and that therefore they look on you with disdain. In the first place, other people probably aren't nearly as aware of your mind state as you are (they're not mind readers, either). Second, it's simply not true that most people see nervousness as something worthy of contempt. Most people have a good deal of sympathy for nervousness, having experienced it themselves at one time or another. There's no reason whatever to assume they will like you any less for it, or harbor anything other than sympathy.

There are so many ways to be wrong about what other people are thinking. Remember the story of Ken, whose friends interpreted his shyness as aloofness—they thought *he* was looking down on *them*. Or take a situation where two people in an audience are smiling at each other as you speak. You assume they're mocking you, when in fact they're laughing about the fact that one of them has the hiccups. Or you leave a party convinced that everyone is just waiting to talk about how ridiculously you behaved. In fact, all anyone says is, "She seems very nice," and that's that. None of this proves that everyone will like you all the time. But it does indicate two things: 1) there's no way to know what people really think, and 2) if you suffer from SAD, it's almost a sure bet that what you imagine people think of you is far worse than what they do think. It's even possible that people are not thinking about you—they may be thinking about what other people think about them.

Ironically, many people with SAD can have close friendships. They will say, "My real friends know me because I trust them." But because people with SAD often isolate themselves and seldom share their inner life with others, the person with SAD has very few opportunities to find out that he or she can actually be liked.

3. Look for Positive Feedback

People with SAD tend to either avoid looking at others or to scan their faces for expressions of negativity: boredom, contempt, or annoyance. If that's what you're looking for, you'll probably convince yourself you've found it. But you can instead make a conscious effort to look for positive signs. Notice when people smile at you or compliment you; try to acknowledge them. It's important to respond to these gestures to make others feel at ease. You invite positive responses through your own positive behavior. If you make eye contact with others and smile, you will almost always get a smile back. Other people are shy, too, and are looking for encouragement from you. Almost all my socially anxious patients dramatically underestimate the positive reactions they can get. They start with the assumption that no one likes them, and they react accordingly. No one likes them much for that. Another self-fulfilling prophecy.

One of my female patients felt particularly anxious around men. She would avoid eye contact and speak to them in a murmur. She was so focused on her own awkwardness that she seldom noticed much about them. I asked her, as an exercise, to start noticing the eye color and shirt color of every man she met. This brought her out of her self-absorption. I also had her deliberately check to see if any of the men were smiling in her direction. To her surprise, many were; when she looked to see their eyes and shirt color, they would notice this and smile back. This taught her to redirect her attention from signs of rejection to signs of acceptance. Again, you tend to get what you're looking for.

You can also acknowledge your own successes. Give yourself credit each time you stretch your comfort level by going to a party, initiating conversations, sitting down next to others, asking them questions about themselves, and being assertive on your own behalf. Reinforcing yourself positively for your own behavior is important—it builds your confidence. Whenever you do anything to help yourself—for example, every time you put one of the techniques in this book into practice—you should acknowledge yourself for your effort. For a long time you've been busy putting yourself down, being your own worst critic, acting like an enemy. Consider switching sides.

4. Pay Attention to What Is Being Said

Many socially anxious people have trouble following what is being said in conversation. That's because they're focusing on what other people think about them, or dwelling on their own anxiety, or planning what they're going to say next to the extent that they totally lose the thread of the conversation, which makes them feel twice as anxious. There is so much chatter going on in your head about yourself and what others think that you have a hard time paying attention to what is being said. An effective way to handle your anxiety is to focus on the *content* of what's being said. If someone is talking about their job, see if you can actually follow the details, whether or not they're of great importance. Shift the focus away from *What does he think of me?* or *Maybe I should tell her about that thing that happened to my sister,* and onto *What's he saying now?* or *Do I agree with that?* One technique that I find useful is to ask the person with SAD to try to find out as much as he can about the other person. Ask a lot questions, empathize with their feelings ("It sounds as if that was exciting for you") and inquire some more. Occasionally rephrase what the other person is saying: "So, you've been working in this job for four years now."

This has the double advantage of taking your mind off your own anxiety while also enabling you to follow the conversation and respond more intelligently. This can dramatically ease your stress in the situation. Not only will it make you less shy, but you will find that people just love talking to someone like you who asks a lot of questions. You might be the most popular person at the party because you are an active listener—you ask more and more questions and show a lot of interest.

Another technique—good for when you're not in the middle of a conversation—is to describe to yourself the physical environment in front of you. If you're sitting at a party, for example, rather than thinking about how anxious you feel, or how embarrassed you are that no one is talking to you, you can simply take a deep breath, relax, and go over what you are seeing: who's in the room, what they're wearing, who's talking to whom, what the furniture or pictures on the wall are like. It lifts your mind out of its obsessive, self-scrutinizing groove, and dissipates your tension. And by the way, there's nothing shameful about sitting by yourself for a while. You may see being alone for the moment as the mark of your unworthiness, your rejection by others. In fact it means little or nothing—you're just being quiet for a while. Accept it and it's no longer a problem.

5. Give Yourself Permission to Be Anxious

One of the most difficult things about anxiety is the feeling that you need to get rid of it. This feeling is almost more of a burden than the anxiety itself. When you become anxious in the presence of others, you immediately feel you have to hide or suppress it. But why? Is it shameful? Is it fatally debilitating? Is it something others will condemn you for? Anxiety is a natural part of life. Everyone feels it at times and everyone understands it. Admitting to yourself (and anyone else around) that you're feeling uncomfortable at the moment is not at all disgraceful. In fact, it can be quite liberating. You no longer have to fake it. You can just be a normal, everyday, anxious person. It's part of learning to be more in the present, allowing "what is" to be.

You may also feel that your anxiety has to be wholly eliminated before you can *do* anything. This is a truly paralyzing belief. If you wait till you're no longer anxious before testing yourself in any social situation, you'll end up avoiding it altogether. You'll never learn that anxiety *can* be allowed, that it's not something to be feared—that in fact it has no terrible consequences beyond itself. Indeed the most important thing you can do to overcome anxiety is to take something you *do* feel anxious about, and do it *while* you feel anxious (more on this shortly). Think of your anxiety as a slightly awkward and loud friend you've brought with you. He may be a little clumsy, he may make things slightly uncomfortable at times, but that's no big deal. You can still hang out with other people even when he's around. The important thing is, *he's not you*. You don't have to control him, and you don't have to let him control you. Just as with all the other anxiety disorders, it's not about eliminating your anxiety. It's about making peace with it.

6. Give Up Your Postmortem

If you're like most SAD sufferers, you spend a good deal of time going over your social failures, fiascos, and shortcomings. If you've just come home from a date or social event that didn't go well, you'll probably start right in on the postmortem: going over everything you did wrong, recalling all the embarrassments and rejections you suffered, reliving each painful moment. But imagine if you decided to just let it go for now. Put off the postmortem until another time. For one thing, there's no urgency; you can certainly put off the rehash for a day or two. But your whole idea that you *need* to assess your performance is an illusion. You think you'll be able to go over your mistakes, learn from them, and correct them next time. It doesn't work like that. Your efforts to manage your anxiety are what got you in trouble in the first place. Going over all your mistakes only feeds your anxiety. It supports your image of yourself as socially inept, a "loser." It would probably be more helpful to go over what was positive about the experience: all the things you did right, the courage you showed in reaching out socially in spite of your fears, the opportunities for self-acceptance being offered to you. If you can look at it all with a sense of humor, so much the better. You'll certainly have plenty of opportunity to do things better next time. But your success will depend on your ability to *accept* your shortcomings—it will not be furthered by self-criticism.

7. Be Realistic about Your Self-Image

You are probably viewing yourself as basically inept, incompetent, uninteresting, or lacking in social skills of any kind. Consider the following: how are you with people you feel comfortable with and trust? Many people with social anxiety can be creative, intelligent, and responsible—once they feel at ease. Is there any evidence of your positive qualities? If so, then you might ask yourself, *When am I at my best?* For example, one man with SAD who thought he came across as boring when in a social situation, was actually very well-educated, had a great sense of humor, and was a decent and caring man.

You can challenge your negative thinking about yourself. What is the evidence for and against your negative view? Are you demanding perfection? Would you be as tough on someone else? Weren't there some things that went well? Isn't there always a next time? Can you give yourself credit for trying—you actually did do something to try to help yourself?

8. Face Your Worst Critic

All of us have in our minds the image of our worst critic. For Ken it was anyone telling him that he was an idiot for feeling anxious. So I thought we should take on his worst critic and defeat him. Here's how it went when Ken and I did a role play:

Worst critic (played by Bob): You must be an inferior person because you feel anxious.
Ken: No, that's your way of thinking. A lot of wonderful and creative people feel anxious. It's part of being human.
Worst critic: You should stop feeling anxious right now.
Ken: That sounds like some kind of moral rule. Am I disobeying the Ten Commandments?
Worst critic: No, but I don't like it.
Ken: Why should that be *my* problem?
Worst critic: Because you should make me feel good all the time. You should always get my approval.
Ken: I don't see any reason why I should make you feel good. That's your job. Sorry that you don't feel well.
Worst critic: Well, I can't stand it when you are anxious.
Ken: You mean you are anxious about my anxiety?

When Ken was able to take on his worst critic he realized how absurd it was. The worst critic was filled with distortions, moral rules, and demands. Ken could choose to let the worst critic be miserable. Why not? The critic has never done anything for Ken.

9. Create a Fear Hierarchy

We now come to some of the specific techniques or exercises you can use to address your social anxiety. In earlier chapters, I explained how to create a fear hierarchy as a way to practice experiencing your fears in a context of safety. You break down your fear of a situation into small steps, and then rank each step according to how much anxiety it arouses in you, assigning it a number from 0 (least fearful) to 10 (most fearful). Then you practice holding each of these steps in your mind for an extended period until your anxiety level—what we call your Subjective Units of Distress, or SUDS level—has subsided. You start with the least threatening and work your way up the list till you get to your worst fear.

I helped Ken develop a fear hierarchy around an especially loaded issue for him: meeting women. Everything about the process of getting to know women and asking them out was terrifying to Ken, but we managed to separate his anxiety into its components. Least threatening was thinking about a woman (rated 1). Being introduced to her was a little more stressful (5). Starting up a conversation was a *lot* more stressful (7). The scariest scenario of all was asking her out in front of other people (10). For each step along the way, I asked Ken to record the result he usually pictured Ken's responses are shown in Table 8.3.

<table>
<tr><th colspan="3">Table 8.3
Ken's Hierarchy of Behaviors
for Asking a Woman Out</th></tr>
<tr><th>Rating</th><th>Behavior</th><th>Thoughts and Fears</th></tr>
<tr><td>1. (Least Distressing)</td><td>Thinking about her</td><td>I might have to do something.</td></tr>
<tr><td>2.</td><td>Looking at her, but she doesn't see me</td><td>She might turn around and notice me.</td></tr>
<tr><td>3.</td><td>Noticing that she sees me looking at her</td><td>She might think I'm gawking at her.</td></tr>
<tr><td>4.</td><td>Going over and standing or sitting next to her</td><td>She might think I'm strange</td></tr>
</table>

5.	Being introduced to her	I won't know what to say after I say hello.
6.	Talking with her when we are alone	I won't know what to say.
7.	Talking with her in front of other people	I won't know what to say. Everyone will think I'm a loser.
8.	Approaching a woman at a party or bar	She'll think I'm too aggressive.
9.	Asking her out with no one around	She's reject me, and I'll feel like a loser.
10. (Most Distressing)	Asking her out in front of other people	She'll reject me, and I will be publicly humiliated. Everyone will think I'm a loser.

10. Image-Test Your Fears

We then worked with Ken's hierarchy. I had him hold the different images (sitting next to a woman, starting a conversation, etc.) in his mind, one by one, and record his SUDS level. With each one it would spike up initially, then gradually decline as his mind habituated to the disturbing image. His homework assignment was to spend thirty minutes each day on this exercise, working through three different steps in the hierarchy. Another way to imagine yourself in the situation is to form a detailed image in your mind of how you will speak—or how you will come across. If you are going to give a speech, you can imagine how you would appear on the video to a stranger—try to give as many details as possible. In one study, forming these images and then watching yourself on a video, dramatically reduced anxiety. This imagery allows you to distance yourself from the experience so that you don't feel as self-conscious.

11. List and Challenge Your Anxious Thoughts

What generally happens as you approach a socially stressful situation is that your mind becomes flooded with fearful thoughts. These thoughts dominate your mind, making it virtually impossible for you to make rational decisions or function effectively. Usually they just bounce around inside your head, piling up so rapidly and chaotically that you have no time to test their validity. That's why I've found it useful to have patients make a list of such thoughts. When you do this, you actually get to see your thoughts written down, one at a time. You can look at them during a quiet moment and consider each one calmly. You have a chance to challenge the *truth* of your anxious thoughts.

As you can see from his list of negative thoughts, Ken's main focus was on the fear of humiliation. Many of these negative thoughts are mind reading (*She'll think I'm a loser*), fortune-telling (*I'll get rejected*), and catastrophizing (*It would be a disaster if I get rejected or if people think I'm a loser*). He is also discounting the positives—after all, doesn't it take a lot of courage to face your fears? He should give himself credit for that.

So, Ken and I decided to challenge these negative thoughts so he could move forward to actually doing some of the exposure—that is, doing what he was afraid to do. Here is what Ken found useful:

Table 8.4
Ken's Fears and Rational Responses

Behavior	Thoughts and Fears	Rational Response
Thinking about her	I might have to do something.	She's nice to think about. She's attractive.
Looking at her, but she doesn't see me	She might turn around and notice me.	I have to look at people. What's so odd about that?
Noticing that she sees me looking at her	She might think I'm gawking at her.	She might think I find her attractive—which might be flattering to her.
Going over and standing or sitting next to her	She might think I'm strange	She might think I'm assertive and that I have the guts to approach her.
Being introduced to her	I won't know what to say after I say hello.	I don't have to be entertaining. I can just ask her about herself—where she's from, what she does, how she likes living here, what she likes to do for fun.

Talking with her when we are alone	I won't know what to say.	(see above)
Talking with her in front of other people	I won't know what to say. Everyone will think I'm a loser.	I can simply make small talk and ask her about herself. Why would anyone think I'm a loser if I'm talking to her? I'm not stupid. My friends like me.
Approaching a woman at a party or bar	She'll think I'm too aggressive.	She might think I'm confident in myself and might like the fact that I'm starting a conversation. After all, she's at a party to meet people.
Asking her out with no one around	She's reject me, and I'll feel like a loser.	It's a sign of confidence and honesty to ask someone out. She might say yes. If she says no, how am I worse off than before? Why should I feel humiliated if for being assertive?
Asking her out in front of other people	She'll reject me, and I will be publicly humiliated. Everyone will think I'm a loser.	If I saw a guy asking a woman out, I would be envious of him—even if he got shot down. I'd think, *He's doing something I wish I could do.*

12. Eliminate Safety Behaviors

Safety behaviors are actions that you think will keep you from going out of control and making a fool of yourself. Examples are looking down, speaking softly, not interrupting other people, not asserting yourself, and holding yourself in a rigid posture. Ironically, these behaviors may make other people think that you are odd and make them look at you with a puzzled expression. The problem with relying on safety behaviors is that you will think that the only way you kept yourself from looking foolish is that you used these behaviors. You will still hold on to your belief that interacting with people is dangerous because you are always on the verge of making a fool of yourself. Giving up safety behaviors is like giving up training wheels on a bicycle—it's scary at first, but it's the only way to ride. So your goal will be *to practice giving up every single safety behavior.* For example, look people *directly* in the face, don't put on a phony smile, let your arms dangle loosely, and interrupt people with your ideas. You will find that nothing terrible happens and that people don't reject you.

You may be reluctant to give up your safety behaviors. That's natural. You have been telling yourself that the only way you can do this is to hold your hands behind your back, clench the glass, speak slowly, look at your notes, or have a drink. But as long as you hold on to these behaviors you will continue to believe that the situation is really dangerous.

13. Practice Your Fears

You can make a good deal of headway with your fears by actually allowing some of the things you're afraid of to happen—even *making* them happen. For example, if you're worried you might freeze up during a presentation at a business meeting, try a little experiment. Stop for a minute, pretend to shuffle around in your notes, and say, "Let's see, I forgot where I was." Then continue. See if anyone notices or cares. Or if you're just standing around ill at ease, fearful that people will perceive your discomfort, you might say to the person next to you, "Gee, these affairs make me feel so awkward." It might start an interesting conversation. You don't have to plunge into your deepest terror; you can simply play your edge. If you do it often enough, your comfort zone will expand considerably. If you worry that your hands might shake, then fake a tremor for a couple of minutes. Again, I'll bet no one notices—and, if they do, why should they care? One man was so afraid that he would get dizzy and faint that I asked him to fake collapsing at a store. He did and people just asked him if he was okay. He got up, assured them he was fine, and then continued shopping. His worst fear turned out to be a minor moment for everyone around him.

Eventually, of course, you'll want to put things to the test—immersing yourself in the situations that most intimidate you and that you most avoid. The good news is that even with the big items, the process is no different. You simply find your comfort edge, go to it, and push a little. If you practice for a while in situations that are minimally threatening, you'll be much better prepared to take on the major challenges. Big noisy gatherings of people. Job interviews. Blind dates. Dinner parties. Giving a speech. Oral exams. Whatever it is that you find most threatening. No matter how scary it seems to you, there are ways of working with it. If you employ all the other steps listed here, putting them together as part of a coherent strategy, you'll have a good chance of success.

The main thing to remember is what we've already touched on. You won't get anywhere obeying the old rules—the ones that tell you you can't handle your anxiety. It's absolutely essential to go out of your way to do things you typically avoid, whether it's saying hello to strangers, asking for a date, speaking up at work, seeking directions, talking in front of groups, or going to a party. You can be gentle with yourself—but it needs to be a gentle *push*. The way to overcome your anxiety is through practice—through doing the things you're afraid to do. That's how your primitive mind—the part of your brain that up to now has been telling you to be afraid—learns what is and is not true danger. That part needs to experience the situation in question and find it safe before it can stop setting off alarms.

Go through your fear hierarchy and begin looking for opportunities to do the next thing on the list that will make you anxious. Keep in mind the new anxiety-free rule: if you are not doing something that is making you uncomfortable, then you are not making progress. For Ken, this required that he initiate a conversation and ask for information. I had Ken say hello to five strangers every day. Most people were pleasantly surprised to see someone so friendly. But when a few people didn't respond, Ken just chalked it up to living in a big city. Practicing your fear—and tolerating your anxiety—is the best way to make progress. If you can do things when you are anxious, then you can do almost anything that you need to do.

14. Exaggerate Your Anxiety

You've been trying desperately to keep your anxiety under control. You try not to let it affect you, and when it does you hide your symptoms. An interesting experiment is to try consciously going to the other extreme. For example, if you're giving a talk and you're afraid people will see you sweating, try dousing some water on your shirt around the armpits. Or let your hands shake violently before you begin. You can then smile and say, "I guess I'm kind of nervous." If all this is too threatening, you can practice in your imagination. If you're having a job interview the next day, for example, try flooding your mind with the scariest thoughts you can. Imagine everything that could possibly go wrong in the interview, and then elaborate on it; make it into the greatest fiasco you can conjure up. By the time you get to the real interview, your anxiety may seem relatively tame.

I'd been telling my patients this for years, and then one day I wondered, *Why not carry out an experiment myself?* I decided to fake having my mind go blank in the middle of a workshop I was giving. I stopped in the middle of a sentence, looked confusedly around, and said, "Hmm, I seem to have lost the thread. What was I talking about?" Some people glanced at their notes; most didn't even change expression. A few said something like, "I don't know, umm, I guess you were talking about worry." "Oh, right," I said, "I was talking about worry," and went on. No one batted an eye. The interesting thing is that this is what people who speak in front of groups fear perhaps more than anything. To all appearances, it had just happened. And yet absolutely nothing came of it. The consequences were zero.

15. Give Yourself Credit

You have been spending your time anticipating the worst and then doing your post-mortem after. But what you really should be doing is giving yourself credit for facing your fears and using the ideas and the techniques that we have been discussing. It's not easy having social anxiety and it's not easy overcoming it. So praise yourself for trying—just as you would if your best friend was struggling hard like you are to move forward.

Try to develop a compassionate kindness toward yourself. No one knows how hard it is for you to have anxiety and to do the things that I have described here. You've been so used to putting yourself down but it's time to give yourself credit for taking on challenges and obstacles. The more you reward yourself for doing the hard things that you are doing, the more likely you will keep your self-help going forward. You deserve your own support.

SUMMING UP YOUR NEW APPROACH
TO YOUR SOCIAL ANXIETY

Now that you have learned the different steps in overcoming your social anxiety, you can rewrite your rule book. You now have an Anxiety-Free Rule Book that you can use every day. It's important to go out of your way to do things that you typically avoid. You only overcome your anxiety—and maintain your improvement—by practicing the things that you have been afraid of. This can include saying hello to strangers, asserting yourself in a restaurant, asking people for directions, complimenting people, speaking up at work or in class, and going to parties.

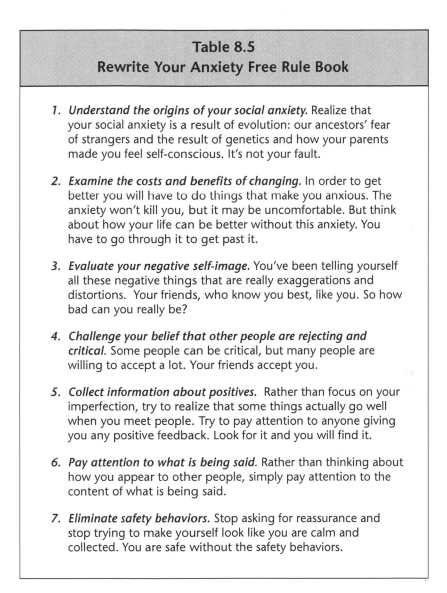

Table 8.5
Rewrite Your Anxiety Free Rule Book

1. *Understand the origins of your social anxiety.* Realize that your social anxiety is a result of evolution: our ancestors' fear of strangers and the result of genetics and how your parents made you feel self-conscious. It's not your fault.

2. *Examine the costs and benefits of changing.* In order to get better you will have to do things that make you anxious. The anxiety won't kill you, but it may be uncomfortable. But think about how your life can be better without this anxiety. You have to go through it to get past it.

3. *Evaluate your negative self-image.* You've been telling yourself all these negative things that are really exaggerations and distortions. Your friends, who know you best, like you. So how bad can you really be?

4. *Challenge your belief that other people are rejecting and critical.* Some people can be critical, but many people are willing to accept a lot. Your friends accept you.

5. *Collect information about positives.* Rather than focus on your imperfection, try to realize that some things actually go well when you meet people. Try to pay attention to anyone giving you any positive feedback. Look for it and you will find it.

6. *Pay attention to what is being said.* Rather than thinking about how you appear to other people, simply pay attention to the content of what is being said.

7. *Eliminate safety behaviors.* Stop asking for reassurance and stop trying to make yourself look like you are calm and collected. You are safe without the safety behaviors.

8. *Exaggerate your symptoms.* Rather than hide your anxiety make it more obvious. Douse water on your shirt so you look like you are sweating, let your hand shake, and even announce that your mind has gone blank. The world will not end if someone thinks you are anxious.

9. *Face your worst critic.* Fight back against the critic that is in your mind. Prove that he is irrational and unfair and is really not worth your time and energy.

10. *Be realistic about your anxiety.* Realize that anxiety is part of being alive—and that you can still talk with people even if you feel anxious. Anxiety is not dangerous—it's simply arousal. And, most of the time, it's based on a false alarm.

11. *Challenge your anxious thoughts.* Your thoughts are irrational. Fight back against them using the evidence, your logical thinking, and think about the advice you would give a friend.

12. *Practice your fears.* Do the things that make you anxious—on purpose. Make a daily plan to face your fears and do the things that you have been avoiding.

    • Set up a hierarchy—start with the least threatening and move up the list.

    • Imagine yourself in the situation—use your imagination to think of yourself successfully facing your fears.

    • Answer your negative thoughts in the situation—recognize your irrational thoughts and challenge them.

13. *Eliminate your post-mortem.* Rather than review your "mistakes" and ruminate about how badly you did, focus on what you are doing now that is productive and what you can do in the future to continue confronting your fears.

14. *Give yourself credit.* Every day is an opportunity to tell yourself that you deserve credit for facing the obstacles in your life. So, be your own best friend and tell yourself to keep up the good work.

CHAPTER 9

"It's Happening Again"
Post-traumatic Stress Disorder

WHAT IS POST-TRAUMATIC STRESS DISORDER?

Sarah had been raised in a strict family where her father was the supreme authority. When Father gave an order, you didn't answer back, you obeyed. Sarah was closer to her mom, but like Sarah and her sisters, her mother was intimidated by Father. She encouraged the girls to stay out of his way and keep from upsetting him. It all sort of worked for Sarah when she was little. She tried to be good: she did well in school and behaved appropriately at home. But as she entered adolescence things changed. She began to have a social life that took her out into the world—a world her father didn't always approve of. She began to form opinions of her own on religion and politics, to dress more independently, to be more outspoken. None of this was very pleasing to her father. Tensions between them began to rise; tempers would smolder and break out in arguments. Once or twice Sarah got in minor scrapes at school, which irked her father to no end. Her mother was not much help—all she wanted was for Sarah to behave, so Father wouldn't be angry and these awful arguments would stop.

One night Sarah came home from a party late. Father wanted to know where she'd been; Sarah refused to tell him. Father grew angrier and angrier; he started shouting. At that point, Sarah realized that he'd been drinking. She yelled back, accusing him of being drunk. Then something in Father seemed to snap. He slapped her hard across the face. She began to scream. He slapped her again and threw her to the floor. Then he stormed out. When she looked in the mirror, she saw that her face was bruised. Sarah was horrified but also felt a strange sense of shame. She decided not to tell her mother about the incident, and the subject was not mentioned.

It turned out this was only the beginning. After that, every time Sarah displeased Father, he would fly into a rage that often ended in violence.

219

He would slap and beat her, calling her stubborn and declaring that if she was going to behave like a tramp she deserved to be treated like one. His drinking was now out in the open, though no one in the family talked about it. One night he came drunk into her room, told her it was a mess, just like her life, and started beating her. Her shoulder was wrenched in the scuffle, and she had more bruises. Still she said nothing to anyone. The only thing her mom said afterward was, "Why do you provoke your father like that? Can't you just do the few little things that would make him happy?" She suggested that Sarah tell her teacher that the bruises were from a household accident, to avoid embarrassment. For reasons she only half understood, Sarah went along with this. But she realized she needed to get out of that house.

Sarah dropped out of school, even though her grades were good. She got a job in the next town and moved in with an older girl. She began to hang out with her friend's crowd, going to parties, hanging out with boys, drinking, and smoking pot. She was pretty, and boys were attracted to her. One night she ended up alone with three older boys she scarcely knew. She was flirting a little, and one of them started coming on to her. She resisted, but he pushed himself on her. The next thing she knew her clothes had been torn off and she was being raped. To her horror, the other two joined in the assault. At some point she heard herself screaming, but it was as if it was coming from someone else, as though the whole thing were happening in a dream or movie. The boys finally left. The room was a wreck. She put herself together and managed to get home with no one seeing her.

She thought of going to the police, but the idea seemed frightening. She told herself that no one would believe her story even if they did find the boys. They'd think she'd been asking for it by fooling around like that. So she kept quiet. She began to have nightmares. She was reluctant to be alone and began to drink and pop pills to get to sleep. Slowly she began to put her life back together but only on the outside. Inwardly the awful experience continued to haunt her. She had to leave her old job and take a less demanding one. For a long time she avoided parties or dating and felt unsafe walking the streets at night. She would scan the bus stop for dangerous looking types and tag along behind other couples for safety. Gradually she learned to cope with these anxieties, but they never seemed far away. She seemed to be living her whole life under a shadow.

Sarah was still having nightmares when I first saw her in my office ten years later. Her father had died three years earlier, and she was estranged from the rest of her family. She was barely hanging on to a low-level office job in the city. She'd hoped to go to college but seemed unable to pull it together. Strangely enough, despite her experience and her continuing terror of being raped, she was almost fatally drawn to the bar scene, hanging out with crowds of guys and often drinking to excess. She'd even been taking part-time gigs as a topless dancer. It was her way of convincing herself she was attractive to men—and perhaps, too, a denial that the assault had affected her. But she refused to date or get involved seriously with a man. Deep down, she told me, she felt like "damaged goods." In her own mind, Sarah was wholly worthless and unlovable, someone who couldn't risk getting close to anyone. And always, day or night, wherever she went, alone or with others, the memory of her past trauma lurked around the edges of her consciousness.

Sarah's condition was a classic case of post-traumatic stress disorder, or PTSD. As the name implies, it's an anxiety disorder brought on by exposure to a life-threatening or injury-threatening experience. The typical emotions associated with it are intense fear, horror, revulsion, shock, and helplessness. You may have been involved in a fire or serious car accident and barely escaped with your life. You may have been the victim of rape or other violence. You may have seen someone killed in front of you—perhaps even a loved one. Or you may have been sexually abused as a child. Whatever the trauma, it continues to disturb you long afterward. You may have dreams or flashbacks in which you re-live the experience. Frightening images may intrude on your consciousness. You have a sense that it is happening again—a feeling of "newness." Often you become hypersensitive to stories or pictures of similar events. You have an overwhelming urge to avoid people, places, activities, or conversations that remind you of your experience. You may begin to feel emotionally detached from those close to you. And you may, for reasons you yourself only dimly understand, be subject to a wide range of symptoms: irritability, hypervigilance, impatience, depression.

PTSD is generally defined as the persistence of these symptoms for at least a month after the event. Though this is somewhat arbitrary, it points to what distinguishes genuine PTSD from normal fallout after a harrowing experience: its long-term persistence. Symptoms of PTSD can last for years or even a lifetime, especially if left untreated. (Aversion to revisiting the trauma often dissuades sufferers from seeking therapeutic help.) The diagnostic test "Do You Have Post Traumatic Stress Disorder?" in Appendix G will help you determine whether your condition should be considered a case of PTSD. It's normal to feel the effects of any distressing experience for a while afterward, but this disorder has some fairly specific symptoms that should help you identify it.

A true case of PTSD is not a trivial matter; its impact can be considerable. There is a greater incidence of alcohol and drug abuse, as well as health problems like gastrointestinal distress, respiratory illness, diabetes, cardiovascular disease, and even cancer. People with PTSD are more than twice as likely to smoke, suffer from obesity, and have poor diet and exercise habits. They have higher rates of unemployment, absenteeism, and disability claims. They are more prone to both depression and suicide, more apt to have failed relationships, and more vulnerable to any of the other anxiety disorders. Having PTSD puts you at increased risk for almost every form of psychological ailment we know of. For those who suffer from this debilitating condition, it's a serious matter.

WHAT BRINGS ABOUT PTSD?

Surveys show that between 40 and 60 percent of the general public has been exposed to a trauma, but only 8 percent of us have PTSD. Why would only a minority of people develop PTSD after trauma?

A lot of factors may make it more likely for you to develop PTSD. These include a history of other psychological problems, a family with psychological problems, repeated exposure to the threat (for example, continued vulnerability to abuse or violence), history of prior trauma, substance abuse history, poor problem-solving skills, and even brain chemistry. In addition, you are more likely to develop PTSD if you "dissociated" (spaced out) during the traumatic event. Prior history of abuse makes you more likely to develop PTSD as an adult. Adults who were abused as children are 7.5 times more likely to develop PTSD as adults.

Women are twice as likely to have PTSD as men (10 percent versus 5 percent) even though males are more likely to be exposed to trauma (60 percent of males and 51 percent of females are exposed sometime during their lives to traumatic events). Genetics plays a role—about 35 percent of the risk for PTSD is inherited. In addition, PTSD, alcohol abuse, and drug dependence share common genetic factors—perhaps one reason why many people with PTSD also use drugs and alcohol to cope with their anxiety.

People with PTSD are more likely to have anxiety sensitivity—that is, they are more likely to focus on their physical sensations or anxious symptoms and to have negative interpretations of these sensations. For example, *My heart is beating rapidly—I must be having some serious physical problems*. Also, your mental coping style also makes you more vulnerable to PTSD. If you rely on worry and rumination (constantly going over in your head, *Why do these things happen to me?*), you are more likely to develop PTSD.

In reality there are a number of factors that must combine to produce a case of PTSD. One of them, of course, is the basic protective function of fear in the human psyche, to which we're all susceptible in some degree. Let's remember that in prehistoric times, human beings were more often prey than predator. Attacks by wild animals were an enormous threat to survival. So were the attacks of other tribes, which could end in wholesale murder, rape, or maiming of victims, not to mention destruction of the social bonds that produce and nurture offspring. One way nature had of keeping us safe from all this was to imprint memories of disaster vividly in the minds of the surviving victims. Any narrow escape, or witnessing of another's ill fate, would result in a strong aversion to situations where such disasters could be repeated. This is where the symptoms of PTSD originate: the bad dreams, insomnia, hypervigilance, and avoidance of similar circumstances all are part of an urgent message planted in our brains by evolution: "Don't let this happen again!"

WHAT IT'S LIKE TO HAVE PTSD

Think of PTSD as an inability to process difficult images, emotions, and thoughts. It's like a failure in "psychological digestion." When you are exposed to a traumatic event—such as a building collapsing—you have images and sensations. These include visual images of the collapsing building, sounds that you heard, smells that you experienced, and sensations that you had at the time (rapid heart beat, sweating). But after the event—in your attempts to recall the experience—the intensity of the experience is too much. You can't process it. The thoughts (*I am going to die*) and the images (the collapsing walls) are so overwhelming that your mind attempts to block them. You can't remember the story and the events in the logical sequence in which these events happened. You are like the little Dutch boy who puts his finger in the dike to prevent the water from leaking through the walls and flooding the town. You fear that one drop of water will lead to a flood and destroy you.

When you have PTSD your memory is disjointed, confused. Sometimes you can't recall clearly what happened first. The images try to get through to your awareness—but you are so frightened of them that you try to suppress them. You try to push them away. Each time you push them away you feel that you are struggling for your mental survival. But each time you push them away you reinforce the idea that remembering is dangerous and terrifying. So you try to keep yourself from experiencing any memory of the events. You can't stand seeing images on TV or hearing people talk about it.

Because your mind has not processed, or "digested," the experience, it is hard for your mind to recognize—"It's all in the past. It's not happening now." In fact, you sometimes feel, *It's happening* now! Your mind is having a panic attack about something that happened in the past—but it seems it's happening all over again. Your feeling of "nowness" of the threat may be triggered by a sound—or even a smell. If you were caught in a fire your terror might be triggered by the smell of smoke. Or if you were raped your terror can be triggered by seeing someone with the same jacket as the rapist. You feel you can never put the past behind you.

Your attempts to suppress the memory continue to fail. So you turn to drugs and alcohol. This keeps you from experiencing the memories for a few hours—but they come back—and your ability to process these memories is even worse. And if you avoid situations that trigger the memories, then you don't have an opportunity to process them and to learn, *I am safe.*

In addition to the intrusive images and thoughts that you have, you may find that your beliefs about yourself and the world have changed. You may now believe, *I am damaged. I can't trust anyone. The world is filled with danger. I am going crazy.* Dr. Ronnie Janoff-Bultmann described these beliefs as "shattered assumptions." Adding to your depressive view of life are your global negative beliefs about yourself—your "mental defeat": *I'm a hollow person. I have no life.*

One characteristic of the disorder is an aggravated tendency to worry. You worry about your sensations, thoughts, emotions, and outside danger. Like many worriers you believe that your worry will make you prepared, prevent something bad from happening—that your worry is realistic. You may find yourself making continual negative predictions—*If I go into that area, I will get hurt again,* or *I will be reminded of what happened, and I won't be able to stand it.* Many worry specifically about their trauma being repeated: another assault or injury awaiting them. Karen, one of my patients who'd been at the World Trade Center the day of 9/11 and who barely survived, for months afterwards remained on the lookout for hijacked planes in the sky or "Arabs" who might be carrying explosives. When she entered a building she would automatically plan her escape route. Your PTSD may cause you to worry primarily about your own mental condition: *Why do I jump at loud noises? Why am I so irritable with my family? Am I losing my mind?* Or you may simply see worry as a way of preventing unspecified disasters from occurring; if you stay alert and prepared, nothing really bad can happen. If you're a PTSD sufferer who worries excessively, you may want to consult Chapter 7 on generalized anxiety disorder (GAD) for some useful techniques.

Those with PTSD often report significant changes in their general outlook. These relate not only to one's own safety, but to how one sees other people, the world, or the meaning of life. One psychologist has spoken of the shattered assumptions that often accompany PTSD. These can be varied, depending on the mind state they are principally associated with:

- *Guilt:* There's something wrong with me. I must have brought this on myself.

- *Shame:* I've been damaged permanently. People will see this and despise me.

- *Uncertainty:* Anything can happen at any time. I'm never safe.

- *Helplessness:* I have no control over my symptoms. I'm a victim of what happened to me.

- *Anger:* I need to get even for this. I'd kill anyone who tries to do it again.

- *Mistrust:* I'll never trust anyone again. People just want to take advantage of you.

- *Hopelessness*: No one can help me with this. No one would understand.

- *Lack of Purpose:* Life has no meaning anymore. There's no reason to go on.

Needless to say, these attitudes are all contributing factors to depression. When a traumatic event has such shattering effects, when one has struggled with its aftermath without apparent success, and when no relief seems available, it is easy to believe that one has suffered a hopelessly devastating reversal of fortune. An important starting point for healing PTSD is seeing that these negative thoughts and attitudes are merely that—thoughts and attitudes. They come from inside you. They are not reality. Distancing yourself from them is your first step toward healing.

AN OVERVIEW OF PTSD

A good way to understand PTSD is to look at Figure 9.1. There are certain predisposing factors—genetics, family history, prior experience to trauma, skills for coping, one's support network, anxiety sensitivity, psychological problems prior to trauma, etc. Then there is the exposure to the traumatic event. Traumatic events include any event where your life (or someone else's life) is threatened—or your integrity as a human being is threatened (for example, torture, rape).

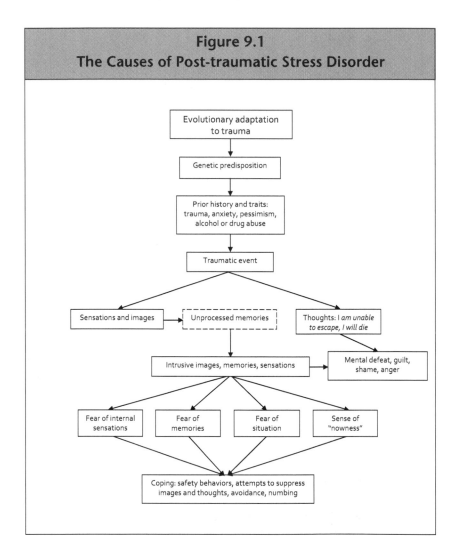

Figure 9.1
The Causes of Post-traumatic Stress Disorder

Let's look at each step in this process. Beginning with evolutionary history, it makes sense that we would have a mental mechanism to terrify us about trauma in order to remind us never to go to that dangerous place again. Terror assures avoidance—and avoidance can assure survival. As with any anxiety problem, there is an inherited component—it doesn't explain everything, but it makes you more susceptible. If you were prone to psychological problems prior to the trauma—or if you have been traumatized before—it makes it more likely that you will develop PTSD. The traumatic event is essential for PTSD—and it may vary in how intense it was, how close you were to the trauma ("Were you in the building when it collapsed?"), how long the trauma lasted, and if it was repeated or ongoing ("Were you in a relationship where you were abused over a long period of time?"). Also, it's important to note the thoughts that were triggered at the time that might make you vulnerable to terror or demoralization later ("I thought I was going to die," "I thought I had lost my dignity as a human being").

The box with the broken line reflects the fact that many sensations, images, and thoughts were not fully processed. They are floating in your mind, not completely clear to you after the event. They keep trying to intrude on your consciousness, but you keep pushing them away. Or they just don't make sense when they come to consciousness. Your memory of the trauma is fragmented, disjointed—the sequence of events is not entirely clear. This is because the intrusive images are not "digested"—your mind struggles against them. Your mind simultaneously experiences the intrusions and struggles to push them away.

As a result of these intrusions and the trauma associated with them, you have fears of your own internal feelings, thoughts, and memories—and you sense when things get really bad—that things are once again happening: *It's happening all over again.* You attempt to cope by pushing thoughts and images away, but this fails. You try to avoid. You use superstitious rituals. You ask for reassurance. And you drink too much. All of these attempts to cope only prolong your PTSD.

THE PTSD RULE BOOK

You're ready now to write your PTSD Rule Book. This is the rule book in your head that you refer to that makes you think that the trauma will never go away and that you are continually in danger. It's your rule book for thinking, feeling, and avoiding.

Table 9.1
PTSD Rule Book

1. Since something terrible happened, then terrible things will happen again.

2. Images and sensations are signs of danger.

3. You have to stop having any memories of what happened.

4. If you feel afraid then it's happening again.

5. Avoid anything that reminds you of the trauma.

6. Try to numb yourself so you don't feel anything.

7. Your life is changed forever.

LET'S TAKE A CLOSER LOOK AT YOUR PTSD RULE BOOK

1. *Since something terrible happened, then terrible things will happen again.* You generalize from the one trauma to the rest of your life. It's as if everything that is bad can be predicted by using this one incident as a basis for everything: *If I was attacked, I will be attacked again.*

2. *Images and sensations are signs of danger.* You use your emotions, physical sensations, and intrusive images as evidence of bad things happening: *I am feeling afraid, therefore it will happen again.* You are tuned in to any increase of your tension, any sweating, any increased heart rate. In fact your body has become a barometer of danger. And you can't escape your body or your mind.

3. *You have to stop having any memories of what happened.* Since your mind is used as a sign of danger, you want to "turn off" your mind. You try to tell yourself to stop thinking, stop feeling, and stop remembering. You might even yell at yourself to convince yourself that you have to suppress these memories. But they keep coming back—so you suppress more.

4. *If you feel afraid then it's happening again.* Your emotions and sensations now tell you, "It's happening right now." You wake up in terror and feel you are being attacked, raped, destroyed. Your sense of past, present, and future are collapsed into one time—*now.*

5. *Avoid anything that reminds you of the trauma.* You try to cope by avoiding any experience remotely reminding you of the past. You change where you go, you avoid traveling at certain times, you avoid certain sounds. You won't watch movies or programs that remind you. You look away. Your world becomes smaller—and feels even more dangerous.

6. *Try to numb yourself so you don't feel anything.* Since remembering and feeling are so terrible, you will try to eliminate any feelings whatsoever. You can do this by drinking or using drugs, hoping to escape from yourself. Or your mind can simply "space out" so that you feel either the world is unreal (derealization) or that you are not real (depersonalization). When you derealize or depersonalize you begin thinking that you are truly insane.

7. *Your life is changed forever.* It's not just the trauma—which was bad enough—now you feel that your whole life has changed. You can't trust anyone, danger can happen at any minute, you have been defeated. Life has lost purpose.

OVERCOMING PTSD

In recent years, there's been enormous progress in helping people overcome the effects of PTSD. Some well-publicized efforts have focused on traumatized war veterans, but of course our understanding of PTSD comes from many sources and applies equally to any devastating experience. One study indicates between 60 and 90 percent improvement after treatment for 15 different PTSD symptoms, while a summary of data from 26 separate studies shows therapy to have been effective in two-thirds of the cases. However because of the inherently disturbing nature of traumatic recollections, as well as the volatility of feelings often released, it is probably advisable to employ the techniques in this book with the help of a trained cognitive-behavioral therapist. He or she can guide you gently and firmly toward greater confidence in facing your fears. With PTSD it is especially important to maintain a feeling of safety, support, and compassion throughout the healing process.

Many people with PTSD simply feel hopeless and depressed about having the disorder. They either aren't aware or don't believe that there are effective treatments. Others may experience symptoms without realizing that they belong to a recognized anxiety disorder—in short, they don't even know they have PTSD. If there's any doubt in your mind, you can assess your condition with the Post-Traumatic Checklist for Civilians (Appendix G). Simply reading the present chapter may help you determine whether you suffer from the disorder. If you do, rest assured that others have experienced the same type of symptoms as you. Those who have undergone treatment have in the vast majority of cases had significant success.

You can use this book on your own as a self-help guide, or as a supplement to therapy. This is not meant to be a rigid procedure, but simply a list of some of the most practical and useful tools you can employ for overcoming PTSD. Here are the steps to overcoming your PTSD.

1. Build Your Motivation

All of our work on anxiety involves some cost. In order to get better you will be recalling in detail the terrible events that upset you. Although you can do this gradually and in the safety of your own home—or, preferably, with a good cognitive therapist—you will feel anxious when you do it. Almost everyone who initially feels anxious practicing the memory of the event also experiences a reduction of their anxiety. But it will be uncomfortable before it gets better. One thing to keep in mind is that you can develop a different approach to your discomfort by recognizing that it will decrease with repeated exposure in a safe and protected environment. Your discomfort can be guided discomfort, so that you learn that gradually facing your fears helps you reprocess the experience in a way that it is less disturbing. But treatment is sometimes unpleasant for short periods of time.

On the other hand, how would your life be better if you no longer had PTSD? Would you be free of nightmares, the sense of danger, the fear of your own memories and sensations? Would you be more likely to pursue close relationships, to travel, or to try new experiences? Would you be less depressed, feel more in control of your life, and feel that the past is finally behind you? Weigh the costs and benefits of getting better.

2. Observe Your Thoughts

Gaining distance on your fearful thoughts is probably the central strategy in overcoming PTSD. We often treat our mind states as pictures of reality. When a fearful image comes into our minds, it arouses real fear—it's as though a photograph of a tiger could bite you. Whatever our thoughts tell us might be out there in the world, we assume is really out there. But thoughts have no necessary connection to the world, especially when generated by our own fevered imaginations. By developing the habit of observing your thoughts in the moment, you can begin to see them as just thoughts. The important thing is not to try and suppress them, to exert any kind of influence over them, to judge them, to "improve" them, to calm them down, or indeed to do anything at all except allow them to be there. They have their own rhythm, arising and passing away according to their own mysterious laws. They are a river flowing gently and slowly through your consciousness. Struggling against them, arguing with them, trying to suppress them—all this only makes you more anxious. It's far more productive to simply watch them without comment.

This is a kind of meditative exercise you can practice any time, especially when your thoughts become a source of agitation. (See Appendix E: Mindfulness) Sit in a quiet place and let the thoughts pass through. Watch them as you would leaves rustling in the branches or waves lapping at the shore. If a thought says, *Something bad is going to happen,* then that's simply what it *says.* It doesn't mean that something bad *is* going to happen. Say to yourself, *This is just a mental event—it's not reality.* Try to look at your thoughts less in terms of their content, and more as events taking place in the mind. The fact is that for all their turbulence, *they pose no danger.* Regardless of what terrors they depict, you are entirely safe in their presence.

3. Evaluate Your Negative Thoughts

You have developed a lot of negative beliefs about your memories, sensations, yourself, and the world. These have added to your anxiety about recalling the event and have demoralized you in your life today. We can use a number of cognitive-therapy techniques to examine and change these beliefs so that you can be less afraid and less depressed. In the tables below, I have outlined some useful responses to these beliefs. You can also identify other negative thoughts that you have and challenge them on your own.

In the table below, you can see some examples of the triggers, negative thoughts, and realistic thoughts that you could have. In Table 9.3, write out your triggers for bodily sensations, your negative thoughts, and more realistic and calming responses.

Table 9.2 Sensations and Images		
Triggers	**Negative Thoughts**	**Realistic Thoughts**
Heart beating rapidly	I'm having a heart attack. I'm losing control.	This has happened many times before and I've gotten over it. I'm simply feeling anxious and my arousal is a little higher.
Feeling spaced out as if the world around you doesn't seem real or that you don't feel real yourself.	I'm going crazy. I'm completely out of control. This will last forever.	You are having an experience of derealization or depersonalization. This is like your mind has a "short circuit" that turns off your anxiety. You are not going crazy—you are simply very briefly pulling away.
Body is shivering or fingers feel cold	Something is terribly wrong with me. Am I dying? Am I having a heart attack?	This is simply a symptom of my anxiety. The shivering and the coldness in my fingers will improve in a few minutes.

Table 9.3 Sensations and Images		
Triggers	**Negative Thoughts**	**Realistic Thoughts**

In addition to your fear of your own sensations you have developed negative ideas about yourself, other people and the world. Look in the table below at some typical negative beliefs ("shattered assumptions") and the realistic thoughts that you can use to challenge them.

Table 9.4 Self, Others, and the World	
Negative Thoughts	**Realistic Thoughts**
I am completely helpless.	You are not helpless, since there are many things in life that you have control of. You can schedule activities that you like to do, you can see friends, you can make plans and carry them out.
I am damaged forever.	Think about all the good qualities that you have and all the things that you could still do. Even though it was a terrible experience, you still have your whole future ahead of you. Everyone has or will suffer losses and disappointments, but we still can go on in our lives.
I can never trust anyone again.	What happened to you was so unusual that it sticks out in your mind. Does it make sense to generalize from one incident or one person to the entire human race? Perhaps you can look at trust in terms of "degrees of trust." Perhaps you can take a little while to get to know someone.

4. Allow Your Anxiety

A major component of PTSD is fear of your own emotions and sensations. When you begin having dark thoughts, uncommon fears, and unusual physical sensations you tend to interpret those very thoughts and sensations as dangerous in themselves, rather than as simply your mind's normal response to a perceived danger. You may become hyperaware of your internal sensations—heart rate, tingling, numbness, bodily tension, aches and pains—and interpret these as signs there's something wrong with you. You may even see them as permanent effects of the trauma. None of this is valid. All these mental and physical symptoms are merely a response to emotions you haven't fully processed yet. Of course this is all very confusing; it's natural to have complicated feelings about traumatic events. But the feelings really pose no danger to you. Anxiety in itself is not a threat, either physically or psychologically.

This is important to recognize, because of a crucial paradox: until you *allow* your anxiety, you cannot be free of it. Your tendency is to think that anxiety is bad and that you have to eliminate it. But this is impossible to do. Your anxiety is already a given fact that you can no longer prevent. Your attempts to eliminate it have just the opposite effect—they reinforce it. And the very impossibility of eliminating anxiety—the frustration of trying to make it go away and *failing*—causes further anxiety. On the other hand, when you relax your effort, when you allow anxiety to occupy its normal place in your awareness, it begins to weaken. It becomes the temporary phenomenon that nature designed it to be. Eventually, inevitably, it goes away.

5. Challenge Your Belief That You Are Still in Danger

The trauma happened in the past—perhaps months or years ago. But you still feel as if you are in danger. The intrusive thoughts, sensations, and images keep reminding you of what happened. But it happened in the past. It is not happening now. You can start challenging the idea that you are in danger now. For example, if you were traumatized by a fire, accident, or explosion—remind yourself of how safe your current situation is. If you were assaulted or raped, remind yourself that this person is no longer here with you. Ask yourself if most people feel safe where you are. Ask yourself how unusual the traumatic event was. And keep in mind that a feeling (of being unsafe) is not the same thing as a fact.

You may think, *Even though I know it's irrational to feel as if I am in danger, I still feel it.* That's natural. But recognizing consciously and rationally that the danger is in the past and that you are safe now is a first step to eventually changing the way you *feel*.

In some cases, the perpetrator of your trauma may still be in your life. It's important for you to respect your own rights and to use every means available through the law to protect yourself. You may be able to get a restraining order. Or you may be able to go to a safe house or place until the danger subsides.

In most cases, though, we have found that our patients with PTSD are realistically in a safer place now but that these thoughts about danger persist.

Table 9.5 Why I Am Safe Now	
Beliefs About Danger	**Why I Am Safe**

6. Retell Your Story

We've now come to some of the specific exercises you can use to overcome PTSD. One of them is to actually tell the story of your trauma in as much *detail* as possible. You will probably notice when you first retell the trauma story that events are disjointed, out of sequence, and that some details are missing. This is because your response to trying to block the trauma has kept you from processing the memory and the events—you have parts of the memory, but not the entire memory at first. As you retell the story and face the fears you may find that the details become clearer, the sequence of events makes more sense, and the story becomes less frightening.

It's good to write it down; though you can also use a voice recorder (some people find it helpful to do both). Try to describe everything that was going on at the time: where you were, the events leading up to the trauma, what was happening around you. If it helps, close your eyes and try to summon a picture in your mind. What were you thinking and feeling? What do you remember of the physical circumstance? What were your sense impressions? The greater the detail, the more you'll be re-creating the actual experience. Though this can be scary, it is the necessary path to healing.

When I asked Sarah to do this, she was hesitant at first. "I just want to forget about it," she told me. "It's hard enough to keep it out of my mind every day. Why dredge it up again?" But as I explained to her, the retelling is an important first step in processing your experience. By practicing exposure you become more tolerant of painful images and sensations. This is how your mind "learns" that the trauma took place in the past and is not being repeated—the key to eventually feeling safe. When you've recorded your recollections, in either audio or written form, use them for repeated practice. I had Sarah listen to the audio tape she'd made for 45 minutes each day. The first few times her anxiety level shot up initially, then began to level off. After a few days the effect was less. After a few weeks she was able to listen with virtually no anxiety whatsoever.

Within the story, there may be certain images or memories that are particularly disturbing. I refer to these as hot spots. For Sarah there were several such moments: the shock of being seized by the wrists; a twisted expression on one of the boy's faces as he pressed close to her; the sound of heavy breathing. Each time Sarah came to one of these points in the narrative she would feel the urge to speed up and rush past it. Certain thoughts would flash through her mind: *They're going to kill me!* or *I'll never be able to have sex again!* Each time she would want to skip over the image that was prompting these thoughts. I urged her to slow down, to focus on these intensely painful moments, especially on what she was feeling and thinking during them. It was difficult, but once she did she found it helped her get to the roots of her fear. Some patients react to such hot spots by disconnecting from their feelings—recounting the facts, but drifting off emotionally. This is what we call dissociation—you're watching the story unfold but you seem to be not really there. You are "spaced out," and the reason for this is to try to block the emotional intensity of the story. When you catch yourself avoiding the impact of a hot spot, for whatever reason, it's a sign your mind is trying to escape something it finds particularly unpleasant. It also tells you that this is a place you need to pay particular attention to. Go over your hot spots repeatedly if necessary, and ask yourself what you are thinking. Sarah thought, *I am going to die.* The areas of greatest discomfort are the areas where you can make the most progress.

Table 9.6 Hotspots in My Story	
Image of the Hot Spot	What It Makes Me Think and Feel

7. Restructure Your Images

Disturbing images have great power when you feel they're beyond your control. One way to dispel that feeling is to consciously change the images in your mind. For example Karen, my World Trade Center patient, had developed a fear of airplanes passing overhead. I asked her to close her eyes and imagine a plane flying in the sky. Then I asked her to alter the image so that the plane flew very, very slowly. Then I had her imagine it moving to the side, going up and down, flipping over, flying backward. It was as though Karen herself were controlling the plane. She found this reduced the scariness of the image. Another patient had been assaulted by a man on the street and been beaten up badly. I had him replay the image in his mind, but making the man small, like a little doll. I had him imagine picking the tiny man up, shaking him, tossing him in the air, throwing him on the ground, and stomping on him. I had him continue this until the new image was as vivid in his mind as the old one. It made him feel less intimidated, more in control. The point was not to fool himself about what had happened, but to see that his fear arose from a somewhat arbitrary picture in his mind. Changing the picture changed the response.

This technique can be particularly effective in cases of abuse. Often abuse victims are left with a core feeling of powerlessness. I encourage these victims to construct statements that address their abuser directly and assert their own power. These might contain language like the following: "You made me think I was weak, that I had no rights. You pushed me around. But it was you who were weak. You turned your own sickness and meanness on me. You blamed me for everything lacking in you, making it seem like my fault. I no longer accept that. I am a good person and a strong person. I deserve to be treated well. You will never do this to me again." You can formulate your own version, but the main thing is to contact a place of strength inside you. The willingness to assert one's own power, even to oneself, is an important step in reclaiming it.

8. Expose Yourself to Feared Sensations

PTSD often involves a fear, not only of threats from outside, but of one's own internal sensations. (We covered this ground extensively in Chapter 5: Panic Disorder.) When the trauma occurred, your body produced certain physiological responses: dizziness, rapid heartbeat, shortness of breath, etc. These sensations are associated in your mind with the initial experience. When they recur in response to your memories, they revive the mind state of that moment. The mere fact that you're having such symptoms re-creates your original terror.

This offers you an important opportunity. As with any fear, you can overcome your anxiety by activating your fearful sensations deliberately and observing that nothing disastrous follows. You may recall the steps involved in overcoming a fear of elevators; one deliberately induces the panicky symptoms and then "stays with" them until one's mind habituates and the panic subsides. One can do the same with PTSD through certain planned exercises. However there are a number of important precautions. One is to make sure you do this in a place that feels safe; preferably with guidance from a therapist (PTSD symptoms can feel volatile). You should also consult a physician or have a health check to make sure you don't have a medical condition that could cause problems: cardiac or lung disease, asthma, proneness to seizures, and the like. If you are pregnant or prone to seizures, you should consult your physician before trying any of these exercises. As long as there's no actual physical problem, merely stimulating your anxiety symptoms should prove quite harmless.

Here are some of the fear-based sensations commonly associated with PTSD, together with exercises to replicate them.

Feared sensation: Dizziness, faintness, rapid heart rate, shortness of breath

- *Exercise:* Shake your head from side to side for 30 seconds; spin around in place; breathe rapidly, or through a straw, for two minutes. Watch responses for 5 minutes.

- *Effect:* Mimics the physiological responses to your original experience. This often stimulates the fearful emotions and panicky thoughts associated with it: *I'm losing my mind!* or *I'm about to die.* When experienced in this safe, controlled situation, the lack of catastrophic consequences reveals these thoughts to be false alarms.

Feared sensation: Depersonalization (the feeling of watching yourself from outside)

- *Exercise:* Stare at yourself continuously in a mirror, or at a spot on the wall, for two minutes.

- *Effect:* Dissolves your sense of self, resulting in a feeling that you are somehow not real. This is a kind of protective mental circuit breaker, designed to disconnect you from fear overload. Its usual effect can be to make you think you're losing your sanity. The exercise demonstrates that, on the contrary, what's happening is a temporary perceptual distortion.

Feared sensation: Derealization (a dreamlike feeling that makes the world seem unreal)

- *Exercise:* Stare continuously at a fluorescent light for one minute, then try to read.

- *Effect:* Produces a feeling of being spaced out, or emotionally removed, as though you were watching a movie. This is another circuit breaker, disconnecting you from your trauma. As you watch the world slowly resume its familiar form, you become conscious of the trick your mind has played. You see that you are not going crazy. The world feels real again.

There are also some simple exercises to dispel these feelings. They're called grounding exercises. Their effect is to bring you back to reality. For example, I sometimes have patients describe all the objects they can see in my office, or the colors of all the books on my shelves. You can also do this by walking very slowly, touching each foot to the ground and noticing the sensations in as much detail as possible. Or you can run your fingers gently across different surfaces, describing in detail what you feel from each. This brings you into direct contact with your experience of the moment, which is a way of bypassing the mind's distortions and illusions. When you are fully present and in contact with your immediate sensations, the games your mind plays begin to recede in your consciousness. You become calmer and clearer, and as a result your fears tend to subside.

9. Create a Fear Hierarchy

A fear hierarchy, as described in some of our previous chapters, is simply breaking down a general fear into its specific components, which are then ranked according to the intensity of your fear about each one. For example, Sarah often ran into situations that reminded her of her assault. One such situation—understandably—was going to a party where there were men drinking. I worked with Sarah on breaking this down into a list of more specific images, which we ranked from least to most frightening: Being invited to the party. Getting dressed to go. Traveling there. Walking into a room and seeing it filled with men. Hearing the sound of male conversation and laughter. Being approached by a man she didn't know. Smelling alcohol on a man's breath. And so on—all the way up to having a man force his attentions on her and having to push him off. We ranked all of these on a 0–10 scale according to how threatening they were. Then I had Sarah sit with each image in her mind, recording her fear level at two-minute intervals. Naturally it would start out at a high level—around 8 or so—and then gradually subside. When the number dropped down below 3, we'd move up to the next step in the hierarchy and repeat the process. Eventually she got to the point where she could run all the way through the hierarchy with relatively little disturbance.

Of course the images in your hierarchy are just pictures in your head, with no real power to harm you. That may be obvious when you're consciously making them up. It's the images that will come to you out of nowhere, the ones that will take you by surprise—the attacker who appears in your nightmares, the sudden whiff of a burning building, the terrifying photo in a magazine—these will be the real challenge. What you need to remember is that *these images are no different.* They're also just pictures in your head. Employing a fear hierarchy trains you to make this connection. It teaches you that all your fears, no matter what their source, are kept alive in your mind. That's where you need to turn your attention.

In cases of PTSD it's often especially hard for people to make the crucial distinction between what is real and what is imagined. What was *once* real is so vivid that the mind believes anything associated with it is also real. But when you're aware in the present moment of what's passing through your mind, you're less likely to be caught up in this illusion.

10. Look at Pictures That Remind You of the Trauma

You have probably noticed that you avoid certain movies or images because they remind you of the trauma. Now we are going to use those images to help you. A common source of terrifying images is the prevalence of violent material in all the major media: movies, TV, newspapers, magazines, the Internet. The bad news is that these images are everywhere. The good news is that because they are everywhere, they can be easily accessed and applied to a therapeutic purpose.

Sarah and I decided to work with a certain movie we'd both seen. It was a gruesome film, depicting a brutal rape and including scenes of torture, humiliation, and revenge. Sarah was understandably hesitant to watch it, but at a certain point in her treatment she decided she was ready to take it on. She prepared by practicing her relaxation and mindfulness exercises and by writing out her positive, empowering thoughts: *I am no longer a victim.* We discussed how it was possible to experience disturbing thoughts from another vantage point, in which they were simply events in the mind. By the time we turned on the video she was feeling guardedly optimistic.

Sarah watched the movie from start to finish. She never left the room, never hid her eyes. Later she admitted that parts of it had pushed her toward the edge, but that every time that happened she was able to distance herself with the recollection: *This is just a movie. There's nothing to be afraid of. My fear has all been created in my mind. Disturbing thoughts can't hurt me.* Just being able to sit through the movie made Sarah feel stronger. She knew that next time she encountered a charged situation, it wouldn't be quite as threatening.

11. If Possible, Revisit the Scene

We took this one step further. We decided Sarah would revisit the building where the rape occurred. This kind of thing is often a big step for people who've been traumatized. Such scenes are usually full of visual or other sensory cues that can touch off painful buried memories. I don't necessarily recommend taking this on unless you're prepared and are pretty sure you can handle it. In Sarah's case, the readiness was everything. She couldn't actually get into the building, which was occupied, but the neighborhood around it was disturbing enough, as she had pictured it in her waking dreams many times. As she approached the building she began to feel nauseated. She felt a kind of pounding in her head. But she was prepared. She took a few deep breaths and looked around. It was broad daylight, people were walking around. The rape had occurred many years ago, the perpetrators were gone. She was safe. She walked around outside awhile, and as she did so she could feel her anxiety level slowly subside just as it had when practicing her fear hierarchy. She left feeling lighter, as though a burden had been lifted.

When she told me this, I said, "Sarah, you should give yourself a lot of credit. You took back your territory."

"More than that," she said, smiling. "I took back myself."

I believe pushing one's limits in this way—habituating oneself to face increasingly charged real-life situations—is by far the most effective way of overcoming PTSD. However I do urge caution in making the jump from imagined situations to real ones, especially with PTSD, for the simple reason that volatile feelings can build up like gas fumes. Sudden exposure can produce more of an explosion than one is ready for. There's a skillful way to prepare yourself for such situations so they can be absorbed at a pace you can handle. That's why I recommend getting the help of a skilled cognitive-behavioral therapist for this part of the PTSD treatment. It can provide you with the benefits of experience—of all we know about the disorder and how others have grappled with it. It can also help guide you along the path to healing at a gentle, steady pace. Any way you regard it, PTSD is a major challenge. You owe it to yourself to have all the resources and support you can muster.

12. Eliminate Your Safety Behaviors

Safety behaviors often play a major role in PTSD. They are the things your mind believes will insulate you from your terrors. Karen, my patient from the World Trade Center collapse, would turn the TV off whenever the news came on. Victims of an assault will sometimes begin carrying pepper spray or even a gun. A patient who'd been in a fire took to positioning himself next to the exit of a theater, while another who'd been in a car crash repeated prayers to himself every time he rode in a vehicle. Some of these behaviors might actually have some protective value (i.e., fastening your seat belt more consistently following an accident), though most do not. Self-medication through drinking and drugs is definitely one that does not. In fact, drugs and alcohol keep you from processing the fear and thus maintain your trauma. But the real problem with safety behaviors is that as long as they continue they reinforce your belief that you're in danger. If the behaviors you're attached to confer no real benefit, it will be greatly in your interest to identify them and work to eliminate them.

The all-important first step is to become conscious of them. Start by making a list. Are there things you have been avoiding—people, places, activities? Are there little "superstitious" gestures you tend to make when anxious—tensing your body, walking close to buildings, repeating a prayer, humming loudly to yourself? Are there feelings you avoid by immersing yourself in distractions—food, entertainment, sex, even work—or by zoning out or sleeping most of the day? Do you steer yourself away from certain images in magazines or TV or public advertisements? And of course what is for many an enormous issue, often difficult to address honestly: are you trying to numb your feelings through drugs or alcohol? It may be hard to answer some of these questions, but if there's something you're in doubt about, it probably belongs on the list. Use Table 9.7 to identify your safety behaviors and beliefs about how they work.

Table 9.7 Safety Behaviors		
Typical Safety Behaviors	**Examples of My Safety Behaviors**	**How I Think these Safety Behaviors Protect Me**
Continually looking for signs of danger		
Avoiding people, places and things		

Looking away from sounds, images, or experiences that remind me of the trauma		
Seeking reassurance		
Repeating prayers or using superstitious behaviors		
Physical tensing (holding my body, holding my breath, walking a certain way, etc.)		
Using alcohol or drugs to make myself feel more calm		
Bingeing on food to take my mind off of memories		
Other behaviors		

The answers to these questions will tell you a great deal about the role safety behaviors play in your PTSD.

When you give up a safety behavior, you're almost certain to feel more anxious. Don't be deterred by this. Your mind has been telling you that the behavior has been keeping you safe; it's natural to feel some alarm when you let go of it. But what your mind has been telling you deserves your profoundest skepticism. It is not the truth. The only way for you to learn this is by giving up the safety behavior and seeing what happens. It's like removing the training wheels from a bicycle. Be prepared for an initial upsurge of anxiety. If you have the patience and determination to stick with it, you'll eventually see that anxiety decline. Nor do you need to do everything at once. Work with your safety behaviors one at a time, enlarging your comfort zone gradually. Don't push yourself into things that are truly unsafe—like walking around dangerous neighborhoods, driving at high speed, or dating men indiscriminately—just to prove a point. Prudence is still a virtue. But so is the ability to tolerate discomfort, especially when it ends up reducing that discomfort.

13. Examine Your Beliefs

As with any anxiety disorder, a number of deep and powerful beliefs support your anxieties. Start by making an honest list of what you really believe, deep down, in connection with your PTSD. Not what you think rationally, but what the deeper, more emotional, more out-of-control part of you thinks, what the voice behind your anxiety disorder is really saying. Then, and only then, construct the answer that a more rational part of you might give in response. The resulting dialogue might take a form something like this:

- *Since something terrible happened, something like it will happen again.* In fact your trauma is in the past; there is no reason to expect it to recur. Your belief comes from your mind's failure to process your experience, leading you to confuse past, present, and future.

- *My agitation is a sign of danger.* Fear, tension, and arousal are normal reactions to your original experience. They arise now because you confuse your situation with real danger. In themselves your feelings constitute no threat. Realizing they are false alarms will neutralize them.

- *I need to forget what happened.* Suppressing your memories is impossible. It's also unnecessary. Your attempt to turn off your mind only increases your fear and guarantees that the bad memories will recur. You need to allow these memories to live in your mind as the harmless thoughts they are.

- *I should avoid anything that reminds me of the trauma.* All this accomplishes is to make your world smaller and seem even more dangerous. It prevents you from recovering. To move on, you need to experience situations that trigger your memories and learn that they're harmless.

- *If I numb myself, I won't have to feel the pain.* True, but only briefly. Drinking, using drugs, "spacing out," or otherwise hiding from unhappy memories are simply ways of anesthetizing your feelings. They rob your life of richness, cause practical problems, and prevent you from healing.

- *My life is changed forever.* It only seems that way because you have not processed your experience. Once you stop confusing past with future, the picture is different. Many people recover from PTSD; it persists as a crippling disorder only as long as you let it.

- *It's happening again.* That was then, this is now. The only thing happening now is that your mind is sending false alarms. The past is gone.

14. Reward Yourself

You have been going through a lot of difficulty both having suffered from PTSD and doing the exercises in this book. It's hard either way. But every time that you do something to help yourself you should reward yourself. Praise yourself for having the courage to do what is hard to do now so it can be easier in the future. Give yourself for credit for making progress the hard way—but the real way. Only you know how difficult this has been for you and only you can do the tough things to get better. Set up your rewards so that you praise yourself immediately for doing these things. If you retell the story until it becomes boring, then tell yourself you are working hard to do what you need to do. If you start doing things that you feared doing, then tell yourself you have more obstacles that most people—and, therefore, you will give yourself more credit.

SUMMING UP YOUR NEW APPROACH TO YOUR PTSD

Now that you have learned about PTSD and used the many techniques described here, you are ready to write a new rule book for PTSD. If you follow these new rules, you will go a long way to conquering your fears and taking your life back from the trauma that has haunted you.

Table 9.8
Rewrite Your PTSD Rule Book

1. *Practice Relaxation.* Set aside time every day for deep muscle relaxation, mindful breathing, or a body scan.

2. *Examine the costs and benefits of changing.* Getting better will require doing some things that are uncomfortable. How will your life be better if you no longer have PTSD?

3. *Be an Observer.* Rather than struggle against sensations, images, and thoughts, just stand back and watch them. Observe that they are temporary. They are mental events, not reality.

4. *Don't struggle, let it be.* Allow thoughts, sensations, and images to come and go like water flowing along a stream. Surrender to the moment.

5. *Evaluate your negative beliefs.* Challenge the negative thoughts that you have about helplessness, guilt, and the lack of meaning in life. What advice would you give a friend?

6. *Challenge your belief that you are still in danger.* It happened in the past, but it sometimes feels as if it is happening now. Remind yourself of how safe you really are.

7. *Retell the story in more detail.* Write out and tape record your retelling of the story of your trauma. Pay attention to the details of sounds, sights, and smells. Try to recall the sequence of how things actually happened.

8. *Focus on the hot spots in your story.* Certain images and thoughts make you feel more anxious. Try to notice what they are and what they mean to you. Slow yourself down and examine the negative thoughts that are associated with these images.

9. *Restructure the image.* Create a new image in which you are triumphant, dominant, and strong. Imagine yourself as the victor and as more powerful than anything and anyone that has traumatized you.

10. *Eliminate safety behaviors.* Notice any superstitious things that you do to make yourself feel safer—like repeating reassurance to yourself, avoiding doing certain things at certain times or places, tensing your body, scanning for danger. Eliminate these behaviors.

11. *Be realistic about anxiety.* Realize that life includes anxiety—because anxiety is necessary for living. Don't think of your anxiety as awful or as a sign of weakness. Everyone has anxiety. It is temporary, it passes, it is part of getting better. You will do things that make you anxious to overcome your anxiety. Go through it to get past it.

12. *Expose yourself to your feared sensations.* You have been afraid of your internal sensations—dizziness, breathlessness, feeling spaced out. Practice the exercises to make yourself intentionally feel these sensations to learn that they are temporary and not dangerous.

13. *Practice your fears.* The best way to overcome your PTSD is to practice the things that make you afraid:

    • Set up a hierarchy.

    • Imagine yourself in the situation.

    • Look at pictures that remind you of the trauma.

    • Answer your negative thoughts in the situation.

    • If possible, revisit the scene.

14. *Reward Yourself.* Remind yourself that you are the one who is doing all this hard work. Give yourself credit. Praise yourself, cheer yourself on, and treat yourself to something special.

A POSTSCRIPT

After Sarah and I did the work together that I've described above, I didn't see her again for about a year. The moment she walked in this time I could tell that something had shifted. She moved and spoke with more confidence, showing a brightness and spark I hadn't seen before. As we spoke, I was gratified to hear of the many changes in her life. She had started working on a college degree, and meanwhile had gotten a part-time job she loved. She was no longer doing exotic dancing or hanging out in bars. Most important of all, she had reclaimed her life as a woman. "I don't need guys to lust after me to feel good about myself anymore," she told me. "There's nothing wrong with me. I feel strong for the first time."

She did report one problem—though on reflection, not such a bad one. "I've met this guy," she told me. "We're really happy. We seem to be in love. But I'm afraid I'll push him away, out of my old fears." We talked about this in a few subsequent sessions. Sarah spoke of her fear of getting hurt, her inclination to reject a man before he rejected her. She said she knew their life together wouldn't all be roses and that she needed to keep her perspective. She felt positive about the relationship, but she was looking for reassurances.

"Sarah," I said. "You're right; life has its ups and downs. There's no guarantee you won't be hurt by this fellow. Maybe you will, maybe you won't. What's important is to be able to handle hurt when it comes."

She thought a moment. "Yes, that's true," she said. "That's what I'm working on."

Then I thought a minute, too. "You know, we all suffer in our lives," I said. "I guess the real question is, will you live a life worth suffering for?"

"Yeah," she said with a smile. "I get that."

249

CHAPTER 10

Final Thoughts

In the course of writing this book, I've had many opportunities to think of the many people who've come to me over the years seeking help. The book itself is a gathering together of all that I've been able to teach these people about living in the shadow of anxiety. What I haven't talked about yet—and would like to say a word about now—is what these brave and wonderful people have taught me.

When I think about this, I'm touched with awe and gratitude. I have learned more from my patients than I could ever have imagined—about suffering, about loneliness, about desperation—but most of all about the courage to overcome those things. It does take courage to feel overwhelming fear and yet go forward in the face of it. I see so many of my patients reaching into the deepest core of their being to face their terrors, release their defenses, and submit to the exacting discipline of reality. From watching this I have developed the deepest respect for the human character—its resilience, its wisdom, its indomitable spirit, its strength. Whenever I'm tempted to become pessimistic or cynical about the human condition, this is what restores my faith.

As I think back over the years, so many examples come to mind. I think of the woman who was so traumatized after a rape that it was all she could do to step out into her yard. I think of the man who lived unhappily alone for years, convinced he was a hopeless misfit, incapable of even starting up a conversation, let alone having a relationship with another person. I remember the woman whose fear of contamination was so great she could not take a bus, eat in a restaurant, or use a public toilet; the man whose health was perfect but who lived in constant terror of a heart attack; the young mother who hadn't slept more than a few hours a night for ten years owing to incessant worry. Most of these people came to me with feelings of hopelessness. They were convinced their anxiety was either the result of a flawed character or part of an incurable condition. Some had battled their symptoms unsuccessfully for years and were coming to me as a last resort. Others had been too ashamed of their condition to reveal it to anyone. In just about every case, they were blocked and intimidated by what they saw as forces beyond their control.

I'm always struck by two things. One is what fundamentally kind, decent, *good* people they really are—no matter what kinds of dysfunctional behavior their condition may have led them to. Deep down they simply wish—as we all do—to be free of their anxiety, to open their hearts to the world, to love, and to be loved. The other thing is what a poor self-image so many of them have developed. Many are actually ashamed of their problems. *There's something wrong with me,* they say in effect, *I'm weak,* or *I'm defective,* or *I'm unworthy.* However likable and sympathetic they seem, however much I am touched by their stories, they see their anxiety as a badge of inferiority, something that makes them essentially unlovable. (Some are even half-convinced that I won't want to treat them once I discover their despicable characters.) The contrast between the way I see them and the way they see themselves is deeply poignant.

Often when these people walk into my office I can sense they're thinking, *Another shrink with a bag of tricks that won't work.* I can well understand that feeling. Many have been struggling for a long time, and I feel a sense of sorrow that they have been plagued with so much suffering. But I also feel excited and hopeful about the opportunity to help them change their lives—because I know they *can.* I don't see myself as the one with the answers, even though many people think of therapists that way. What I try to do is to get people to look for answers within themselves. I know they can find those answers because I've seen it happen countless times. However debilitating their anxiety has been, they have the opportunity to come to grips with it and shake off its tyranny. They have the power to heal themselves.

One thought I often have in such situations is, *There but for fortune go I.* A therapist is as human as his patients. In working with them he cannot help but learn about himself as well. Sometimes my patients test me—as did the woman whose physical abuse by a boyfriend had left her with a reservoir of resentment toward men. She came to me with a lot of distrust and half-concealed anger. Yet that kind of anger makes sense, and I have learned not to personalize it. My job is to listen, to hear the pain of those who feel rejected, and to offer help—not to criticize or argue or justify myself. Only by listening could I earn this patient's trust. I have learned that as a therapist I must be prepared to go through some pain, rejection, and disappointment myself.

What matters for both my patients and me is the understanding that we're all in the same boat. We all know suffering. Yet the goal for all of us is *to live a life worth suffering for*. By accepting our anxiety, by ceasing to battle against it, we find what it has to teach us. We begin to release the resistance that prolongs it. This is the path to freedom. It's not always the easy path, but it's the only one that leads out of suffering rather than deeper into it.

The various steps along that path have been described in this book. By now you are familiar with them.

It's that your anxiety is almost always based on a set of false beliefs about danger. You overestimate danger in crossing a bridge, flying in an airplane, meeting new people, touching "unclean" surfaces, and danger about unforeseen catastrophes that never occur. You are constantly predicting danger. And it almost never happens.

Your anxiety is also based on the false belief that you need to predict danger, know for sure, control everything, and avoid risk and regret. You are so conscientious about being cautious that you have been sacrificing your life in order to avoid bad things from happening. And because nothing bad has really happened—at least for some time—you think, *Maybe it's working!*

You have beliefs about avoiding risk that put you at great risk. In fact, these beliefs risk the quality of your life.

You also have false beliefs about anxiety. You think that unless you do something right now your anxiety will escalate, go out of control, and ruin your day. You are walking around with a hammer, nailing down your anxiety the minute it pops up. But you continue to hit yourself in the head.

Banging away at your anxiety won't work. And it won't feel very good, either.

We have seen how these false beliefs persist because you follow a rule book. Your anxiety may feel unique to you, but I can guarantee you that there are literally billions of people in this world who follow rules very much like your own. It's as if all of us, speaking hundreds of languages, separated by thousands of miles, who never meet one another, show up, look at our rule books and wonder, *Where did you get that? That's my rule book!*

The irony is that it is not your rule book—it is *our rule book*. Our ancestors, going back hundreds of thousands of years, developed the Anxiety Rule Book to survive. We go around reading it today and believing it—not recognizing that we are not being chased by tigers and wolves—we are being chased by our own thoughts and feelings.

The odd thing about false beliefs about danger and protecting yourself is that we really think we need these beliefs. We think that we are safer because we don't touch the contamination, avoid flying, hold on tightly to the seat, avoid making eye contact. We actually think that all of our safety behaviors have prevented bad things from happening.

This is like an alcoholic who thinks that the next drink will cure his alcoholism. It won't work.

The key to overcoming fear is to practice your fear—to go to the center of it, to allow it to happen, to live alongside it.

This is the part of the task that requires courage. If you've read any of the six chapters on specific anxiety disorders, you understand what is involved. It requires courage because it asks you to confront, rather than run away from, the thing you fear, to open yourself to your anxiety when every fiber of your being tells you not to. It may seem wholly counterintuitive. You may wonder, *How can doing something that makes me* more *frightened help me reduce my fear?* Strange indeed—yet it's been proven that this is what *works*. No matter what the mind thinks will keep it safe, its true safety lies not in hiding from fear or struggling to suppress it, but in accepting it and learning to live with it comfortably.

Each cure is a triumph.

But overcoming your fears is not easy. You know better than I do, I am sure.

You will learn that by practicing your fear, you prove to yourself that you can really tolerate the discomfort—and that it will decrease with time. Your anxiety goes down. It doesn't last forever.

It's like hopelessness. It's temporary. Even hopelessness goes away.

You may think, *But what if I am* the one *who actually does get contaminated, humiliated, or killed?* There is no guarantee against awful things happening. All of us face this every day. And terrible things will happen anyway. We will all die. But while we are living we can choose to live a complete life—which means a life that has some risks. Reasonable risks, but risks nonetheless.

The alternative is not living a life. The alternative is hiding, sheltering yourself, continually asking for reassurance, and holding yourself back. Waiting for life to happen will never work.

You must choose.

You may get frustrated along the way. You may try these exercises, but the anxiety may persist. In fact, I will predict that the anxiety will persist. Sometimes it will get even *worse*. It's like being out of shape, going to the gym, and feeling the pain of the exercise for the first few weeks. You say to yourself, *What's the use?* But persistence is 90 percent of the game. Repeating your fears, practicing your discomfort, acting against your negative thoughts, doing the opposite of what you feel like doing—will lead to change. Progress is not perfection, and progress doesn't happen all at once. Every day that you do something that is uncomfortable that you feared before is progress. You are showing yourself that you can choose to act against your fears. Every day is a step in that direction.

The other thing to remember is the importance of self-compassion. While you need to stop fleeing from discomfort, you also need to be kind to yourself. The Dalai Lama has a wonderful way of putting it: "Send lovingkindness toward your pain." In all the hard and challenging work you will be doing—and it will be hard at times—it's important to be your own supporter, *not* your critic. Self-judgment is probably the greatest enemy you face. No matter how often you try and fail, your effort alone is progress. However difficult the work may seem at times, your willingness to do it is a blessing you are bestowing on yourself, not the demand of some stern taskmaster. You are rebuilding your life. It is a noble undertaking for which you deserve all the credit, encouragement, and compassion you can give yourself.

The image comes to mind of a woman patient I was once seeing. She was feeling such a deep sense of shame and guilt over a rape she had suffered that it was almost paralyzing. She could see how others might be blameless in such a situation, she could feel deep compassion for them— but not for herself. Her experience only proved how unworthy she really was. I asked her, as I sometimes do, to imagine the compassionate side of herself as a voice speaking to her, a kind of guardian angel. It was a soft and gentle voice, open-hearted, telling her she was loved and cared for. It told her she was always welcome, always at home, never alone. It told her she was safe. I asked her to think about this deeply for a while, to really let this voice sink in. She closed her eyes and was silent for a long time. Then I reminded her where this voice came from. It came from within *her*. It was a part of her that she could open to if she wished. Just as she could feel love and compassion for a perfect stranger, she could love herself. She could be her own guardian angel.

She took a deep breath and opened her eyes, which had welled with tears. "Yes," she said, smiling. "I understand."

APPENDIX A

Progressive Muscle Relaxation

An inevitable by-product of mental anxiety is tension in the body. The constant presence of fear in the mind gives the body the message that it needs to be constantly on edge, alert for danger. This produces arousal of all sorts: muscle tension, increased heart rate, higher blood pressure, aches and pains, clenching of the jaw, sweating, tremors, shallow breathing—even fatigue. These effects are not only unpleasant in themselves, they add to your overall anxiety level, and thus become part of a downward spiral. In addition to the cognitive-behavioral techniques offered in this book, there are some simple methods you can use to address physical tension and become more relaxed. It may take you a while to master the routine, but anyone can do it. If tension and anxiety are your daily companions, the effort is well worth your time.

"TENSE-AND-RELEASE" RELAXATION

This is a series of relaxation techniques applied to the different muscle groups. Its main purpose is to help you become aware of the difference between tension and relaxation, to feel that difference in your body. Begin by either sitting in a comfortable chair or lying down on a couch or bed. Breathe deeply for a few moments. Then tighten each muscle group in the following sequence, holding the tension for five seconds or so before releasing.

1. *Lower arms:* Tighten the fist and pull it up; release.

2. *Upper arms:* Tense against the side of the body; release.

3. *Calves:* Extend leg, point foot up; release.

4. *Thighs:* Push legs tightly together; release.

5. *Stomach:* Tighten and push back toward spine; release.

6. *Thorax:* Inhale into the lungs, hold rigid for a count of 10; exhale and release.

7. *Shoulders:* Hunch upward toward the ears; release.

8. *Neck:* Push head back and hold there; release.

9. *Lips:* Purse together without clenching teeth; release.

10. *Eyes:* Squint tightly with eyes closed; release.

11. *Eyebrows:* Furrow tightly together; release.

12. *Forehead:* Raise; release.

Next, breathe deeply for a few moments. Then begin the above sequence again. This time tense each muscle group while you count to 5 and then say *release* silently to yourself as you relax that part of you. Pause 15 or 20 seconds in between each muscle group. During the sequence, do the following:

1. Notice the difference in the body between tension and relaxation.

2. Feel each muscle group grow more relaxed, soft, and "warm."

3. Continue breathing easily.

The next step is an exercise that connects your breathing to your physical relaxation. Closing your eyes and continuing to sit or lie comfortably, count slowly down from 5 to 1. Time each count with an exhalation if possible. Allow a couple of breaths between each count. In between each count, notice the following:

1. Feel the relaxation spread down from the top of your head through your face and neck.

2. Feel it spread down through your shoulders, arms, and torso.

3. Feel it spread down through your legs and feet.

4. Feel it spread throughout your body, allowing it to become more and more deeply relaxed.

Repeat this several times, or as long as you need to. Next, coordinate the process with your breathing. Focus on a particular area of the body as you inhale; then as you exhale, say "relax" silently to yourself with each out breath. Do this for a few minutes. Finally, reverse the counting, going up from 1 to 5, and opening your eyes on the count of 5. With each count, feel yourself becoming more alert, while staying relaxed. There *is* such a thing as being both relaxed and alert. Practice this until you get the hang of it.

Go through these exercises twice a day. It's important to be regular about it; it will make a difference. Practice at first should not be during stressful situations. Later, when you are accustomed to the routine, it may be appropriate to use the exercises in moments of stress or agitation.

"RELEASE ONLY" RELAXATION

When you have become familiar with the above process, you may be able to achieve the same results without the tension phase. Focus on each muscle group, just as above, merely noting whether tension is present at any level. Relax each group, allowing 30 to 45 seconds for each. Let the mind go blank, or think relaxing thoughts. Once each muscle group feels fully relaxed, proceed to the next. If a group does not feel fully relaxed, go back to the tense-and-release formula. Once all the muscle groups feel fully relaxed, you can complete the process as above, first counting down from 5 while repeating *relax* in conjunction with your outbreath, then counting back up again.

"CUE-CONTROLLED" RELAXATION

This is the final phase of your exercises. Do the "release-only" relaxation until you are fully relaxed. Then take a few deep breaths, beginning each outbreath with the word *relax,* spoken silently to yourself while you scan the body for tension. This will be the pattern you carry out into the world, into your normal life. Whenever tension appears (a traffic jam, an unpleasant exchange), the word *relax,* repeated silently, will be your signal to your body to let go of its tension. Practice this cuing 10 to 15 times a day (more if you're able) in a variety of settings. Certain cues may become standard: glancing at your watch, stopping at a red light, a ringing phone. It may be useful to stick small colored dots around your home or workplace (on a mirror, a desk or lamp, the phone, etc.), as prompts for relaxation. All this will be an important adjunct to the work you are doing to overcome your anxiety. When you see the cue, think *relax,* and when you breathe out, think *relax.*

APPENDIX B

Insomnia

One of the most troubling consequences of anxiety—and of the depression frequently linked to it—is insomnia. Some people experience difficulty falling asleep (onset insomnia, usually linked to anxiety), while others tend to wake prematurely (early morning insomnia, linked to both anxiety and depression). Usually when anxiety and depression lift as a result of treatment, insomnia decreases and sleep becomes more restful. However, there are a number of cognitive-behavioral interventions that may be used to address your insomnia directly. This appendix will outline some of these interventions. However, before undertaking any of them, you should record some baseline information concerning your sleep patterns. You can then compare any changes in these patterns with the baseline measures.

Sleep Diary						
Enter the information each night for the time you go to bed, the time it takes for you to fall asleep, the number of times you wake during the night, the time you finally get out of bed, the total hours of sleep, and any medications for sleep that you take.						
Date	Time to Bed	Time to Sleep	Number of Times Awake During the Night	Time Out of Bed	Total Hours of Sleep	Medications Taken

An issue to be addressed at the outset is sleep medication. In general, your sleep problems are related to how various factors impact your circadian rhythms. These are the daily hormonal changes that influence when you feel sleepy and when you feel awake. It's important to let those natural rhythms assert themselves. Therefore, in order for the cognitive-behavioral approach to have its proper effect, you may consider getting off whatever sleeping pills you may be taking. Sleeping pills artificially alter your circadian rhythms; they will interfere with the techniques outlined here. Actually, research shows that cognitive-behavioral therapy is far more effective than sleeping pills in reversing insomnia. (Pills rarely work other than for the short-term.) Before you make any changes in medication, consult your physician.

It takes a certain amount of time for progress to be felt—perhaps weeks. Because your disturbed sleep patterns have taken a long time to learn, it may take you a while to unlearn them. Do not expect immediate results.

HOW TO OVERCOME YOUR INSOMNIA

1. *Develop regular sleep times.* Try to arrange your life so that you go to bed and get up at about the same times. This may mean sometimes retiring or rising irrespective of how tired you are.

2. *Avoid naps.* Naps may feel good and make you feel as if you're catching up on sleep, but they can throw off your circadian rhythms. You need to retrain your brain to fall asleep and wake up at certain consistent times. So, eliminate naps.

3. *Use the bed only for sleep.* Insomnia is often stimulated by increased arousal just before bedtime or while lying in bed awake. Many insomniacs use their beds for reading, watching television, phone calls, or just plain worrying. As a result, the bed becomes associated with arousal and anxiety. It's important that the bed be used only for sleep. Read or talk on the phone in another room. Discourage friends from calling after you are in bed.

4. *Avoid anxiety arousal during the hour before bedtime.* Avoid arguments and challenging tasks before you go to bed. You don't want to be revved up. Have a wind-down time for the hour before bed. Do something relaxing or boring. Don't exercise before going to bed.

5. *Get your "worry-time" and "to-do" lists over with earlier.*
   Most insomnia is due to excessive mental activity. You are
   simply thinking too much before you go to bed. You may be
   lying in bed thinking about what you have to do tomorrow.
   Or you may be thinking about what happened today. *Too much
   thinking.* Set aside a worry time *three hours or more before* you
   go to bed. Write out your worries, ask yourself if there is some
   productive action you need to take, make up a to-do list, plan
   what you will do tomorrow or this week, accept limitations
   (you won't get everything done, it will be imperfect, and there
   will be some uncertainty). If you are lying in bed that night,
   worrying about things, get out of bed, write down the worry,
   and set it aside for tomorrow morning. You don't need to know
   the answer right now.

6. *Discharge your feelings.* Sometimes insomnia is due to
   harboring emotions and feelings that are bothering you. It is
   useful to set aside "feeling time" several hours before you go
   to bed and write out your feelings. For example, *I was really
   anxious and angry when Bill said that to me.* Try to mention as
   many feelings as you can in your writing. Try to make sense of
   your feelings. Have compassion for yourself, validate your right
   to have feelings and recognize that it is okay to feel anxious
   some of the time. Then set this aside. Do this three hours or
   more before you got to bed.

7. *Reduce or eliminate liquid intake in the evening.* Sleep is often
   disturbed by urinary urgency. Avoid caffeine products, heavy
   foods, fats, sugar, alcohol, etc. in the evening. If necessary,
   consult a nutritionist to plan a diet that encourages sound sleep.

8. *Get out of bed if you're not sleeping.* If you are lying awake
   at night for more than fifteen minutes, get up and go in the
   other room. *Write down your negative thoughts and challenge
   them.* Typical automatic negative thoughts are *I'll never get to
   sleep, If I don't get enough sleep, I won't be able to function, I need
   to get to sleep immediately,* and *I'll get sick from not getting enough
   sleep.* The most likely consequence of not getting enough sleep
   is that you will feel tired and irritable. Although these are
   uncomfortable inconveniences, they are not catastrophic.

9. ***Don't try to force yourself to fall asleep.*** This will only increase your frustration, and, in turn, your anxiety. A more effective attitude is to let go of the attempt to fall asleep; paradoxically, a very effective way of increasing sleep is to practice *giving up* trying to fall asleep. You can say to yourself, *I'll give up trying to get to sleep and just concentrate on some relaxing feelings in my body.*

10. ***Practice repeating your anxious thoughts.*** Like any feared situation or thought, if you repeat it long enough, it becomes boring. You can practice this thought slowly, standing back in your mind as if you are just "observing the thought," and repeat it slowly and silently in your mind hundreds of times. Imagine that you are almost a zombie repeating this thought. Don't try to reassure yourself, stay with the thought, go slowly.

11. ***Eliminate Safety Behaviors.*** To combat your sleep anxiety, you may have been resorting to superstitious behaviors, such as checking the clock, counting, keeping your body motionless, or repeating injunctions to yourself like *Stop worrying.* Try to become aware of these, and give them up. You could, for example, turn the clock away from your bed. Or you could just allow whatever comes into your mind to be there, without trying to control it.

12. ***Challenge your negative thoughts.*** The whole process of going to sleep is complicated by the fact that your mind develops a whole range of negative thoughts about it. These thoughts then prevent you from sleeping. If you question their validity, they will have less power to cause you anxiety. Here are some typical thoughts of the insomniac, together with what a reasonable response to them might look like:

    • *Negative thought:* I've got to fall asleep right now, or I won't be able to function tomorrow.

    • *Rational response:* Actually, there's no urgency. You've done without sleep before. You'll be a little tired, which is uncomfortable and inconvenient, but hardly the end of the world.

- *Negative thought:* It isn't normal to have this kind of insomnia. It means there's something wrong with me.

- *Rational response:* Unfortunately, insomnia is quite common. Almost everyone experiences it sometimes. No one will think the worse of you for having it.

- *Negative thought:* I could will myself to go to sleep if I tried hard enough.

- *Rational response:* Trying to force yourself to sleep never works. It increases anxiety, which only fuels your insomnia. It's better to let go of the attempt, and give in to *not* sleeping. Then you can relax a little.

- *Negative thought*: I need to remember all the things I'm lying awake thinking about.

- *Rational response:* If something is worth remembering, get out of bed, write it down, and go back to bed. There's plenty of opportunity to plan things tomorrow.

- *Negative thought:* I never get enough sleep.

- *Rational response:* This is probably true for most people, but it's simply uncomfortable and inconvenient. It's not the end of the world.

SLEEP RESTRICTION THERAPY: A POWERFUL ALTERNATIVE

There's a more dramatic treatment for insomnia that is sometimes effective. It's called sleep restriction therapy. It's based on the idea that you need to retrain your brain to adjust to a circadian rhythm. This is more challenging than the program outlined above, but sometimes it's what works best. It may involve the use of special "bright light" to establish a regular pattern of light and darkness. This can come from sunlight (if controlled by shades or blinds), high-intensity lamps, or certain commercially produced bright lights designed for this purpose. (These are available from Apollo Light, at www.apollolight.com, or Sunbox, at www.sunbox.com, as well as other manufacturers.)

The steps involved in sleep restriction therapy are as follows:

1. *Go without sleep for 24 hours.* This is quite a difficult first step, and many people will feel quite exhausted from it. But it may help you reestablish your circadian rhythms. If you cannot bring yourself to go without sleep for 24 hours, then you can start with the second step, "Start with your minimum sleep time."

2. *Start with your minimum sleep time.* Look at your baseline information. What's the minimum amount of sleep you've had over the preceding week? If it's four hours, plan to begin by sleeping only four hours, no matter how tired you are. If you plan to get up at 7 A.M., then go to bed at 3 A.M.

3. *Increase sleep time gradually.* Add 15 minutes per night to your sleep. Go to bed 15 minutes earlier each night. For example, if you went to bed at 3 A.M., then go to bed at 2:45 A.M. the next night and 2:30 A.M. the night after.

4. *Don't demand eight hours.* Many of us don't really need a full 8 hours. See if you're developing less fatigue and more alertness during the day before leveling off. Although sleep restriction therapy seems quite difficult to many people, it can be highly effective. After you have completed sleep restriction therapy, you may use the 12 steps outlined earlier for healthy sleep. An occasional night of insomnia is to be expected for all of us, but developing the proper sleep habits is quite important. Improving your sleep can have a significant impact on your anxiety and depression.

APPENDIX C

Diet and Exercise

DIET: THE FOUNDATIONS OF HEALTHY EATING

Your anxiety can have a great effect on your eating patterns. It can lead you to overeat and gain weight, with attendant health consequences such as heart conditions, diabetes, high cholesterol, etc. On the other hand, it can lead you to fast or starve yourself for long periods, causing fluctuations in blood sugar, weakness or dizziness, and a host of problems stemming from poor nutrition. Anxiety can upset the balance of your diet causing unhealthy proportions of carbohydrates, sweets, salty foods, or fats. If you are anxious, you are more likely to prefer eating higher levels of carbohydrates, sweets, and comfort foods. We are going to review the basic principles of a good, heart-healthy, balanced diet. Don't let your anxiety determine your eating. However, it also works the other way around: maintaining a healthy, balanced diet will help you gain control of your anxiety. Any kind of imbalance in your diet can throw your system off-kilter; whenever that happens, your anxiety level is apt to rise. So any program designed to address anxiety—such as the one outlined in this book—should include some dietary guidelines for maintaining good eating habits. This appendix will review some of the more helpful guidelines.

Although you may believe you know what a healthy diet is, I have found that a lot of my patients are misinformed. Some people think that they can skip meals, deprive themselves of food, eat only one kind of food, or avoid entire food groups.

You should read the labels on food items that you purchase in the grocery store. Pay attention to calories, servings per container, saturated fat, and other dietary information. The following are guidelines for healthful eating—both in what you eat and how you eat.

1. *Eat a heart-healthy diet.* You should eat a diet that is low in saturated fat. This includes lean meats (chicken or turkey without the skin, roast beef or fish). Replace butter or margarine with olive oil or canola oil. Use skim or 1 percent milk rather than whole milk. Use nonfat rather than whole milk yogurt. Limit cakes, pastries, and pies—they are high in calories and saturated fat. Limit your salt intake. Processed foods, canned

foods, and fast foods are very high in salt. Look at the labels. Women should eat a sufficient amount of calcium each day to prevent osteoporosis.

2. *Variety.* Eat foods from all five food groups—fruits, grains, dairy, meats, vegetables, together with an appropriate amount of fat or oils—which will give you a good complement of the various vitamins and minerals. (For basic information about food groups, consult the website www.mypyramid.gov.)

3. *Balance.* Make sure you're getting proper proportions of carbohydrates, fats, and protein in your diet. Many fad diets designed around getting thin recommend either great concentrations or great reductions in one or more of these. Nonetheless, on the whole, our bodies need some of each to function efficiently.

4. *Moderation.* Think about portion sizes. One serving of meat or poultry is the size of a deck of cards! A portion of rice or pasta is one cup—when was the last time a restaurant served you only one cup? Set appropriate limits to your consumption and stick to them. Multiple helpings and constant snacking can wreak havoc with any diet plan. Also, reduce or eliminate your consumption of products that contain caffeine such as coffee, tea, soda, and chocolate.

5. *Pace.* Many people have a tendency to concentrate their consumption in heavy meals. Our Stone Age bodies are not meant to do this. It's best to eat smaller amounts more frequently: the three traditional meals and two healthy snacks in between. If each meal is relatively low in calories, fats, and sugar, you'll have fewer cravings and less of a tendency to overeat at a big meal.

6. *Consistency.* Maintaining a consistent blood glucose level throughout the day is particularly important in reducing anxiety. The basic strategy for this is to eat the same amount of carbohydrates at each meal. (Carbohydrates are found in many foods other than bread and pasta, such as milk products, rice, and fruit.

To find out more about your particular needs, consider consulting a registered dietitian. Information on how to find one in your area can be had at www.eatright.org, the Website of the American Dietetic Association.

YOUR EATING HABITS

Developing good eating habits is in many ways the key to a healthy diet. This has to do not only with what you eat, but how and when you eat it, what your mind state is while eating, and the sum total of how you think and behave around food. To assess your own eating habits, go through the following list. It describes six habits of healthy eating, along with tips on how to develop each of them.

1. *Eat steadily throughout the day.* Plan to have at least five small meals a day: breakfast, lunch, and dinner, and a few healthy snacks. Don't skip meals or go for long periods without eating; this only adds to your craving and binge tendencies—and to your anxiety.

2. *Eat a balanced diet with foods from the different groups.* Read the guidelines above, and get more information from reliable sources. Keep track of what and how much you eat, and record the effects on your mood and general well-being.

3. *Don't eat too fast.* Slow down: don't just gobble your food. Chew slowly and take smaller bites, putting your fork or spoon down in between. Enjoy each bite; make your pleasure in eating last longer.

4. *Don't eat too much.* Stop eating before you become full. Wait a while after consuming a portion before helping yourself to seconds. Give the feeling of repletion a chance to kick in.

5. *Pay attention to your eating.* Eat mindfully (this goes with eating slowly). Avoid too much distracting conversation or activity. Don't watch TV or sit at the computer, and see if you can eat without reading. Be aware of the taste and texture of food, all the sensations involved in eating.

6. *Maintain a consistent eating pattern.* Don't let your moods, anxiety, or depression alter your eating habits. Follow your dietary plan no matter how you're feeling. If you've lost your appetite, eat smaller amounts more frequently.

EXERCISE: HELPING YOUR BODY FEEL BETTER

There's considerable research to support the usefulness of exercise in helping you cope with your anxiety. A program of regular exercise can have positive effects on a wide range of anxiety disorders. Benefits are both short-term (you feel better right afterward) and long-term (you feel better over months and years). Exercise helps you stay in shape physically, builds your confidence, increases your vigor, and improves your appearance. Aerobic exercise is particularly important in terms of your cardiovascular system, though other kinds, such as weight training, have considerable health benefits as well. Moreover, regular exercise helps discharge the nervous energy that builds up when anxiety is present.

There are two basic approaches to getting regular exercise. One is to build it into your daily routine. For example, walk or bike to work if possible, or make a habit of walking up the stairs of the building where you work or live. You can take your dog for long walks twice a day (the dog will usually appreciate it). Wherever possible, you can walk instead of drive to a shopping mall, a neighbor's house, or a town center. Outdoor work activities such as gardening, hand mowing, brush cutting, or splitting wood can help you keep fit, though they're sometimes a little short on the aerobics. But any exercise is probably good.

The other approach is to consciously devise a program of exercise for yourself. You might take up jogging, bicycling, or hiking. You might join a health club and schedule time there three or four days a week. Dance classes can be terrific exercise (you don't have to be a world-class dancer to enjoy them either). If you're into sports such as tennis, volleyball, or soccer, you can probably find friends or groups to play with. Tai chi, yoga, or martial arts classes can give you a good workout, and even a brisk walk around the neighborhood, if done regularly, can be salutary. There's no shortage of options: it's just a question of selecting the type of exercise that's right for your age and physical condition. It shouldn't be anything stressful or beyond your limits. On the other hand, it's good to push yourself a little, just as you've done with your exercises to overcome anxiety. Proper exercise is about playing your edge.

It's not hard to devise an exercise program that works in theory. However the best exercise program is the one you actually do.

If you're like most people, the biggest problem you'll have with exercise is your own resistance to it. Without special motivation, our bodies often seem gripped by a certain inertia, a tendency to do only what is minimally required (like a trip to the refrigerator). When resistance strikes, how will you respond? Chances are you'll start finding excuses for not exercising regularly. Just as we learned with anxiety, it helps to become aware of your resistance, to recognize your excuses for what they are. The more conscious of them you are, the more clarity and discipline you'll be able to muster.

Let's take a look at some of the more common excuses for avoiding exercise. Let's consider at the same time what the voice of reality might say in response to each.

1. ***I'm too busy.*** All you need is thirty minutes. You probably fritter away more than that each day in between tasks. Spend a half hour doing something that's good for you and feel better for it. If you're not prioritizing your life, you're undermining your goals.

2. ***I don't live near (or can't afford) a health club.*** You don't need a health club to get proper exercise. People were in better shape before there were health clubs. You can do sit-ups, or stretches, or jog around the neighborhood, or a dozen other things—all for free.

3. ***I can't do anything too hard.*** This just won't wash. There's always some form of exercise that's appropriate; no one's asking you to run a supermarathon. Getting in shape has to do with finding your physical limits and gently but firmly extending them.

4. ***I'll look silly.*** No one cares what you look like; they have other things on their minds. People will admire you for having the discipline to exercise. Besides, what's more important, your vanity or your physical and mental well-being?

5. ***I just don't seem motivated.*** My answer to this is: "So what?" You're making a choice that will have consequences for you.

You can still choose to do things you're not excited about if you think it will improve your life. With exercise, the motivation often comes afterward.

6. *I get too tired.* You're probably tired because you haven't been exercising. In the long run, unless you have some medical condition, exercise will improve your stamina. Being a little more tired at first is nothing terrible; it means you're making progress. Chances are you'll sleep better.

7. *I'm planning to start, but this isn't the right time.* This one is really insidious. Who are you kidding? The fact is, it's never the right time. The more you put things off, the less likely you are to do them. Living in the future is a good way to botch it up. The only time to do anything is now.

8. *My problems are too big to be solved by exercise.* By exercise alone? Perhaps. But exercise will improve your mood, increase your confidence, improve your health, and calm your mind. These are real solutions to problems, and not trivial ones. You might be surprised at how effective they can be.

Note that every one of these excuses is a thought running through your mind. Each one stands for a self-limiting belief that you're holding on to. Deal with these thoughts exactly as you've been dealing with the anxious thoughts you've confronted in our exercises. Be aware of them, hold them to the light, examine the assumptions they're based on, and challenge them. Since none of them are serving your interests, there's no reason they should have any power over you.

APPENDIX D

Medications

Before you consider any medications, you should have your physician conduct a complete medical examination. Inform him or her of any medications (including over-the-counter drugs, alternative supplements, etc.) that you are taking. Some anxiety symptoms may be due to a medical condition, while other medications may interact negatively with the ones for anxiety. Inform your doctor if you are misusing alcohol since drinking can interact negatively with some of these medications. Do not try to self-medicate.

Most anxiety disorders can be helped at some point with medication, although it may not be the ultimate means of getting better. People who have a specific phobia (such as fear of flying, heights, or some other specific stimulus) are better off not taking medication. This is because anti-anxiety medication can interfere with getting over a specific phobia—you need to feel fear during exposure in order to overcome the phobia, and medication tends to dull or suppress that fear. Medications can have a positive impact in all the other anxiety disorders, but once they're discontinued, there's a good chance the symptoms will return.

This is why I recommend the kinds of treatment outlined in this book. Cognitive-behavioral therapy has longer-lasting effects. You may wish to take medication at first, in order to reduce some of the symptoms of arousal (rapid heartbeat, sweating, muscle tension, etc.), but no medication will teach you the skills you need to control your anxiety permanently. Pills don't teach you skills.

This is what cognitive-behavioral therapy can do.

Nonetheless, it's good to know what the chief options are for medication. You can discuss them with your therapist or with a physician.

BENZODIAZEPINES

Benzodiazepines are the fastest-acting anti-anxiety medications. These include Xanax, Klonapin, Ativan, Valium, and others. They can start working almost immediately—usually within thirty minutes. Your doctor may want to start your treatment with a benzodiazepine to give you some short-term relief. However, most patients will want to taper off after a couple of weeks in order to avoid side effects or even addiction. Some patients will continue using benzodiazepines for a few months, along with cognitive-behavioral therapy and other anti-depressant medications. Avoid alcohol while using benzodiazepines. Side effects include lethargy, sedation, and difficulty concentrating.

Benzodiazepines are useful for short-term relief of anxious arousal in panic disorder, generalized anxiety disorder (GAD), and social anxiety disorder (SAD). A typical course of treatment might be to start you on a benzodiazepine and also on another class of medications—for example, SSRIs (see below). You should only reduce the dosage of your benzodiazepines under your doctor's direction, since too rapid withdrawal of the medication can result in a significant increase of anxiety.

SELECTIVE SEROTONIN REUPTAKE INHIBITORS

Selective Serotonin Reuptake Inhibitors (SSRIs) are often identified as anti-depressant medications, though they're now widely used for the treatment of anxiety disorders as well. They can be used for panic disorder, obsessive-compulsive disorder (OCD), generalized anxiety disorder (GAD), social anxiety disorder (SAD), and post-traumatic stress disorder (PTSD). The most commonly prescribed SSRIs are Prozac, Zoloft, Paxil, Luvox, Celexa, and Lexapro. Unlike the benzodiazepines, which work within thirty minutes in most cases, the SSRIs take much longer to become effective—usually two to eight weeks. Your doctor may gradually increase the dosage of your medication in order to allow you to adjust to the dosage and avoid side effects (such as decreased sex drive, headache, and insomnia). Many side effects will disappear or become less unpleasant after a couple of weeks as you habituate to the medication, although some people do continue to have them even with continued use. (Side effects are also related to the dosage level you're taking.) Sometimes your doctor may use a lower dosage of an SSRI and add an additional medication that can increase the effectiveness of both drugs. However, you should not take an SSRI if you're also taking a MAOI (see below), such as Nardil or Parnate. With any medication, make sure you consult directly with your doctor when reducing or discontinuing it.

TRICYCLIC ANTIDEPRESSANTS

Tricyclic antidepressants (TCAs) are an older class of drug that can be quite useful for anxiety—especially for panic disorder. Examples of TCAs include Anafranil, Aventyl, Adapin, Ludiomil, Surmontil, and Tofranil. TCAs are less commonly prescribed today because of possible side effects, including dry mouth, constipation, sedation, weight gain, and feeling overly stimulated.

BETA-BLOCKERS

Beta-blockers are medications often used for the treatment of high-blood pressure (hypertension)—but they can also be used short-term for "performance anxiety." Beta-blockers lower the anxious physical arousal that some people fear. Some find beta-blockers helpful for public speaking or musical performances. Commonly prescribed beta-blockers include Inderal and Tenormin. These should only be used under your doctor's direction.

MONOAMINE OXIDASE INHIBITORS

Monoamine Oxidase Inhibitors (MAOIs) are a class of medications that can be helpful for anxiety disorders. These medications were initially used for the treatment of depression, but they have also been shown to be effective with anxiety. Common MAOIs include Parnate and Nardil—but these require strict restrictions on the kinds of foods and beverages you consume. Serious negative reactions can occur with MAOIs when they interact with substances in certain foods and beverages, so you should follow directions carefully when using them. They can also have serious negative effects when combined with other medications.

ANTIPSYCHOTIC MEDICATIONS

Antipsychotic medications are sometimes used to reduce agitation and obsessive thinking. Using these medications does not imply that you are "psychotic"—in fact, an older name for them was "major tranquilizer." Your doctor may want to use these medications if you have difficulty stepping back from your anxiety, or seeing how extreme or rigid your ideas are (as in cases of obsessive-compulsive disorder). More recent antipsychotic medications have fewer side effects than the older antipsychotics. Most commonly prescribed are Zyprexa, Clozapine, Risperdal, Geodon, Abilify, and Seroquel. You should have close medical supervision with these medications. Possible side effects include weight gain, insulin resistance, and dizziness.

Refer to the table below for a listing of commonly used medications for anxiety. Always consult with your doctor, and always read the information that accompanies your medication.

Trade Name	Generic Name	Common Side Effects
Benzodiazepines Target Anxiety Disorders: Generalized Anxiety Disorder, Panic Disorder, Social Anxiety Disorder		
Ativan Klonopin Librium Serax Tranxene Valium Xanax	Lorazepam Clonazepam Chlordiazepoxide Oxazepam Clorazepate Diazepam Alprazolam	Common side effects of benzodiazepines: sedation, dizziness, unsteadiness, weakness, disorientation, nausea, drowsiness, headaches, change in appetite, weight gain/loss, sleep disturbance, fatigue, lethargy, ataxia, confusion, blurred vision, dry mouth, dehydration, constipation, various gastrointestinal complaints, increased and decreased libido, sexual dysfunction, depression.
Selective Serotonin Reuptake Inhibitors (SSRIs) Target Anxiety Disorders: Panic Disorder, Social Anxiety Disorder, Post-Traumatic Stress Disorder, Generalized Anxiety Disorder, Obsessive-Compulsive Disorder		
Celexa Lexapro Luvox Prozac Paxil Zoloft	Citalopram Escitalopram Fluvoxamine Fluoxetine Paroxetine Sertraline	Common side effects of SSRIs: abdominal pain, insomnia, somnolence, agitation, restlessness, anxiety, nervousness, drowsiness, fatigue, dizziness, tremors, dry mouth, impotence, nausea, sweating, weight gain, decreased appetite, changes in libido, abnormal ejaculation, male sexual dysfunction, asthenia, gastro-intestinal complaints, diarrhea, constipation.

Tricyclic Antidepressants

Target Anxiety Disorders: Panic Disorder, Post-Traumatic Stress Disorder, Generalized Anxiety Disorder, Obsessive-Compulsive Disorder (Anafranil only)

Adapin	Doxepin	Common side effects of tricyclics: dry mouth, blurred vision, constipation, drowsiness, fatigue, skin rash, nausea, vomiting, restlessness, insomnia, dream and sleep disturbances, nightmares, numbness, tingling, weight gain/loss, increased appetite, anorexia, sweating, chills, tremors, dizziness, nervousness, increased appetite, abnormal thinking, depression, hypo-/hypertension, disorientation, anxiety, panic, hypomania, stroke, arrhythmias, coma, seizures, hallucinations, delusions, confused states, testicular swelling, breast enlargement, palpitations, bone marrow, exacerbation of psychosis, myocardial infarction, impotence, increased/decreased libido, ejaculatory failure.
Sinequan	Clomipramine	
Anafranil	Nortriptyline	
Aventyl	Amitriptyline	
Pamelor	Desipramine	
Elavil	Trimipramine	
Endep	Imipramine	
Laroxyl	Protriptyline	
Norpramin		
Surmontil		
Tofranil		
Presamine		
Vivactyl		

Beta-Blockers

Target Anxiety Disorders: Performance Anxiety, Panic Disorder

Inderal	Propranolol	Common side effects of beta-blockers: insomnia, fatigue, weakness, irregular heartbeats, dizziness, nausea, diarrhea, shortness of breath, rash, loss of appetite, weight gain, depression, anxiety, fever, fainting, swelling of hands, lower legs, ankles or feet, cold extremities, impotence, changes in sexual libido.
Tenormin	Atenolol	

Antidepressants – Monoamine Oxidase Inhibitors (MAOIs) Target Anxiety Disorders: Panic Disorder, Social Anxiety Disorder, Post-Traumatic Stress Disorder		
Marplan Nardil Parnate	Isocarboxazid Phenelzine Tranylcypromine	Common side effects of MAOIs: orthostatic hypotension, dizziness, constipation, diarrhea, abdominal pain, headache, tremors, dry mouth, weakness, fatigue, drowsiness, nausea, sleep disturbances, weight gain/loss, sexual disturbances, sweating, skin rash, blurred vision, manic reaction, acute anxiety reaction, restlessness or insomnia, chills.
Antipsychotic Medications		
Abilify Clozaril Geodon Risperdal Seroquel Zyprexa	Aripiprazole Clozapine Ziprasidone Risperidone Quetiepine Olanzapine	Common side effects of antipsychotic medications: nausea, vomiting, constipation, insomnia, somnolence, increased duration of sleep, sedation, headache, weakness, fatigue, dizziness, drowsiness, dry mouth, cold symptoms, fever, cough, runny nose, increase/decrease in weight, restlessness, tremors, rash, involuntary movement, twitching or jerking of extremities, tardive dyskinesia, irregular heartbeats, rapid heart rate, irregular blood pressure, blurred vision, muscle pain, muscle spasms or stiffness, increased salivation and drooling, anxiety, extrapyrimidal symptoms, postural hypotension, back pain, orthostatic hypotension, increased prolactin levels, NMS, personality disorders.

Updated information on a wide range of medications can be found on the following websites:

http://www.nlm.nih.gov/medlineplus/druginformation.html
http://www.pdrhealth.com/home/home.aspx

Almost all medications will have side effects. The question is, how common are these side effects, how serious are they likely to be, and how do you balance this risk against the effects of the drug on your anxiety. You should make a list of any negative reactions that you've had to medications in the past. You should also make a written list of all of your current prescriptions, over-the-counter medications, and alternative or "natural" remedies. Give both these lists to your physician. Some medications increase the potency of other medications. Some medications may interact negatively with other medications.

Only you working together with your physician can make the right choice for you. Self-medication is never a good idea. People get in trouble trying to be their own doctor.

APPENDIX E

Mindfulness

If you suffer from an anxiety disorder, this appendix could provide another practical tool for dealing with it. I strongly urge any reader who has not already done so to investigate its benefits.

What is mindfulness? One thing should be obvious from everything I've said in this book: much of the suffering our anxiety causes us is created in our minds. Since this is true, it may be worth asking a basic question: is there a way to change the way our minds function? When we fear something that reason tells us we have no cause to fear, and when that fear disrupts our lives, darkens our moods, restricts our activities, spoils our pleasures, and threatens our very health and survival, we might want to consider whether or not there is an alternative. Could there be some sort of technique or practice that would allow our minds to see more clearly what's happening outside them, without the distortions and delusions they always seem to cast?

People from many traditions all over the world who have looked into this question—spiritual teachers, psychologists, religious figures, medical authorities—have insisted that there is. Mindfulness is nothing mystical or exotic. It's simply a way of experiencing the world (including your inner world) in which you are fully aware *in the present moment* of what is happening. To be fully aware means not to be thinking, judging, or trying to control what is going on. All these are departures from awareness. For example, when I am mindful of my breath, I simply notice it as it rises and falls. I focus my attention on it without trying to control it, or judge whether I am doing it correctly. I am simply in the moment, noticing and experiencing it.

This practice is at the heart of many forms of Eastern meditation, especially Buddhist forms. But one does not need to be a Buddhist, or even to know the first thing about Buddhism, in order to practice it. Mindfulness is simply a way of observing one's experience *directly*, instead of through a fog of concepts, ideas, and opinions. It provides a clarity that exists only when thought is suspended. Best of all, it is a technique available to anyone. One does not need to be a meditation master in order to experience its benefits. To prove that this is so, you can try a little mindful breathing yourself in the next five minutes.

Begin by sitting in a comfortable position. It doesn't have to be cross-legged—it can be kneeling on a cushion or sitting in a chair. It's helpful if your spine is erect. Close your eyes. Start by bringing your attention to your breath. Notice how it goes in and out, rises and falls. It does this by itself: you don't have to "do" anything to make it happen. Continue observing the breath, moment by moment, as it flows onward. What you will notice next (probably within seconds) will be the mind wandering away from the breath into the world of thought. Perhaps you will be distracted by some worry of yours, perhaps apprehension around how you will perform, perhaps a feeling that you need to be doing something instead of just sitting here. Or, hearing certain sounds, you may start wondering what's causing them or what they mean. You may begin to think about tonight's dinner, yesterday's ball game, or how things are going at work. It doesn't matter what the content of the thought is. The key is this: as soon as you become aware that the attention has wandered, bring it gently but firmly back to the breath, back to the moment. Do this without comment or judgment; just bring it back. As many times as the mind drifts off, simply notice this and restore your attention to the breath. Do this for as long as you like. As you practice mindfulness, you'll probably be both able and motivated to do it for longer periods.

If you are an anxiety sufferer, practicing mindfulness can help you address the root causes of your worry—your fear, your tension, your mistaken belief that you are in continual danger. It will help you stay in the present, where anxiety does not exist (anxiety is built out of past and future). It will calm your mind and relax your body. If you keep at it, you may find the strength of your anxiety diminishing considerably.

None of this may seem at first to have much to do with the major "issues" of your life. But it does. That's because the practice of mindfulness is connected in a very deep way with our thoughts—or rather with the relationship we have with our thoughts. Being in the present moment means being attuned to whatever is going on: our breath, the sound of a clock ticking, a pain in the back. But what's happening in the moment *also includes our thoughts.* Thoughts are events to which we can direct our attention. Like the sensations of our breath, thoughts arise in the mind and pass away, coming in and out of existence with no apparent effort on our part.

We don't often treat our thoughts that way. We treat them as though they were reality or rather pictures that infallibly describe reality. If we think something is so, it *is* so. We form an abstract concept like, *This traffic is unbearable,* or *My life is a mess,* and accept it as truth. If we think of someone as a good or a bad person, then that's what they are. Conceptual thinking drives us—never more completely and powerfully than when we are anxious. We worry that something terrible is going to happen, and presto, the threat is real. We assume that our anxiety is informing us of all the things "out there" in the world that we need to be concerned about. Anxiety, more than almost any other human process, depends on the belief that our thoughts are accurate descriptions of reality.

But we can view our thoughts in a different way. We can see a thought as *just a thought*—an event in the mind, with no necessary connection to what goes on in the world at all. Rather than getting caught up in the *content* of our thoughts, we can simply notice them in the moment—just as we did with our our breath. It's possible, in short, to be *mindful of our thoughts*. This changes our entire relationship with them. When we see our thoughts as part of the flow of consciousness, when they're simply phenomena passing through the mind rather than descriptions of reality, their power over us suddenly looks a lot smaller. Instead of reacting with *Uh oh, this is awful,* or *I've got to do something right away,* we can say *Ah yes, there's that thought again.* Watching our thoughts come and go, we realize how ephemeral they are, how tenuously connected to anything important. We don't have to "obey" them any more.

If you suffer from anxiety, this is a useful insight. One way to apply it is to notice, when doing the mindfulness exercise described above, all the thoughts that come into your mind. Probably a good many of them will come under the category of anxieties or worries, ranging from trivial to serious. *Am I doing this right? Is it going to get boring? Will the ache in my back go away? Will that root canal I'm having next week be painful? Can I get that report in on time? Can I afford my mortgage payments? Will my partner leave me? Am I going to get cancer? Am I a despicable person? Is my life a mess?* Try studying these anxious thoughts as you would the leaves of a plant, waves in the ocean, or flames in a bonfire. Detach yourself for the moment from their content and just see how *interesting* they are. Stay present with them. If you do, you will almost surely notice a change in the urgency with which they present themselves to you. Your mind will begin to calm down, your breathing will become deeper, and a feeling of peace will begin to seep into your consciousness.

If you do this once or twice a day over a period of days or weeks, you'll probably notice a couple of things. One is that the frequency of your anxious thoughts will begin to lessen on its own. The other is that you'll feel less agitated when such thoughts do appear. The object is not to try and extinguish your anxious thoughts—that would have the opposite effect of strengthening them—but simply to become more aware of them. As you get used to watching your anxieties come and go, your mind will become habituated to them, just as it does when performing some of the fear hierarchy exercises described in this book. Anxiety will become less of a dreaded enemy and more of a familiar companion. You'll start to learn from it. You'll begin to understand what it means to experience anxiety and *not* be seized by it, *not* identify with it, *not* buy into what it's telling you.

If this much works for you, you might consider making mindfulness a consistent presence in your life. A regular meditation practice is generally useful. Classes and workshops that provide basic meditation instruction are given almost everywhere in the country, while long-term retreats are available for those who wish to go deeper. Basic principles and techniques are pretty universal; differences in approach are less important than what the approaches have in common. One thing you'll quickly see is that the topic is highly relevant to the issues discussed in this book. Developing the quality of mindfulness should be helpful to anyone interested in mastering their anxiety.

APPENDIX F

Depression and Suicide

The topic of depression is a vast one—well beyond the scope of this book. (Someday soon I hope to publish a self-help book on the subject.) But depression is also an important factor when it comes to an anxiety disorder. All the anxiety disorders we've examined can lead to depression, especially when the condition is severe and the sufferer has struggled for a long time without apparent success. The symptoms of depression can intermingle with those of anxiety, making it hard to know which condition is being experienced and what the appropriate treatment is. And a given individual may be predisposed to both conditions, for either psychological or biological reasons—even in terms of body chemistry. So any comprehensive approach to anxiety must take into account the nature and consequences of anxiety-based depression. In this appendix I'll merely touch on some highlights and offer a few suggestions for dealing with this debilitating condition.

What is depression? There is no one symptom that defines depression. It may consist of sadness, lack of energy, loss of interest, indecisiveness, self-criticism, regrets, hopelessness, irritability, withdrawal, changes in appetite, and sleep disturbance. Your particular symptoms are often accompanied by specific negative thoughts about yourself, the future, and your present experience. For example, you may think, *I don't enjoy anything, I can't get anything done, Nothing I do works out, I'm a loser,* and *No one could accept me.*

Nonetheless, there are some very concrete steps you can take that can get you started. Trusting in the possibility that your outlook *can* change is the first crack in the wall. Here are some of the specific steps that will begin the process.

OVERCOMING DEPRESSION

Keep Track of Your Moods

Depression may seem like a single gray shadow cast over your life. In reality, your outlook is changing all the time, day and night, moment to moment, depending on what you're doing and what's going on around you. One woman said, "I feel terrible all the time." I asked her to keep track of her negative moods on a scale from zero to ten for every hour of the day, noting her activities at the time. She found her depression was not nearly as monolithic as she imagined. It was at its worst when she was sitting at home, ruminating about how terrible her life was. By contrast, it was much better when she was working, exercising, or talking with friends (even talking about her depression was an improvement). She was not at the point yet where she could say it ever quite lifted, but the fact that it could fluctuate so much suggested there was something to work with.

Schedule Pleasant Activities

You may feel your depression makes it impossible to look forward to anything. Acknowledge the feeling—but don't allow it to paralyze you. Do pleasurable things for yourself even when you don't feel like it. I often encourage depressed patients to simply get out and enjoy themselves—or at least to maintain activities that *would* be enjoyable under better circumstances. These might include outdoor trips, socializing on weekends, visits to a museum—or just simple things like warm baths, music, movies, or reading. Giving yourself over to small pleasures you can enjoy in the moment will ultimately affect your overall mood.

It's also useful to plan ahead with a positive outlook. Have a schedule of activities on your calendar that you can look forward to—a kind of reward menu of interesting or exciting events over the next day, week, month, or year. You might set out to explore the city, town, or countryside where you live. You might join a hiking club or investigate local bike trails. You might take a drawing class (any class is usually an opportunity to meet new and interesting people) or start learning a musical instrument. As you look ahead to these activities, you'll find them competing for space with the dismal scenarios in your mind. Life will begin to seem more like a series of ups and downs, rather than unbroken doldrums. It will begin to seem like something with possibilities.

Stay Connected

Connectedness to other people is a major bulwark against depression. When you're depressed, there's often a tendency to isolate yourself. You withdraw from relationships because you don't feel up to social interaction, because you feel ashamed of your condition or simply because you're in a bad mood. This worsens the problem. People who stay connected to their friends, who are willing to engage, who are open to new relationships, are far more likely to recover from their depression. Rather than being a reason for withdrawing, your depressed state offers an excellent chance to get involved in groups or organizations, to renew old friendships, to socialize regularly. Initially, you may not feel like doing any of these things. You may think, *I am a burden to my friends*—challenge this by calling them and talking about the positive things that you are planning and try to be supportive to them. Or, you might think, *I haven't called them in a long time. They will be annoyed with me.* Test this out by calling a number of friends, tell them you've been busy, and apologize and make some plans with them.

Get Outside Yourself

Self-absorption is depression's ally. It keeps you stuck in the rut of self-pity and negative thinking. Trying new things and new experiences is a good way to break out of this rut. I've seen people derive tremendous benefits from throwing themselves into things like yoga, meditation, music lessons, hiking, biking, cooking lessons, dance, reading clubs, reconnecting with old friends, tours, joining teams, religious groups, researching interesting topics—almost anything you can think of. Personal growth is often lampooned, but it's a marvelous remedy for depression.

One of the best things of all—something I can't recommend too highly—is doing something for others. Nothing will change your attitude toward your own life so much as addressing others' needs; it often helps you put your own problems in perspective. One patient of mine who was terribly depressed about his work found that what got him out of it was working with homeless people. "I just started to feel differently about myself," he told me. "I stopped focusing on myself all the time and became a lot happier." Volunteering, working with disadvantaged people, or simply reaching out to those you know personally who are having difficulty can be a most remarkable medicine. I've seen people utterly transformed by such experiences. You can also volunteer your time to help animals. One woman who felt lonely and isolated volunteered at a local animal shelter and found being around animals and people who cared made her feel better.

Practice Self-Compassion

You need someone on your side to encourage you during your darkest hours. Someone who will fight for you. Someone who is always there for you. If you are like a lot of depressed people, you have been your own worst enemy at times. So I will ask you to make believe that you are your own best friend.

If your own best friend were feeling down, what would you say to support her or him? How would you cheer them on? If they felt like a loser, what would you say to them to make them feel cared for and loved?

You need to have yourself on your side.

If you're like most depressed people, that hasn't generally been your role. You're probably your harshest critic, your most pessimistic advisor, the underminer of all your efforts to be happy.

Usually a basic element in depression is a lack of self-acceptance. People who don't feel good about themselves have a hard time feeling good about their lives. In battling depression, it's important to become aware of the many ways in which you judge yourself for your supposed shortcomings and to release those judgments. You may have made mistakes in your life; like all of us, you have many imperfections. Nonetheless, you are a human being worthy of love and compassion. None of your mistakes or shortcomings can change that in any way. If you begin to practice kindness toward yourself in all your thoughts and actions, you'll have a lot less to be depressed about.

Examine Your Negative Thoughts

If you've followed the procedures in this book, you'll have done this extensively with your anxious thoughts. It's no different with depression. The thought might be *I'll never get over this*. In fact you don't know that, since you haven't tried everything. Or it might be *I'm a total loser*. But in fact there are probably many things about you that others like. Or you may tell yourself that you're depressed all the time, when in fact your moods are fluctuating constantly. The fact is, none of your gloomy assessments of the situation are necessarily accurate. They're simply thoughts your mind has created. And as we've seen, the best way to free yourself from their tyranny is to become aware of them *as thoughts*.

Years ago I had a patient who was feeling anxious and depressed about her marriage, which was ending. She was an intelligent, personable, and kind woman. I had found sailing and windsurfing to be exciting sports for myself so I suggested that she take sailing lessons. She did. Then she began meeting people every week to crew on boats. She eventually crewed for a week in the U.S. Virgin Islands. She met a young man there, and they began corresponding, dating, and sailing together.

Eventually, a couple of years after she finished therapy, I received an e-mail from her with a photo. She had gotten married to the sailor and they were literally sailing his boat around the world.

I know it sounds like a fairy tale.

But sometimes dreams come true.

I have learned from my patients (who teach me every day) that nothing is unsolvable if we work together to find the solution.

SUICIDE

Suicide may be considered the ultimate outcome of depression, especially when left untreated over time. And since severe and chronic anxiety is highly correlated with depression, it becomes a good predictor of eventual suicidal risk. If an anxiety disorder has led you into depression, and if that depression has in turn led you to thoughts of harming or killing yourself, it's important to seek help right away. The first step would be to consult a trained professional who will help you evaluate your suicidal risk. The following questions are pertinent:

1. What are your reasons for living and for dying? Do the former outweigh the latter?

2. Have you tried to harm yourself in the past? If so, do you think you actually wanted to die, or did you really wish to send someone a message about your suffering?

3. When you have thoughts of suicide, do you feel resigned to carry them out or do you feel that they are disturbing to you?

4. Have you made plans to commit suicide or written a suicide note?

5. Have you overtly threatened suicide?

6. When you think of suicide, do you feel spaced out or in a trance?

7. Are you taking the medication your doctor prescribes?

8. Are you drinking in excess or using nonprescription drugs?

9. Can you promise you won't do anything to harm
   yourself until you have spoken to a professional?

Behind the suicidal impulse lies hopelessness. People who are profoundly depressed invariably express feelings of hopelessness, either because they have suffered great losses, have struggled with their problems for a long time without success, or have an abysmally poor self-image. Yet with the proper therapeutic treatment (supplemented with medication) feelings of hopelessness can be eradicated. You may still have problems, but your belief in your ability to cope with your problems can be strengthened dramatically.

For those who feel hopeless, this is a good thing to know. Start by questioning your hopelessness itself. Why are you hopeless? Is it because you think your depression will never lift? Why do you think that? Perhaps you've tried a number of medications and found them ineffective. I can practically guarantee you that you haven't tried all the possible combinations of medications. Many psychiatrists will try out dosages of different types of drugs, adjusting the amounts, measuring side effects, and testing various combinations. Sometimes it takes the right combination to succeed, even where no one drug or even class of drugs is the answer in itself. Some medications are specifically helpful in inhibiting suicidal tendencies temporarily, until other treatments can have time to be effective. (See Appendix D: Medications) There are also more dramatic treatments that have proven effective, such as electroconvulsive, magnetic, or biological treatments. Despite past concerns over electroconvulsive treatment (ECT), over 90 percent of those receiving it say they would do it again. In fact, no treatment for depression has proved more effective. One should consider all these possibilities before concluding the situation is irremediable.

Perhaps your hopelessness stems from the fact that you've tried certain psychotherapies (or other approaches such as prayer, exercise, natural healing, exercise, meditation, or spiritual counseling) that haven't worked. It's the same as with medication: all these things have the potential to be helpful, but no one of them in itself may be the answer. Effective treatment for depression will usually involve a number of approaches, especially when intelligently coordinated by you, with the help of whatever support system you're able to put together. The more resources you can bring to bear the better, but don't be discouraged merely because a particular one of them hasn't proven to be a panacea.

My own feeling, based admittedly on my own professional bias but also on many years of clinical experience, is that intensive cognitive-behavioral therapy is one of the best defenses against the risk of suicide. It's important to find a good cognitive-behavioral therapist, trust the guidelines he or she sets out for you, and stick with the program. It can be done. I know because I've seen it many times, including with patients who arrived in the office feeling as hopeless as possible. You can locate a certified cognitive therapist through the Website www.academyofct.org (or in the United Kingdom, www.babcp.com).

A final word to anxiety sufferers, particularly those whose hopelessness stems from a belief that they'll never get over their OCD, panic disorder, or whatever particular form of anxiety they suffer from: your belief may be due to the way you think about your anxiety. If you're thinking in terms of a *complete cure,* you're probably not getting the right picture. Anyone who expects to live a life without anxiety is going to be disappointed. Anxiety is part of the human condition. "Getting better" doesn't mean eradicating anxiety but rather learning to function and be happy in spite of it. By working with a qualified cognitive-behavioral therapist, following the appropriate self-help procedures (such as the ones in this book), and continuing to practice exposure to anxious situations, most people are able to make dramatic progress. In my experience, there's really no valid reason for hopelessness at all. I've learned from my patients that no problem is unsolvable when we work together to find the solution.

Diagnostic Tests

CHAPTER 5: PANIC DISORDER

<table>
<tr><td colspan="2">Agoraphobic Cognitions Questionnaire (ACQ)</td></tr>
<tr><td colspan="2">Below are some thoughts that may pass through your mind when you are nervous or frightened. Please indicate how often each thought occurs when you are nervous. Rate from 1–5 using the scale below.

When I am anxious . . .</td></tr>
</table>

1 = never occurs	2 = rarely occurs	3 = occurs half of the time	4 = usually occurs	5 = always occurs

Thoughts	Rating
I am going to throw up.	
I am going to pass out.	
I must have a brain tumor.	
I will have a heart attack.	
I will choke to death.	
I am going to act foolish.	
I am going blind.	
I will not be able to control myself.	
I will hurt someone.	
I am going to have a stroke.	
I am going crazy.	
I am going to scream.	
I am going to babble of talk funny.	
I am going to be paralyzed by fear.	
Other ideas not listed (please describe and rate them)	
TOTAL SCORE=	

Total your score for the first 14 items (exclude Item 15). Then divide by 14. The average score for people with agoraphobia is 2.3.

© Chambless, D. L., Caputo, G. C., Bright, P., & Gallagher, R, "Assessment of Fear in Agoraphobics: The Body Sensations Questionnaire and the Agoraphobic Cognitions Questionnaire," Journal of Consulting and Clinical Psychology, 52 (1984) 1090–1097.

CHAPTER 6: OBSESSIVE-COMPULSIVE DISORDER (OCD)

Maudsley Obsessional-Compulsive Inventory		
Instructions: Please answer each question by putting an X in the "True" or "False" column. There are no right or wrong answers, and no trick questions. Work quickly and do not think too long about the exact meaning of the question.		
Actions	**True**	**False**
1. I avoid using public telephones because of possible contamination.		
2. I frequently get nasty thoughts and have difficulty in getting rid of them.		
3. I am more concerned than most people about honesty.		
4. I am often late because I can't seem to get through everything on time.		
5. I don't worry unduly about contamination if I touch an animal.		
6. I frequently have to check things (e.g., gas or water taps, doors, etc.) several times		
7. I have a very strict conscience.		
8. I find that almost every day I am upset by unpleasant thoughts that come into my mind against my will.		
9. I do not worry unduly if I accidentally bump into somebody.		
10. I usually have serious doubts about the simple, everyday things I do.		
11. Neither of my parents was very strict during my childhood.		
12. I tend to get behind in my work because I repeat things over and over again.		
13. I use only an average amount of soap.		
14. Some numbers are extremely unlucky.		

15. I do not check letters over and over again before posting them.		
16. I do not take a long time to dress in the morning.		
17. I am not excessively concerned about cleanliness.		
18. One of my major problems is that I pay too much attention to detail.		
19. I can use well-kept toilets without any hesitation.		
20. My major problem is repeated checking.		
21. I am not unduly concerned about germs and diseases.		
22. I do not tend to check things more than once.		
23. I do not stick to a very strict routine when doing ordinary things.		
24. My hands do not feel dirty after touching money.		
25. I do not usually count when doing a task.		
26. I take rather a long time to complete my washing in the morning.		
27. I do not use a great deal of antiseptics.		
28. I spend a lot of time every day checking things over and over again		
29. Hanging and folding my clothes at night does not take up a lot of time.		
30. Even when I do something very carefully I often feel that it is not quite right.		

Reprinted from Behaviour Research and Therapy, 15, Hodgson & Rachman, "Obsessional-Compulsive Complaints," p. 395 (1977), with permission from Elsevier Science.

Scoring for the Maudsley Obsessional-Compulsive Inventory

I have listed below the items for the various subscales, scoring +1 for True (T) and -1 for False (F). For each subscale, count the total number of answers that match those listed below. (Some items can appear on more than one subscale.)

Checking	Cleaning	Slowness	Doubting
2-T	1-T	2*-F	3-T
6-T	4-T	4-T	7-T
8-T	5-F	8*-F	10-T
14-T	9-F	16-F	11-F
15-F	13-F	23-F	12-T
20-T	17-F	25-F	18-T
22-F	19-F	29-F	30-T
26-T	21-F		
28-T	24-F	*Note: These two items load on this factor in the opposite direction from what would be expected.	
	26-T		
	27-F		
Score:	Score:	Score:	Score:

Total			
1-T	9-F	17-F	25-F
2-T	10-T	18-T	26-T
3-T	11-F	19-F	27-F
4-T	12-T	20-T	28-T
5-F	13-F	21-F	29-F
6-T	14-T	22-F	30-T
7-T	15-F	23-F	
8-T	16-F	24-F	

Score:

Adapted from *Behaviour Research and Therapy, 15,* Hodgson & Rachman, "Obsessional-Compulsive Complaints," p. 391 (1977), with permission from Elsevier Science.

The average total score for college students without OCD is 6.3. The average scores for people with OCD on the total scale is 18.8 and on the subscales are as follows: checking (4.7), washing (3.4), doubting (4.8), slowness (2.6).

In addition to completing the form above, you should note examples of OCD tendencies such as fears of contamination, losing control (fear of hurting or offending others), fears of illness, needing to set things straight or in order, excessive washing or rituals for washing or eating, needing to repeat an action, or repeated words, melodies, or images that intrude into your mind. You should take this test over again after you have completed your self-help on your OCD.

CHAPTER 7: GENERALIZED ANXIETY DISORDER (GAD)

Leahy Anxiety Checklist	
Rate the feelings in the left column with the number that most accurately describes how you have been feeling generally during the past week. Use the scale below. When you are finished, add the numbers in the right column to get your generalized anxiety score.	

0 = not at all	1 = slightly true	2 = somewhat true	3 = very true

Feeling	Score
1. Feeling shaky	0
2. Unable to relax	1
3. Feeling restless	1
4. Get tired easily	1
5. Headaches	1
6. Shortness of breath	0
7. Dizzy or light-headed	0
8. Need to urinate frequently	2
9. Sweating (unrelated to heat)	1
10. Heart pounding	2
11. Heartburn or upset stomach	3
12. Easily irritated	3
13. Startled easily	2
14. Difficulty sleeping	0
15. Worried a lot	1
16. Hard to control worries	1
17. Difficulty concentrating	1
Generalized Anxiety Score:	20
Scores between 5 and 10 reflect mild anxiety, 11 and 15 moderate anxiety, and 16 and above severe anxiety.	
© 1999 Robert L. Leahy	

Penn State Worry Questionnaire (PSWQ)

Enter the number that best describes how typical or characteristic each item is of you, putting the number next to the item.

1_____ 2 _____ 3 _____ 4 _____ 5_____

Not at all typical   Somewhat typical   Very typical

Characteristic	Score
If I don't have enough time to do everything, I don't worry about it. (R)	2 4
My worries overwhelm me.	4
I do not tend to worry about things. (R)	2 4
Many situations make me worry.	4
I know I shouldn't worry about things, but I just cannot help it.	3
When I am under pressure I worry a lot.	3
I am always worrying about something.	2
I find it easy to dismiss worrisome thoughts. (R)	2 4
As soon as I finish one task, I start to worry about everything else I have to do.	2
I never worry about anything. (R)	1 5
When there is nothing more I can do about a concern, I don't worry about it anymore. (R)	2 4
I've been a worrier all my life.	4
I notice that I have been worrying about things.	3
Once I start worrying, I can't stop.	2
I worry all the time.	3
I worry about projects until they are done.	4
Your Total Score:	56

(R) indicates a reverse score. Thus, to reverse score your question, if you give an answer of 1 ("Not at all typical"), score it as a 5. Add up your scores on the test—and be sure to note which items are reversed scored (see above for how to reverse score your responses). People with some problems with worry on the average score above 52 and really chronic worriers score above 65. "Nonanxious" people average around 30. It is also quite possible to score below the clinical range (somewhere between 30 and 52) but still feel that your worries are bothering you.

CHAPTER 8: SOCIAL ANXIETY DISORDER (SAD)

Liebowitz Social Anxiety Scale		
Fear or Anxiety	**Avoidance**	
0 = none	0 = never (0–10%)	
1 = mild	1 = occasionally (10–33%)	
2 = moderate	2 = often (33–67%)	
3 = severe	3 = usually (67–100%)	
Action	**Fear or Anxiety**	**Avoidance**
1. Using the telephone in public (P)	2	2
2. Participating in small groups (P)	1	1
3. Eating in public places (P)	2	2
4. Drinking with others in public places (P)	0	0
5. Talking to people in authority (S)	2	1
6. Acting, performing, or giving a talk in front of an audience (P)	3	3
7. Going to a party (S)	2	1
8. Working while being observed (P)	2	1
9. Writing while being observed (P)	1	1
10. Calling someone you don't know very well (S)	1	1
11. Talking with people you don't know very well (S)	2	1
12. Meeting strangers (S)	2	2
13. Urinating in a public bathroom (P)	2	2
14. Entering a room when others are already seated (P)	2	2

15. Being the center of attention (S)	1	1
16. Speaking up at a meeting (P)	0	0
17. Taking a test (P)	0	0
18. Expressing disagreement or disapproval to people you don't know well (S)	1	1
19. Looking at people you don't know very well in their eyes (S)	3	2
20. Giving a report to a group (P)	2	2
21. Trying to pick up someone (P)	2	2
22. Returning goods to a store (S)	2	2
23. Giving a party (S)	1	1
24. Resisting a high pressure salesperson (S)	1	1
Total score:	37 (P)	32 (S)
Performance (P) anxiety score:	19	18
Social (S) anxiety score:	18	14

You can evaluate your final score using these cutoff points:

55-65 Moderate social phobia

65-80 Marked social phobia ⟵

80-95 Severe social phobia

Greater than 95 - Very severe social phobia

Michael R. Liebowitz, "Social Phobia," Modern Problems in Pharmacopsychiatry 22 (1987): 141. Reproduced with permission of S. Karger AG, Basel.

CHAPTER 9: POST-TRAUMATIC STRESS DISORDER (PTSD)

Do You Have Post-Traumatic Stress Disorder?	
Exposure to Trauma	• You experienced or witnessed an event that involved actual or threatened death or serious injury, or a threat to yourself or others. • You experienced fear, helplessness, or horror.
Intrusive Recollection	• Distressing recollections of the event • Distressing dreams of the event • Acting or feeling as if the traumatic event were recurring—for example, a sense of reliving the experience, illusions, hallucinations, and flashback episodes • Distress when experiencing internal or external cues that symbolize or resemble an aspect of the traumatic event • Physiologic reactivity upon exposure to internal or external cues that symbolize or resemble an aspect of the traumatic event
Avoidance or Numbing	• Efforts to avoid thoughts, feelings, or conversations associated with the trauma • Efforts to avoid activities, places, or people that arouse recollections of the trauma • Inability to recall an important aspect of the trauma • Markedly diminished interest or participation in significant activities • Feeling of detachment or estrangement from others • Restricted range of affect (e.g., unable to have loving feelings) • Sense of foreshortened future (e.g., does not expect to have a career, marriage, children, or a normal life span)
Hyperarousal	• Difficulty falling or staying asleep • Irritability or outbursts of anger • Difficulty concentrating • Hypervigilance • Exaggerated startle response
Adapted from American Psychiatric Association. (2000). Diagnostic and statistical manual of mental disorders DSM-IV-TR (Fourth ed.). Washington, D.C.: American Psychiatric Association.	

Post-Traumatic Checklist for Civilians

Below is a list of problems and complaints that people sometimes have in response to stressful life experiences. Enter the number that best indicates how much you have been bothered by that problem in the last month.

1 = Not at all	2 = A little bit	3 = Moderately	4 = Quite a bit	5 = Extremely

Response	Rating
1. Repeated, disturbing *memories, thoughts,* or *images* of a stressful experience from the past?	
2. Repeated, disturbing *dreams* of a stressful experience from the past?	
3. Suddenly *acting or feeling* as if a stressful experience were *happening again* (as if you were reliving it)?	
4. Feeling *very upset* when *something reminded* you of a stressful experience from the past?	
5. Having *physical reactions* (e.g., heart pounding, trouble breathing, or sweating) when *something reminded* you of a stressful experience from the past?	
6. Avoid *thinking about* or *talking about* a stressful experience from the past or avoid *having feelings* related to it?	
7. Avoid *activities* or *situations* because *they remind you* of a stressful experience from the past?	
8. Trouble *remembering important parts* of a stressful experience from the past?	
9. Loss of interest in things that you used to enjoy?	
10. Feeling *distant* or *cut off* from other people?	
11. Feeling *emotionally numb* or being unable to have loving feelings for those close to you?	
12. Feeling as if *your future* will somehow be *cut short?*	
13. Trouble *falling* or *staying* asleep?	
14. Feeling *irritable* or having *angry outbursts?*	

15. Having *difficulty concentrating?*	
16. Being *"super alert"* or watchful on guard?	
17. Feeling *jumpy* or *easily startled?*	

Scores on the scale can vary from 17 to 85. Most people with scores of 44 or above are diagnosed as having PTSD. Even scores below 44 can indicate that traumatic experiences continue to impact your quality of life.

Weathers, Litz, Huska, & Keane; National Center for PTSD—Behavioral Science Division. This is a government document in the public domain.

APPENDIX H

How to Identify Your Anxious Thinking

Many of us who are anxious have a biased, negative way of thinking about things. We are constantly seeing threats and danger. Whereas someone else might just think, *Oh, that would be a minor inconvenience if that happened,* you might think it would be awful. We refer to these negative thoughts that occur spontaneously as "automatic thoughts." They seem plausible to you at the time, but they also may reflect a biased way of thinking.

One of the first things that you can do to handle your anxious thinking is to catch your negative anxious thoughts. For example, let's say that you are at a party and you notice that you are feeling anxious. You begin thinking the following negative thoughts:

- People will think that I look like a fool.
- It would be awful if anyone thought that.
- I couldn't stand it.
- I must be an idiot.
- I have nothing going for me.

Well, you are off and running with your anxiety.

We have found that people who are prone to anxiety and depression have typical ways of thinking—we call these cognitive distortions. This simply means that you have a bias toward negative thinking. We can categorize your negative thoughts into specific styles. For example, if you think that someone thinks that you are boring (but you really don't have direct evidence of this), you are probably mind reading.

Take a look at the list below and see if you are using any of these distorted ways of thinking.

1. *Mind reading.* You assume that you know what people think without having sufficient evidence of their thoughts: *He thinks I'm a loser.*

2. *Fortune-telling.* You predict the future negatively; things will get worse, or there is danger ahead: *I'll fail that exam,* or *I won't get the job.*

3. **Catastrophizing.** You believe that what has happened or will happen will be so awful and unbearable that you won't be able to stand it: *It would be terrible if I failed.*

4. **Labeling.** You assign global negative traits to yourself and others: *I'm undesirable,* or *He's a rotten person.*

5. **Discounting positives.** You claim that the positive things you or others do are trivial: *That's what wives are supposed to do—so it doesn't count when she's nice to me,* or *Those successes were easy, so they don't matter.*

6. **Negative filtering.** You focus almost exclusively on the negatives and seldom notice the positives: *Look at all of the people who don't like me.*

7. **Overgeneralizing.** You perceive a global pattern of negatives on the basis of a single incident: *This generally happens to me. I seem to fail at a lot of things.*

8. **Dichotomous thinking.** You view events or people in all-or-nothing terms: *I get rejected by everyone,* or *It was a complete waste of time.*

9. **Shoulds.** You interpret events in terms of how things should be, rather than simply focusing on what is: *I should do well. If I don't, then I'm a failure.*

10. **Personalizing.** You attribute a disproportionate amount of the blame to yourself for negative events, and you fail to see that certain events are also caused by others: *The marriage ended because I failed.*

11. **Blaming.** You focus on the other person as the *source of* your negative feelings, and you refuse to take responsibility for changing yourself: *She's to blame for the way I feel now,* or *My parents caused all my problems.*

12. **Unfair comparisons.** You interpret events in terms of standards that are unrealistic. For example, you focus primarily on

others who do better than you and find yourself inferior in the comparison: *She's more successful than I am,* or *Others did better than I did on the test.*

13. **Regret orientation.** You focus on the idea that you could have done better in the past, rather on what you can do better now: *I could have had a better job if I had tried harder,* or *I shouldn't have said that.*

14. **What if?** You keep asking a series of questions about "what if" something happens, and you fail to be satisfied with any of the answers: *Yeah, but what if I get anxious?* or *What if I can't catch my breath?*

15. **Emotional reasoning.** You let your feelings guide your interpretation of reality: *I feel depressed; therefore, my marriage is not working out.*

16. **Inability to disconfirm.** You reject any evidence or arguments that might contradict your negative thoughts. For example, when you have the thought *I'm unlovable,* you reject as *irrelevant* any evidence that people like you. Consequently, your thought cannot be refuted: *That's not the real issue. There are deeper problems. There are other factors*

17. **Judgment focus.** You view yourself, others, and events in terms of evaluations as good/bad or superior/inferior, rather than simply describing, accepting, or understanding. You are continually measuring yourself and others according to arbitrary standards and finding that you and others fall short. You are focused on the judgments of others as well as your own judgments of yourself: *I didn't perform well in college,* or *If I take up tennis, I won't do well,* or *Look how successful she is. I'm not successful.*

It can be helpful to you to write down your anxious thoughts and see if you are using specific distortions. For example, are you prone to mind reading (*He thinks I look nervous*) or fortune-telling (*My mind will go blank*) or personalizing (*She yawned so I must be boring*)? Sometimes your negative thoughts can fall into more than one category. Take a look at the table below and see how you can categorize some typical anxious thoughts. You can use this table on a daily basis to begin tracking your habits of anxious thinking. In Appendix I, I will show you how to change your thinking to be more realistic—and more practical.

Keeping Track of My Anxious Thoughts		
Situation	**Anxious thought**	**Thought distortion**
Thinking of talking to someone at a party	She will think I'm an idiot.	Mind reading
Same situation	If I get rejected it would be terrible.	Catastophizing
Thinking I might have a panic attack	If I had a panic attack, I would lose all control.	Fortune telling, Catastrophizing, all or nothing thinking
Making a mistake on a project at work	I must be an idiot.	Labeling

Keeping Track of My Anxious Thoughts		
Situation	**Anxious thought**	**Thought distortion**

From *Treatment Plans and Interventions for Depression and Anxiety Disorders* by Robert L. Leahy and Stephen J. Holland. Copyright 2000 by Robert L. Leahy and Stephen J. Holland.

Use Your Emotional Intelligence

A big part of your anxiety is how you think, feel, and react to your anxious feelings. For example, imagine if you are going through a breakup in a relationship and you feel sad, angry, and worried about the future. But you also have a good friend, Tricia, who is warm and caring and listens to you talk about your mixed feelings. When you talk with her you feel that you can express yourself, you feel she understands and cares about your feelings and, so, you feel validated: *At least I know that she understands how I feel.* And when you talk with her you realize that she's gone through a breakup, too. She knows what it's like. So, you feel, *I'm not the only person who has felt this way.* You also begin to think, *Tricia has been through this and she seems to be doing okay, so maybe these feelings won't last forever.* When you are talking with her and you recall how painful it all feels *right now,* you start to cry, and Tricia comforts you and says, "I know how hard it feels. This is a difficult time for you." After a short while you stop crying. And then you think, *I can lose control and cry and nothing terrible happens. In fact, I feel even closer to Tricia right now. I feel she understands me.*

If you have experienced having a friend like Tricia, you are very fortunate. Someone like her can help you feel that you can express your feelings, get validation, experience compassion, understand that you are not alone, and realize that when you have a painful feeling, it won't last forever. Tricia helps you use your emotional intelligence. She helps you understand that your feelings are part of being human. She helps put things in perspective and helps you feel that you are not alone.

But many people who are prone to anxiety have a very different experience about their feelings. They think:

- I can't express my feelings. I have no one to talk to.

- No one understands how hard it is for me.

- My feelings just don't make sense.

- I feel embarrassed and guilty over my feelings.

- I think that if I allow myself to have these feelings, I'll lose control.

- My feelings are dangerous—I could go crazy if I allow myself to feel this way.

- I've got to get control. I've got to get rid of these feelings immediately.

All of these thoughts will make you feel worse about the way you feel. You feel alone, overwhelmed, confused, guilty, and embarrassed. You try to control your feelings, but you can't get rid of them. This makes you feel more anxious about your anxiety. Feeling bad about feeling bad will make you feel *even worse*.

The good news is that we can help you come to terms with your anxious feelings and help put the way you feel into perspective.

THE WORST WAYS TO HANDLE YOUR ANXIETY

When you feel anxious you may be using some of the worst strategies to get rid of your feelings. For example, you may drink too much, eat too much, misuse drugs, get lost in Internet pornography, repeat rituals and compulsions, get angry at yourself or at the world, or even bang your head against the wall or cut yourself. Ironically, all of these distractions from your anxiety may help you feel better immediately. But they make things worse in the long term. Trying to handle your anxiety using these strategies is like trying to cure alcoholism by having another drink. You will end up with twice as many problems.

For example, if you use alcohol or drugs to handle your feelings you set off opposite processes in your brain—you feel better and then your brain kicks in to compensate—and you feel worse. Alcohol, of course, is a central nervous system depressant. It will depress you and make you more anxious as the alcohol wears off—and then you will need another drink. You are then on a roller-coaster going nowhere.

Or, if you binge eat you may temporarily distract yourself from your anxiety, but it only reinforces your self-destructive eating habits. You feel more out of control, you gain weight, you feel the urge to purge, and you reinforce the idea, *The only way to get rid of these feelings is to binge*. That's a hopeless strategy.

Look at the figure below and see if any of this makes sense in how you try to handle your anxiety. Are there problematic thoughts and strategies that you are using? Would you be better off if you developed a different way of living with your feelings?

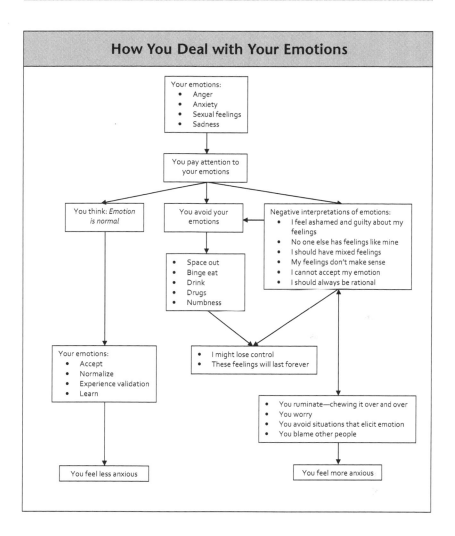

HOW TO COME TO TERMS WITH YOUR ANXIETY

Just as we have rule books for dealing with each of the anxiety disorders, we also can develop a rule book for dealing with your anxiety. The first goal is to recognize that you need to have a different relationship to your feelings. Rather than trying to get rid of your feelings, you can put them in perspective. Here's how.

1. Anxious feelings are part of being alive.

2. All of us feel anxious some of the time. You are not alone.

3. Your anxiety does make sense. Think about all of the things we have been talking about in this book—evolution, genetics, false alarms, anxious rule books, etc.

4. Your anxiety is temporary and not dangerous.

5. There is nothing to feel guilty or ashamed about. There is nothing immoral or malicious about feeling anxious. You don't have to control your anxiety—you only have to live with it.

6. You can still do productive things even if you are anxious.

Okay. Let's take a closer look at each of these new rules about your anxiety.

1. Anxious feelings are part of being alive.

Nature has built into all of us the capacity to feel anxious at times. In this book, we have gone over the reasons that evolution built into us the fear of heights, closed spaces, contamination, humiliation, and being attacked. Many of our anxious feelings are false alarms, but that is part of being alive.

2. All of us feel anxious some of the time. You are not alone.

We feel anxious when we get up in front of a group of people to talk, when we are behind in our work, or when we think that our relationship or our health is in jeopardy. We are not made to be cool, rational, and above it all at all times. Anyone who tells you that he is never anxious is probably not telling the complete truth. About 50 percent of the general public has a history of anxiety, depression, or substance abuse. Anxiety is the common cold of life.

3. Your anxiety does make sense. Think about all of the things we have been talking about in this book—evolution, genetics, false alarms, anxious rule books, etc.

Once you realize that there are very good reasons why evolution has built all of these fears into us, you can realize that your anxiety is "the right response at the wrong time." Your fear of heights or fear of public speaking was very adaptive for your ancestors. It helped them survive. There is no deep secret to discover. Your anxiety is based on software in your brain that worked for your ancestors. After all, they survived. They were adaptive. They avoided danger. They ran from the tigers, avoided dangerous strangers, and kept themselves from being contaminated. They hoarded food and clothing so they wouldn't die during the winter. Three cheers for anxiety!

4. Your anxiety is temporary and not dangerous.

Anxiety is always temporary. I have never had a patient who has "panic attacks" come to my office with one. You may think, *If I do this, my anxiety will last all day and overwhelm me.* But check it out: most of the time your anxiety only lasts a few minutes. It goes away on its own. Anxiety is simply arousal—very much like jogging is a bit of arousal. Or sex is a lot more arousal. Maybe your anxiety is not as sexy as sex, but it is arousal nonetheless.

5. There is nothing to feel guilty or ashamed about. There is nothing immoral or malicious about feeling anxious. You don't have to control your anxiety—you only have to live with it

No one is worse off because of your anxiety. You are not "doing this to other people." You wouldn't feel guilty or ashamed if you had indigestion or a headache. You are simply experiencing the false alarms that automatically go off in your head. The anxious thoughts and sensations happen to you—you are not sitting there on Tuesday afternoon at 3 o'clock trying to be anxious. But you can learn some new ways to think about your anxiety and respond to it. That's why you are reading this book and applying these techniques.

Your anxiety is not like a flood of water coming over the dam threatening to destroy the community. The more you try to control it by telling yourself to stop feeling anxious, the more anxious you will feel. We have gone over a lot of techniques that allow you to welcome your anxious thoughts and arousal. It's like being diplomatic with guests that you have invited over. They don't always behave the way you like, but you tolerate them. You can stand back and observe, detach yourself, don't take your anxiety too personally. Think about your anxiety as a temporary visitor.

6. You can still do productive things even if you are anxious.

Sometimes we think, *I can't do anything because I am anxious.* Well, you have been doing a lot of things even though you have felt anxious. You can choose to act against your anxiety. Sometimes you think, *I can't exercise because I feel tired.* Then you think, *I want to lose weight.* So, you go out and you exercise. Even though you felt tired, you did it anyway. Anxiety is not a deterrent to living a life. The more you do things that are productive while you are anxious, the less afraid of anxiety you will be. Do it anyway.

APPENDIX J

How to Deal with Your Anxious Thoughts

Now that you have begun to identify some of your negative thoughts and put them into the different categories (for example, mind reading or fortune-telling), you can start using some of the techniques from cognitive therapy to test and challenge them. Keep in mind that you are not trying to "stop thinking," and you are not trying to suppress your thoughts. You are simply going to put them to the test. You might find out that your anxious thoughts are extreme, invalid—even silly.

Let's take a closer look at how to handle these anxious, negative thoughts.

1. *Recognize the difference between a thought and a feeling.* Imagine that you are walking down the street in the dark and you hear three men walking quickly behind you. You feel anxious and afraid because you think, *They are going to attack me.* The anxious feeling is your emotion and the thought is your interpretation of what is happening, *I am going to be attacked.* However, if you had the thought, *These are some people coming from a medical convention* you would have a different feeling—one of indifference.

2. *Your thoughts lead you to feel anxious.* You can notice that your anxiety is often the result of seeing threats that might not be realistic. For example: *I feel anxious because I think I'll fail.* Start by monitoring your negative anxious thoughts. Write down your thoughts when you are anxious. If you notice you are feeling anxious and thinking, *I am going to make a fool of myself* and *I will lose control,* write down these thoughts and keep a record of them. We will then see how these thoughts may or may not be unrealistic.

3. *Distinguish thoughts from facts.* For example: I can believe that it is raining outside, but that doesn't mean it's a fact. I need to collect evidence—go outside—see whether it's raining.

4. *Identify and categorize distorted automatic thoughts.* Use the Keeping Track of My Anxious Thoughts form in Appendix H to put your negative thoughts into the categories outlined there. For example, *I am always failing* (over-generalizing) or *I'm an idiot* (labeling).

5. *Rate your confidence in the accuracy of your thoughts, as well as the intensity of your feelings.* For example: I feel anxious (80 percent) because I think I'll fail (95 percent).

6. *Cost-benefit analysis.* Weigh the costs and benefits of your anxious thoughts. Example of thought: *I need people's approval.* Costs: *This thought makes me shy and anxious around people, and lowers my self-esteem.* Benefits: *Maybe I'll try hard to get people's approval.* Conclusion: *I would be much better off if I didn't think this way.*

7. *Examine the logic of your thoughts.* Are you jumping to conclusions that don't follow logically from premises? For example, *I'm a failure because I did poorly on that test.*

8. *What is the evidence for and against your thought?* Are you jumping to conclusions without sufficient information? Are you only looking for evidence that supports your thoughts, not evidence that might refute them?

9. *Distinguish possibility from probability.* It may be possible that you will have a heart attack if you are anxious, but what is the probability? If you were a betting person, would you bet on the bad thing happening, or would you bet against your prediction?

10. *What would it mean (what would happen, why would it be a problem) if X occurred?* What would happen next? And what would that mean—what would happen, why would it be a problem? For example, If my heart beats rapidly it would get worse and worse and then I would have a panic attack, and then I would collapse, go unconscious, and go into a coma.

11. ***Double standard technique.*** *Ask* yourself, *Would you apply the same thought (interpretation, standard) to others as you do to yourself? Why/why not?* For example, if a friend was giving a talk and her mind went blank momentarily, would you think she was a fool?

12. ***Weigh the evidence for and against your thought.*** Example of thought: I'll get rejected. Evidence in favor: I'm anxious (emotional reasoning), Sometimes people don't like me. Evidence against: I'm a decent person, Some people like me, There's nothing rude or awful about saying hello to someone, People are here at the party to meet other people. Conclusion: I don't have much convincing evidence that I'll get rejected. Nothing ventured, nothing gained.

13. ***Examine the quality of the evidence.*** Is your evidence actually good? Would your evidence stand up to scrutiny by others? Are you using emotional reasoning and selective information to support your arguments?

14. ***Keep a daily log of evidence for and against your thoughts.*** Record evidence in a daily log of behaviors/events that confirm or disprove a thought. For example, if you think you are going to have a panic attack, keep a record of your anxiety levels throughout the day. Or if you think that you will only say stupid things around other people, keep a record of anything positive, neutral, or negative that you say.

15. ***Look for alternative interpretations of events.*** For example, If someone doesn't like me, it might simply be that the two of us are different. Or perhaps the other person is in a bad mood or shy or involved with someone else. If I am feeling anxious, maybe it's just physical arousal, not a sign of losing total control.

16. ***Prove to yourself that this is not really a problem.*** List all the reasons why the current situation is not a problem: Even if my face blushes, it's not a problem because I can still talk, I can still think, and I can still do everything I've always done.

17. *Be your own defense attorney.* Imagine that you have hired yourself as an attorney to defend yourself. Write out the strongest case you can in favor of yourself, even if you don't believe it.

18. *Carry out an experiment.* Test a thought by engaging in behavior that challenges the thought. For example, for the thought *I'll be rejected,* approach ten people at a party.

19. *Put things in perspective.* What would you still be able to do even if a negative thought were true? Or how does your situation compare to that of someone with, say, a life-threatening illness?

20. *Argue with yourself.* Make believe that the positive and negative are two characters in an argument. Do a role play with the negative thoughts. Engage in a role-play argument: negative you says, "You'll fail the exam"; positive you replies, "There's no evidence that I'll fail." Continue in this manner.

21. *Act as if the thought is not true.* In actual situations, act as if you do not believe your negative thoughts. For example, if you are anxious at parties, go up to ten people and introduce yourself. If you are afraid of having a panic attack in a theater, go inside, sit down, and make believe that you are acting in a play as a character who is confident. Stay "in character."

22. *Make it less awful.* Decatastrophize a possible bad outcome by putting it into perspective—Why would this not be so awful after all? For example, *If I had a panic attack, why would it not be awful? Well, panic attacks are self-limiting, I've had them before, it's simply arousal.*

23. *Examine the "feared fantasy."* Ask yourself, *What is the worst possible outcome of X?* How would you handle it? What behaviors could you control even if it happened? If you made a mistake on something, what is the worst outcome that could happen? How probable is that? What is the best outcome and the most probable outcome?

24. *Examine your past predictions.* Do you fail to learn from false predictions? Have you generally made negative predictions in the past that have not come true? Are you negatively biased? Have these predictions turned into self-fulfilling prophecies? For example, you have predicted that you would get rejected at a party, so you said nothing when you went to the party—and no one liked you.

25. *Test your predictions.* Make a list of specific predictions for the next week and keep track of the outcomes.

26. *Examine past worries.* Have you worried about things that you no longer think about? List as many of these as possible and ask yourself, *Why are these no longer important to me?*

27. *Challenge your need for certainty.* You can't have certainty in an uncertain world. If you are trying to rule out absolutely all possibility of negative outcomes, you will be unable to act. Which things do you do every day that don't require certainty (for example, driving in traffic, eating in restaurants, talking with people, doing your job).

28. *Practice acceptance.* Rather than trying to control and change everything, perhaps there are some things you can learn to accept and make the best of. For example, perhaps you won't be perfect in your job, but perhaps you can learn to appreciate what you can do.

29. *Invite your thoughts in as a visitor.* Imagine that your negative thought is a visitor that comes to your party. The party is all the other thoughts running around in your head. Just ask the thought to have a seat, get itself a drink, and enjoy the party. You don't have to get rid of the thought or struggle with it. Just let it be.

30. *Make your thoughts into a movie.* Imagine your negative thoughts are characters in a movie that you are watching. Just watch the movie. Don't try to change the script. Don't argue with the thoughts. Just watch them. The movie will come to an end.

31. ***Identify your maladaptive rules and assumptions.*** Look at the contents of your rule book (shoulds, musts, and if-then statements). For example, *I should succeed at everything I do, If people don't like me, it means there's something wrong with me,* and *I must be approved by everyone.*

32. ***Challenge your maladaptive rules and assumptions.*** Are you setting unrealistic expectations for yourself? Are your standards too high? Too low? Too vague? Do your standards give you room for a learning curve? Would you apply these rules to everyone else? For example, would you think that someone is a loser simply because he was anxious? Would you think someone is irresponsible if she didn't check everything?

33. ***Borrow someone else's head.*** Instead of getting trapped by your way of reacting, try to think of someone you know who you think is highly adaptive. How would this person think and act under these circumstances?

34. ***Develop new more adaptive assumptions.*** Develop new, realistic, fair, and more humane rules for yourself. For example, *I'm worthwhile regardless of what others think of me* instead of *If people don't like me, it means there's something wrong with me.* What are the costs and benefits of these more adaptive assumptions? Costs: *Maybe I'll get conceited and alienate people.* Benefits: *Increased self-confidence, less shyness, less dependence on others, more assertiveness.* Conclusion: *This new assumption is better than the one that I have to get other people to like me in order to like myself.*

35. ***Use coping imagery.*** Try to develop an image of yourself coping competently with a feared person or situation. Imagine yourself going into a crowded area and feeling confident and strong. Or imagine exposing yourself to situations you fear and coming out triumphant.

36. ***Restructure the frightening images.*** Think of situations and people that make you anxious, and change your image of them so they are less threatening to you. Miniaturize the frightening image. For example, develop an image of a feared person or thing as much smaller and weaker than you, instead of bigger and more powerful.

37. **Practice the feared image.** Desensitize yourself to the feared image—engage in repeated exposure to a feared image or situation in order to diminish its capacity to frighten you. For example, if you fear people laughing at you, practice imagining someone laughing for thirty minutes. You will find that this will make you bored.

38. **Use coping cards.** Write out instructions to yourself for use in times of difficulty (e.g., "Don't worry about my anxious arousal. It's arousal. It's not dangerous. Anxiety doesn't mean I'm going crazy. I can tolerate it"). Put these statements, along with reminders and so on, on a coping card that you can refer to easily.

39. **Anticipate problems.** List the kinds of problems that might come up and develop rational responses and ways of coping. For example, you worry that you might lose your job. List a number of things that you could do to solve that problem should it occur.

40. **Inoculate yourself to stress.** Think about your worst negative thoughts and write out how you would challenge them. For example, your worst negative thought is, *I am a complete failure.* Write out a rational response: *I have succeeded at a number of things in my life, and it's not the end of the world to fail at something.*

41. **Reward yourself.** List all the positive thoughts you have about yourself. Make a praise card and carry it around with you. On the card, list positive self-statements, "Good for me for practicing my self-help," "I am facing my fears," "I am making progress."

Parts are adapted from *Treatment Plans and Interventions for Depression and Anxiety Disorders* by Robert L. Leahy and Stephen J. Holland. Copyright 2000 by Robert L. Leahy and Stephen J. Holland.

ACKNOWLEDGMENTS

Once again I want to thank my agent, Bob Diforio, for his constant support and encouragement. I also want to thank Patty Gift of Hay House for her positive and effective approach to making this project possible and Dan Breslaw, my editor at Hay House, for making the book more targeted and clear.

I also want to thank the many patients that I have seen over the years. I have learned from them how life looks from the perspective of fear and despair. Thank you for trusting me and for all that I have learned from you. I am often impressed with the wisdom that people have when they find their own way to solve a problem—often helping me with how to help others. Therapists should always think of their patients as teachers.

This book owes a great deal to the magnificent contributions of cognitive-behavioral therapists throughout the world. I wish to thank the following people whose work I have found most helpful: Anke Ehlers, Thomas Borkovec, David Barlow, Chris Brewin, Gillian Butler, David A. Clark, David M. Clark, Michel Dugas, Christopher Fairburn, Melanie Fennell, Edna Foa, Mark Freeston, Paul Gilbert, Leslie Greenberg, Ann Hackman, Allison Harvey, Steven Hayes, Richard Heimberg, John Kabat-Zinn, Robert Ladouceur, Marsha Linehan, Warren Mansell, Isaac Marks, Douglas Mennin, Susan Nolen-Hoeksema, Lars Ost, Costas Papageorgiou, Christine Purdon, Jack Rachman, Steven Reiss, John Riskind, Paul Salkovskis, Roz Shafran, Debbie Sookman, Gail Steketee, Steven Taylor, and Adrian Wells. I am most fortunate to consider many of these people my friends. Thank you again and again.

Of course, special gratitude goes to my mentor, colleague, and friend of the past 27 years, Aaron T. Beck, founder of cognitive therapy and a true giant of our time.

I also wish to thank my colleagues at the American Institute for Cognitive Therapy (AICT) who have been kind enough to allow me to share these ideas with them and to test them out with their patients. Among my colleagues at AICT, Lisa Napolitano and Dennis Tirch have expanded my understanding and appreciation of mindfulness, acceptance, and dialectical behavior therapy—often in our heated debates at case conferences. Laura Oliff has always been the test of clinical wisdom as to what actually makes sense with real patients. In addition, my editorial and research assistant, Poonam Melwani, has been indispensable throughout this project.

319

My friend, Philip Tata, from London has been a great source of support for me for many years and he has been instrumental in facilitating my participation in British and world conferences and in helping me learn from our excellent British colleagues. Cheers to you, Philip!

Finally, my wife Helen has been patient with me as I have persisted on this and other writing projects. All of this was written at our weekend home in rural Connecticut where we are constantly reminded that nature—and what is natural—is the greatest source of calm and perspective. It's hard to feel anxious when you are in awe of fall foliage or are kayaking through the wetlands. Often we find that serenity is all around us—if only we will look.

REFERENCES

Chapter 1

E. Jane Costello et al., "Psychiatric Disorders in Pediatric Primary Care," *Archives of General Psychiatry* 45 (1988): 1107.

E. Jane Costello and Adrian Angold, "Epidemiology," in *Anxiety Disorders in Children and Adolescents*, ed. John March (New York: Guilford Press, 1995), 109-124.

Robert L. DuPont et al., "Economic Costs of Anxiety Disorders," *Anxiety* 2, No. 4 (1996): 167.

Gregg Easterbrook. *The Progress Paradox: How Life Gets Better While People Feel Worse*. (New York: Random Huse, 2003).

Martin C. Harter, Kevin P. Conway, and Kathleen R. Merikangas, "Association between Anxiety Disorders and Physical Illness," *European Archives of Psychiatry and Clinical Neuroscience* 253, No. 6 (2003): 313.

Ronald C. Kessler et al., "Lifetime and 12-month Prevalence of DSM-III-R Psychiatric Disorders in the United States. Results from the National Comorbidity Survey," *Archives of General Psychiatry* 51 (1994): 8.

Ronald C. Kessler et al., "Lifetime Prevalence and Age-of-Onset Distributions of DSM-IV Disorders in the National Comorbidity Survey Replication," *Archives of General Psychiatry* 62 (2005): 593.

Ronald C. Kessler et al., "Prevalence and Treatment of Mental Disorders, 1990 to 2003," *New England Journal of Medicine* 352, No. 24 (2005): 2515.

Anthony C. Kouzis and William W. Eaton, "Psychopathology and the Initiation of Disability Payments," *Psychiatric Services* 51, No. 7 (2000): 908.

Christopher Lasch, *Haven in a Heartless World: The Family Besieged* (New York: Basic Books, 1977).

Martin Marciniak et al., "Medical and Productivity Costs of Anxiety Disorders: Case Control Study," *Depression and Anxiety*, 19, No.2 (2004): 112

Thomas H. Ollendick, Neville J. King, and Peter Muris, "Fears and Phobias in Children: Phenomenology, Epidemiology and Aetiology," *Child and Adolescent Mental Health* 7 (2002): 98.

David Shaffer et al., "Psychiatric Diagnosis in Child and Adolescent Suicide," *Archives of General Psychiatry* 53 (1996): 339-348.

Jean M. Twenge, "The Age of Anxiety? The Birth Cohort Change in Anxiety and Neuroticism, 1952-1993," *Journal of Personality and Social Psychology*, 79, No. 6 (2000): 1007.

Jean M. Twenge, Liqing Zhang, and Charles Im, "It's Beyond my Control: A Cross-Temporal Meta-Analysis of Increasing Externality in Locus of Control, 1960-2002," *Personality and Social Psychology Review*, 8, No. 3 (2004): 308.

Jean M. Twenge ,Brittany Gentile, C. Nathan DeWall, Debbie Ma, Katharine Lacefield, David R. Schurtz, Increases in psychopathology among young Americans, 1938-2007: A cross-temporal meta-analysis of the MMPI Unpublished paper, San Diego State University, 2008 US Census data

Chapter 2

Simon Baron-Cohen, *Mindblindness: An Essay on Autism and Theory of Mind* (Cambridge, MA: MIT Press, 1995).

Simon Baron-Cohen et al., "Recognition of Mental State Terms: Clinical Findings in Children with Autism and a Functional Neuroimaging Study of Normal Adults," *British Journal of Psychiatry* 165 (1994): 640-649.

Peter Carruthers and Andrew Chamberlain, eds., *Evolution and the Human Mind: Modularity, Language and Meta-Cognition* (New York: Cambridge University Press, 2000).

Tim F. Chapman, "The Epidemiology of Fears and Phobias," in *Phobias: A Handbook of Theory, Research and Treatment*, ed. Graham C. L. Davey (New York: Wiley, 1997), 415-434.

David A. Clark, *Cognitive-Behavioral Therapy for OCD* (New York: Guilford, 2003).

David A. Clark, *Intrusive Thoughts in Clinical Disorders: Theory, Research, and Treatment* (New York: Guilford, 2005).

David M. Clark, "Anxiety Disorders: Why they Persist and How to Treat them," *Behaviour Research and Therapy* 37 (1999): S5

William R. Clark and Michael Grunstein, *Are We Hard-Wired? The Role of Genes in Human Behavior* (New York: Oxford University Press, 2000).

Charles Darwin, *The Expression of the Emotions in Man and Animals* (Chicago: University of Chicago Press, 1872/1965)

Irenaus Eibl-Eibesfeldt, *Human Ethology: Foundations of Human Behavior* (Hawthorne, New York: Aldine de Gruyter, 1989).

John H. Flavell and Eleanor R. Flavell, "Development of Children's Intuitions about Thought-Action Relations," *Journal of Cognition and Development* 5, No. 4 (2004): 451.

Eleanor J. Gibson and Richard D. Walk, "The Visual Cliff," *Scientific American* 202 (1960): 64.

Paul Gilbert, "The Evolved Basis and Adaptive Functions of Cognitive Distortions," *British Journal of Medical Psychology* 71 (1998): 447.

Jeffrey A. Gray, *The Neuropsychology of Anxiety: An Enquiry into the Functions of the Septo-Hippocampal System* (Oxford: Clarendon, 1982).

Jeffrey A. Gray, *The Psychology of Fear and Stress* (2nd ed.) (New York: McGraw-Hill, 1987).

John M. Hettema, et al., "A Twin Study of the Genetics of Fear Conditioning," *Archives of General Psychiatry* 60 (2003): 702.

Joseph E. LeDoux, *The Emotional Brain: The Mysterious Underpinnings of Emotional Life* (New York: Simon and Schuster, 1996).

William Manchester, *World Lit Only by Fire. The Medieval Mind and the Renaissance: Portrait of an Age* (Boston: Back Bay Books, 1993).

Isaac M. Marks, *Fears, Phobias and Rituals: Panic, Anxiety, and their Disorders* (New York: Oxford University Press, 1987).

Ross G. Menzies and Lisa Parker, "The Origins of Height Fear: An Evaluation of Neoconditioning Explanations," *Behaviour Research and Therapy* 39 (2001): 185.

Harald Merckelbach and Peter J. de Jong, "). Evolutionary Models of Phobias," in *Phobias: A Handbook of Theory, Research and Treatment*, ed. Graham C. L. Davey (New York: Wiley, 1997), 323-347.

Arne Ohman and Susan Mineka, "Fears, Phobias, and Preparedness: Toward an Evolved Module of Fear and Fear Learning," *Psychological Review* 108 (2001): 483.

Josef Perner, *Understanding the Representational Mind* (Cambridge, MA: MIT Press, 1991).

Steven Pinker, *The Blank Slate: The Modern Denial of Human Nature* (New York: Viking, 2002).

Richie Poulton and Ross G. Menzies, "Non-Associative Fear Acquisition: A Review of the Evidence from Retrospective and Longitudinal Research," *Behaviour Research and Therapy* 40 (2002): 127.

Richie Poulton and Ross G. Menzies, "Fears Born and Bred: Toward a More Inclusive Theory of Fear Acquisition," *Behaviour Research and Therapy* 40 (2002): 197.

Jennifer J. Quinn and Michael S. Fanselow, "Defenses and Memories: Functional Neural Circuitry of Fear and Conditioning Responses," in *Fear and Learning: From Basic Processes to Clinical Implications*, eds. Michelle G. Craske, Dirk Hermans, and Debora Vansteenwegen (Washington, DC: American Psychological Association Press, 2006), 55-74.

Paul Rozin and James W. Kalat, "Specific Hugers and Poison Avoidance as Adaptive Specializations of Learning," *Psychological Review* 78 (1971): 459.

Martin E. P. Seligman, "Phobias and Preparedness," *Behavior Therapy* 2 (1971): 307; Martin E. P. Seligman and Joanne L. Hager, Eds., *Biological Boundaries of Learning* (New York: Appleton-Century-Crofts, 1972).

John Tooby and Leda Cosmides, "Psychological Foundations of Culture," in *The Adapted Mind: Evolutionary Psychology and the Generation of Culture*, ed. Jerome H. Barkow, Leda Cosmides, John Tooby (New York: Oxford University Press, 1992), 19-136.

Adrian Wells, "A Cognitive Model of GAD: Metacognitions and Pathological Worry," in *Generalized Anxiety Disorder: Advances in Research and Practice*, ed. Richard G. Heimberg, Cynthia L. Turk, and Douglas S. Mennin (New York: Guilford, 2004), 164-186.

Edward O. Wilson, *Sociobiology: The New Synthesis* (Cambridge: Belknap Press, 1975).

Chapter 3

Aaron T. Beck, Gary Emery, and Ruth L. Greenberg, *Anxiety Disorders and Phobias: A Cognitive Perspective* (New York: Basic Books, 1985).

David M. Clark, "Anxiety Disorders: Why They Persist and How to Treat Them," *Behaviour Research and Therapy* 37 (1999): S5.

Christopher G. Fairburn, Zafra Cooper and Roz Shafran, "Cognitive Behaviour Therapy for Eating Disorders: A "Transdiagnostic" Theory and Treatment," *Behavior Research and Therapy* 41, No. 5 (2003): 509.

Allison Harvey, Edward Watkins, Warren Mansell, and Roz Shafran, *Cognitive Behavioural Processes across Psychological Disorders: A Transdiagnostic Approach to Research and Treatment* (New York: Oxford University Press, 2004).

Naomi Koerner and Michel J. Dugas, "A Cognitive Model of Generalized Anxiety Disorder: The Role of Intolerance of Uncertainty," in *Worry and its Psychological Disorders: Theory, Assessment and Treatment*, ed. Graham C. L. Davey, and Adrian Wells (Hoboken, NJ: Wiley, 2006), 201-216.

Isaac M. Marks, *Fears, Phobias and Rituals: Panic, Anxiety, and their Disorders* (New York: Oxford University Press, 1987).

Christine Purdon, Karen Rowa, and Martin M. Antony, "Thought Suppression and its Effects on Thought Frequency, Appraisal and Mood State in Individuals with Obsessive-Compulsive Disorder," *Behaviour Research and Therapy* 43, No. 1 (2005): 93.

John H. Riskind, "Looming Vulnerability to Threat: A Cognitive Paradigm for Anxiety," *Behaviour Research & Therapy* 35, No. 8 (1997): 685.

Paul Salkovskis et al., "An Experimental Investigation of the Role of Safety-Seeking Behaviours in the Maintenance of Panic Disorder with Agoraphobia," *Behaviour Research and Therapy* 37 (1999): 559.

Adrian Wells, "Anxiety Disorders, Metacognition and Change," in *Roadblocks in Cognitive Behavioral Therapy*, ed. Robert L. Leahy (New York: Springer, 2003), 69-90.

Adrian Wells, *Cognitive therapy of Anxiety Disorders: A Practice Manual and Conceptual Guide* (New York: Wiley, 1997).

Chapter 4

American Psychiatric Association, *Diagnostic and Statistical Manual of Mental Disorders*, 4th-TR ed. (Washington, DC: Author, 2000).

Albert Bandura, Dorothea Ross, and Sheila Ross, "Imitation of Film-Mediated Aggressive Models," *Journal of Abnormal & Social Psychology* 66, No.1 (1963): 3.

Peter A. Di Nardo, "Etiology and Maintenance of Dog Fears," *Behaviour Research and Therapy* 26, No. 3 (1988): 241.

Elevator and Escalator Safety Foundation, "History of Elevator Safety," Elevator and Escalator Safety Foundation, http://www.eesf.org/safetrid/elevhist.htm.

Mats Fredrikson et al., "Gender and Age Differences in the Prevalence of Fears and Specific Phobias," *Behaviour Research and Therapy 26* (1996): 241.

John Garcia, Kenneth W. Rusiniak, and Linda P. Brett, "Conditioning Food-Illness Aversions in Wild Animals," in *Operant Pavlovian Interactions*, eds. Hank Davis & Harry M. B. Hurwitz (New York: Wiley, 1977).

Jeffrey A. Gray, *The Neuropsychology of Anxiety: An Enquiry into the Functions of the Septo-Hippocampal System* (New York: Clarendon Press/Oxford University Press, 1982).

Jeffrey A. Gray, *The Psychology of Fear and Stress*, 2nd ed. (New York: McGraw-Hill, 1987).

Jerome Kagan, "Temperamental Contributions to Social Behavior," *American Psychologist* 44, No. 4 (1989): 668.

Kenneth S. Kendler et al., "The Genetic Epidemiology of Irrational Fears and Phobias in Men," *Archives of General Psychiatry* 58, No. 3 (2001): 257.

Ross G. Menzies and J. Christopher Clarke, "The Etiology of Childhood Water Phobia," *Behaviour Research & Therapy* 31, No.5 (1993): 499.

O. H. Mowrer, "A Stimulus-Response Analysis of Anxiety and its Role as a Reinforcing Agent," *Psychological Review* 46, No 6 (1939): 553.

New York City Department of Buildings. "Elevator Safety," New York City Government, http://www.nyc.gov/html/dob/html/news/elevator_safety.shtml.

Lars-Göran Öst, "Rapid Treatment of Specific Phobia," in *Phobias: A Handbook of Theory, Research and Treatment*, ed. Graham C. L. Davey (Hoboken, NJ: Wiley, 1997), 227-246.

David Ropeik, and George Gray, *Risk: A Practical Guide for Deciding What's Really Safe and What's Really Dangerous in the World Around You, Appendix 1* (Houghton-Mifflin: Boston, 2002).

Martin E. Seligman, "Phobias and Preparedness," *Behavior Therapy* 2, No. 3 (1971): 307.

Murray Stein, Kerry Jang, and John W. Livesley, "Heritability of Social Anxiety-Related Concerns and Personality Characteristics: A Twin Study," *Journal of Nervous and Mental Diseases* 190, No. 4 (2002): 219.

Andrew J. Tomarken, Susan Mineka, and Michael Cook, "Fear-Relevant Selective Associations and Covariation Bias," *Journal of Abnormal Psychology* 98, No. 4 (1989): 381.

Chapter 5

Michael E. Addis et al., "Effectiveness of Cognitive-Behavioral Treatment for Panic Disorder versus Treatment as Usual in a Managed Care Setting: 2-Year Follow-Up," *Journal of Consulting and Clinical Psychology* 74, No. 2 (2006): 377.

American Psychiatric Association, *Diagnostic and Statistical Manual of Mental Disorders*, 4th-TR ed. (Washington, DC: Author, 2000).

Roger Baker et al., "Emotional Processing and Panic," *Behaviour Research and Therapy* 42, No. 11 (2004): 1271.

David H. Barlow, *Anxiety and its Disorders: The Nature and Treatment of Anxiety and Panic* (New York: Guilford, 1988).

Sabine Kroeze et al., "Automatic Negative Evaluation of Suffocation Sensations in Individuals with Suffocation Fear," *Journal of Abnormal Psychology* 114, No. 3, 466.

Jill T. Levitt et al., "The Effects of Acceptance versus Suppression of Emotion on Subjective and Psychophysiological Response to Carbon Dioxide Challenge in Patients with Panic Disorder," *Behavior Therapy* 35, No. 4 (2004): 747.

Seung-Lark Lim and Ji-Hae Kim, "Cognitive Processing of Emotional Information in Depression, Panic, and Somatoform Disorder," *Journal of Abnormal Psychology* 114, No. 1 (2005): 50.

Richard J. McNally, *Panic Disorder: A Critical Analysis* (Guilford: New York, 1994).

Norman B. Schmidt et al., "Does Coping Predict CO-Sub-2-Induced Panic in Patients with Panic Disorder?," *Behaviour Research and Therapy* 43, No. 10 (2005): 1311.

Jasper A. J. Smits et al., "Mechanism of Change in Cognitive-Behavioral Treatment of Panic Disorder: Evidence for the Fear of Fear Mediational Hypothesis," *Journal of Consulting and Clinical Psychology* 72, No. 4 (2004): 646.

Myrna M. Weissman et al., "Panic Disorder and Cardiovascular/ Cerebrovascular Problems: Results from a Community Survey," *American Journal of Psychiatry* 147, No. 11 (1990): 1504.

Joan Welkowitz, "Panic and Comorbid Anxiety Symptoms in a National Anxiety Screening Sample: Implications for Clinical Interventions," *Psychotherapy: Theory, Research, Practice, Training* 41, No. 1 (2004): 69.

Chapter 6

Jose A. Amat et al., "Increased Number of Subcortical Hyperintensities on MRI in Children and Adolescents with Tourette's Syndrome, Obsessive-Compulsive Disorder, and Attention Deficit Hyperactivity Disorder," *American Journal of Psychiatry* 163, No. 6 (2006): 1106.

American Psychiatric Association, *Diagnostic and Statistical Manual of Mental Disorders*, 4th-TR ed. (Washington, DC: Author, 2000).

Nader Amir, Laurie Cashman, and Edna B. Foa, "Strategies of Thought Control in Obsessive-Compulsive Disorder," *Behaviour Research & Therapy* 35, No. 8 (1997): 775.

Fernando R. Asbahr et al., "Obsessive-Compulsive Symptoms among Patients with Sydenham Chorea," *Biological Psychiatry* 57, No. 9 (2005): 1073.

Susan G. Ball, Lee Baer and Michael W. Otto, "Symptom Subtypes of Obsessive-Compulsive Disorder in Behavioral Treatment Studies: A Quantitative Review," *Behaviour Research & Therapy* 34 (1996): 47; Robert L. Leahy and Stephen J. Holland, *Treatment Plans and Interventions for Depression and Anxiety Disorders* (New York: Guilford, 1996).

David A. Clark, "Unwanted Mental Intrusions in Clinical Disorders: An Introduction," *Journal of Cognitive Psychotherapy* 16, No. 2 (2002): 123.

Diana L. Feygin, James E. Swain, and James F. Leckman, "The Normalcy of Neurosis: Evolutionary Origins of Obsessive-Compulsive Disorder and Related Behaviors," *Progress in Neuro-Psychopharmacology & Biological Psychiatry* 30, No. 5 (2006): 854.

R. J. Hodgson and S. J. Rachman, "Obsessional-Compulsive Complaints," *Behaviour Research and Therapy* 15 (1977): 389.

Robert L. Leahy, "On My Mind," *The Behavior Therapist* 30 (2007): 44–45.

Robert L. Leahy and Stephen J. Holland, *Treatment Plans and Interventions for Depression and Anxiety Disorders* (New York: Guilford, 2000).

James T. McCracken and Gregory L. Hanna, "Elevated Thyroid Indices in Children and Adolescents with Obsessive-Compulsive Disorder: Effects of Clomipramine Treatment," *Journal of Child and Adolescent Psychopharmacology* 15, No. 4 (2005): 581.

Obsessive Compulsive Cognitions Working Group, "Cognitive Assessment of Obsessive-Compulsive Disorder," *Behaviour Research & Therapy* 35, No. 7 (1997): 667.

Christine Purdon, "Thought Suppression and Psychopathology," *Behaviour Research and Therapy* 37 (1999): 1029.

Christine Purdon and David A. Clark, "Obsessive Intrusive Thoughts in Nonclinical Subjects: II. Cognitive Appraisal, Emotional Response and Thought Control Strategies," *Behaviour Research and Therapy* 32 (1994): 403.

Stanley Rachman, "Obsessions, Responsibility and Guilt," *Behaviour Research and Therapy* 31 (1993): 149.

Stanley Rachman, "A Cognitive Theory of Obsessions," *Behaviour Research and Therapy* 35 (1997): 793.

Stanley Rachman, *The Treatment of Obsessions* (New York: Oxford University Press, 2003).

Stanley Rachman and Padmal de Silva, "Abnormal and Normal Obsessions," *Behaviour Research &* Therapy 16, No. 4 (1978): 233.

Paul M. Salkovskis and Joan Kirk, "Obsessive-Compulsive Disorder," in *Science and Practice of Cognitive Behaviour Therapy,* eds. David M. Clark & Christopher G. Fairburn (New York: Oxford University Press, 1997) 179-208.

Paul Salkovskis et al., "Multiple Pathways to Inflated Responsibility Beliefs in Obsessional Problems: Possible Origins and Implications for Therapy and Research," *Behaviour Research and Therapy* 37, No. 11 (1999): 1055.

Gail S. Steketee, *Treatment of Obsessive Compulsive Disorder* (New York: Guilford Press, 1993).

Steven Taylor, "Cognition in Obsessive Compulsive Disorder: An Overview," in *Cognitive Approaches to Obsessions and Compulsions: Theory, Assessment and Treatment*, eds. Randy O. Frost and Gail Steketee (New York: Pergamon, 2002), 1-14.

Daniel M. Wegner and Sophia Zanakos, "Chronic Thought Suppression," *Journal of Personality* 62 (1994): 615.

Myrna M. Weissman et al., "The Cross National Epidemiology of Obsessive Compulsive Disorder: The Cross National Collaborative Group," *Journal of Clinical Psychiatry* 55, No. 3, Suppl. (1994): 5.

Adrian Wells, *Emotional Disorders and Metacognition: Innovative Cognitive Therapy* (New York: Wiley).

K. Elaine Williams, Dianne L. Chambless, and Anthony Ahrens, "Are Emotions Frightening? An Extension of the Fear of Fear Construct," *Behaviour Research & Therapy* 35, No. 3 (1997): 239.

Chapter 7

American Psychiatric Association, *Diagnostic and Statistical Manual of Mental Disorders*, 4th-TR ed. (Washington, DC: Author, 2000).

James E. Barrett, et al. "The Prevalence of Psychiatric Disorders in a Primary Care Practice," *Archives of General Psychiatry* 45, No. 12 (1988): 1100.

Robin M. Carter et al., "One-Year Prevalence of Subthreshold and Threshold DSM-IV Generalized Anxiety Disorder in a Nationally Representative Sample," *Depression and Anxiety* 13, No. 2 (2001): 78.

John M. Hettema, Michael C. Neale, and Kenneth S. Kendler, "A Review and Meta-Analysis of the Genetic Epidemiology of Anxiety Disorders," *American Journal of Psychiatry* 158 (2001): 1568.

Kenneth S. Kendler and Carol A. Prescott, *Genes, Environment, and Psychopathology: Understanding the Causes of Psychiatric and Substance Use Disorders* (New York: Guilford, 2006).

Barbara L. Kennedy and John J. Schwab, "Utilization of Medical Specialists by Anxiety Disorder Patients," *Psychosomatics* 38, No. 2 (1997): 109.

Robert L. Leahy, "An Investment Model of Depressive Resistance," *Journal of Cognitive Psychotherapy: An International Quarterly* 11 (1997): 3.

Robert L. Leahy and Stephen J. Holland, *Treatment Plans and Interventions for Depression and Anxiety Disorders* (New York: Guilford, 2000).

See Table 11-2 in S. Molina and T. D. Borkovec, "The Penn State Worry Questionnaire: Psychometric Properties and Associated Characteristics," in *Worrying: Perspectives on Theory Assessment and Treatment*, eds. Graham C. L. Davey and Frank Tallis (Chichester, England: Wiley, 1994), 265–283.

Adrian Wells, "Meta-Cognition and Worry: A Cognitive Model of Generalized Anxiety Disorder," *Behavioural and Cognitive Psychotherapy* 23 (1995) 301.

Adrian Wells and Gerald Matthews, "Modelling Cognition in Emotional Disorder: The S-REF model," *Behaviour Research and Therapy* 34, No.11-12 (1996): 881.

Kimberly A. Yonkers et al., "Phenomenology and Course of Generalised Anxiety Disorder," *British Journal of Psychiatry* 168 (1996): 308.

Chapter 8

American Psychiatric Association, *Diagnostic and Statistical Manual of Mental Disorders*, 4th-TR ed. (Washington, DC: Author, 2000).

Susan M. Bögels and Warren Mansell, "Attention Processes in the Maintenance and Treatment of Social Phobia: Hypervigilance, Avoidance and Self-Focused Attention," *Clinical Psychology Review* 24 No. 7 (2004): 827.

Monroe A. Bruch and Jonathan M. Cheek, "Developmental Factors in Childhood and Adolescent Shyness," in *Social Phobia: Diagnosis, Assessment, and Treatment*, ed. Richard G. Heimberg (New York: Guilford, 1995), 163-184.

Monroe A. Bruch and Richard G. Heimberg, "Differences in Perceptions of Parental and Personal Characteristics between Generalized and Nongeneralized Social Phobics," *Journal of Anxiety Disorders* 8, No. 2 (1994): 155.

Gillian Butler et al., "Exposure and Anxiety Management in the Treatment of Social Phobia," *Journal of Consulting & Clinical Psychology* 52, No. 4 (1984): 642.

Charles S. Carver and Michael F. Scheier, *Attention and Self-Regulation: A Control Theory Approach to Human Behavior* (New York: Springer, 1981).

David M. Clark and Adrian Wells, "A Cognitive Model of Social Phobia," in *Social Phobia: Diagnosis, Assessment, and Treatment*, eds. Richard G. Heimberg et al. (New York: Guilford, 1995), 69-93.

Irenaus Eibl-Eibesfeldt, *Love and Hate: The Natural History of Behavior Patterns* (New York: Henry Holt & Company, 1972).

Erin A. Heerey and Ann M. Kring, "Interpersonal Consequences of Social Anxiety," *Journal of Abnormal Psychology* 116, No. 1 (2007): 125.

Craig S. Holt et al., "Situational Domains of Social Phobia," *Journal of Anxiety Disorders* 6, No. 1 (1992): 63.

Debra A. Hope et al., "Thought Listing in the Natural Environment: Valence and Focus of Listed Thoughts among Socially Anxious and Nonanxious Subjects" (Poster presented at the annual meeting of the Association for Advancement of Behavior Therapy, Boston, 1987).

Jerome Kagan, Nancy Snidman, and Doreen Arcus, "On the Temperamental Categories of Inhibited and Uninhibited Children," in *Social Withdrawal, Inhibition, and Shyness in Childhood*, eds. Kenneth H. Rubin and Jens B. Asendorpf (Mahwah, NJ: Erlbaum, 1993), 19-28.

Kenneth S. Kendler and Carol A. Prescott, *Genes, Environment, and Psychopathology: Understanding the Causes of Psychiatric and Substance Use Disorders* (New York: Guilford, 2006).

Ronald C. Kessler et al., "Lifetime and 12-month prevalence of DSM-III-R Psychiatric Disorders in the United States. Results from the National Comorbidity Survey," *Archives of General Psychiatry* 51, No. 1 (1994): 8.

Hi-Young Kim, Lars-Gunnar Lundh, and Allison Harvey, "The Enhancement of Video Feedback by Cognitive Preparation in the Treatment of Social Anxiety: A Single-Session Experiment," *Journal of Behavior Therapy and Experimental Psychiatry*, 33, No. 1 (2002): 19.

Michael R. Liebowitz, "Social Phobia," *Modern Problems in Pharmacopsychiatry* 22 (1987): 141. Reproduced with permission of S. Karger AG, Basel.

Rosemary S. L. Mills and Kenneth H. Rubin, "Socialization Factors in the Development of Social Withdrawal," in *Social Withdrawal, Inhibition, and Shyness in Childhood*, eds. Kenneth H. Rubin and Jens B. Asendorpf (Mahwah, NJ: Erlbaum, 1993), 117-148.

Lynne Murray et al., "The Effects of Maternal Social Phobia on Mother-Infant Interactions and Infant Social Responsiveness," *Journal of Child Psychology and Psychiatry* 48, No. 1 (2007): 45.

Robert Plomin and Denise Daniels, "Genetics and Shyness," in *Shyness: Perspectives on Research and Treatment*, eds. Warren H Jones, Jonathan M Cheek, and Stephen R Briggs (New York: Plenum, 1986), 63-80.

Franklin R. Schneier et al., "Social Phobia: Comorbidity and Morbidity in an Epidemiologic Sample," *Archives of General Psychiatry* 49, No. 4 (1992): 282.

Jane M. Spurr and Lusia Stopa, "Self-Focused Attention in Social Phobia and Social Anxiety," *Clinical Psychology Review* 22, No. 7 (2002): 947.

Chapter 9

American Psychiatric Association, *Diagnostic and Statistical Manual of Mental Disorders*, 4th-TR ed. (Washington, DC: Author, 2000).

Edward B. Blanchard et al., "Psychometric Properties of the PTSD Checklist (PCL)," *Behaviour Research and Therapy* 34, No. 8 (1996): 669.

Rebekah Bradley et al., "A Multidimensional Meta-Analysis of Psychotherapy for PTSD," *American Journal of Psychiatry* 162 (2005): 214.

Naomi Breslau et al., "Traumatic Events and Posttraumatic Stress Disorder in an Urban Population of Young Adults," *Archives of General Psychiatry* 48, No. 3 (1991): 216.

Timothy D. Brewerton, "Eating Disorders, Trauma, and Comorbidity: Focus on PTSD," *Eating Disorders: The Journal of Treatment & Prevention* 15, No. 4 (2007): 285.

Chris R. Brewin and Emily A. Holmes, "Psychological Theories of Posttraumatic Stress Disorder," *Clinical Psychology Review* 23, No. 3 (2003): 339.

Anke Ehlers and David M. Clark, "A Cognitive Model of Posttraumatic Stress Disorder," *Behaviour Research and Therapy* 38 (2000): 319

Anke Ehlers et al., "Predicting Response to Exposure Treatment in PTSD: The Role of Mental Defeat and Alienation," *Journal of Traumatic Stress* 11, No. 3 (1998): 457.

Edna B. Foa and Michael J. Kozak, "Emotional Processing of Fear: Exposure to Corrective Information," *Psychological Bulletin* 99 (1986): 20.

Nick Grey, Emily Holmes, and Chris R. Brewin, "Peritraumatic Emotional "Hot Spots" in Memory," *Behavioural and Cognitive Psychotherapy* 29 (2001): 367.

R. Janoff-Bultmann, *Shattered Assumptions: Toward a new psychology of trauma.* (New York: Free Press, 1992).

B. Kathleen Jordan et al., "Problems in Families of Male Vietnam Veterans with Posttraumatic Stress Disorder," *Journal of Consulting and Clinical Psychology* 60 (1992): 916.

Ronald C. Kessler et al., "Posttraumatic Stress Disorder in the National Comorbidity Survey," *Archives of General Psychiatry* 52, No. 12 (1995): 1048.

Birgit Kleim, Anke Ehlers, and Edward Glucksman, "Early Predictors of Chronic Post-Traumatic Stress Disorder in Assault Survivors," *Psychological Medicine* 37, No. 10 (2007): 1457.

Miles McFall and Jessica Cook, "PTSD and Health Risk Behavior," *PTSD Research Quarterly* 17, No. 4 (2006): 1.

Richard J. McNally, "Psychological Mechanisms in Acute Response to Trauma," *Biological Psychiatry* 53, No. 9 (2003): 779.

Emily J. Ozer et al., "Predictors of Posttraumatic Stress Disorder and Symptoms in Adults: A Meta-Analysis," *Psychological Bulletin* 129, No. 1 (2003): 52.

Patricia A. Resick and Monica K. Schnike, *Cognitive Processing Therapy for Rape Victims: A Treatment Manual* (Newburk Park, CA : Sage, 1993).

Ebru Salcioglu, Metin Basoglu, and Maria Livanou, "Effects of Live Exposure on Symptoms of Posttraumatic Stress Disorder: The Role of Reduced Behavioral Avoidance in Improvement," *Behaviour Research and Therapy* 45, No. 10 (2007): 2268.

Jitender Sareen et al., "Physical and Mental Comorbidity, Disability, and Suicidal Behavior Associated with Posttraumatic Stress Disorder in a Large Community Sample," *Psychosomatic Medicine* 69, No. 3 (2007): 242.

Regina Steil and Anke Ehlers, "Dysfunctional Meaning of Posttraumatic Intrusions in Chronic PTSD," *Behaviour Research & Therapy* 38, No. 6 (2000): 537.

K. Chase Stovall-McClough and Marylene Cloitre, "Unresolved Attachment, PTSD, and Dissociation in Women with Childhood Abuse Histories," *Journal of Consulting and Clinical Psychology* 74, No. 2 (2006): 219.

Steven Taylor, *Clinician's Guide to PTSD: A Cognitive-Behavioral Approach* (New York: Guilford, 2006).

Edward A. Walker et al., "Health Care Costs Associated With Posttraumatic Stress Disorder Symptoms in Women," *Archives of General Psychiatry* 60 (2003): 369.

Frank W. Weathers, Jennifer A. Huska, Terence M. Keane, *PCL-C for DSM-IV* (Boston: National Center for PTSD – Behavioral Science Division, 1991).

Frank W. Weathers et al., "The PTSD Checklist: Reliability, Validity, & Diagnostic Utility (paper presented at the annual meeting of the International Society for Traumatic Stress Studies, San Antonio, TX, October, 1993).

Adrian Wells, "Anxiety disorders, Metacognition and Change," in *Roadblocks in Cognitive Behavioral Therapy*, ed. Robert L. Leahy (New York: Springer, 2003), 69-90.

Adrian Wells, "A Cognitive Model of GAD: Metacognitions and Pathological Worry," in *Generalized Anxiety Disorder: Advances in Research and Practice*, ed.

Richard G. Heimberg, Cynthia L. Turk, and Douglas S. Mennin (New York: Guilford, 2004), 164-186.

Hong Xian et al., "Genetic and Environmental Influences on Posttraumatic Stress Disorder, Alcohol and Drug Dependence in Twin Pairs," *Drug and Alcohol Dependence* 61 (2000): 95.

Rachel Yehuda and Cheryl M. Wong, "Pathogenesis of Posttraumatic Stress Disorder and Acute Stress," in *Textbook of Anxiety Disorders*, eds. Dan J. Stein and Eric Hollander (Washington, DC: American Psychiatric Publishing, 2001), 373-386.

INDEX

Note: Page numbers in italics indicate references to tables.

compulsive disorder); Rituals
delaying, 146, *149, 152*
examples of, 119
explanation of, 118
modifying, *152*
as safety behaviors, 130
Conceptual skills, 21–22
Control, 5, 46–47, 53–54, 68, 124, 127,
309–310
Control, letting go of, 46–*49, 56,* 177, *183*
Controlling situations
anxiety and, 34–37, 46–47, 53–54
examples of, 31, 36, 46
explanation of, 31
with GAD, 160, 163–165, *164*
limitations and, 174
"magical thinking" and, 35
obsessions and, 31
with panic disorder, *94,* 107
safety behaviors and, 35, 40
Coping
cards, 317
imagery, 316
statements, 81
strategies, 111–112
Costs/benefits
of anxiety, 3–4
of OCD, *132–133, 149–150*
of panic disorder, *99*
of PTSD, 230, 247
of SAD, 204, *217*
of specific phobias, *70*–71
of thoughts, 312, 316
Courage, 251, 254
Crime, 5
Criticism, 189–190
Crowds, fear of, 1–3, 91–92
"Cue-controlled" relaxation technique,
258

D
Dalai Lama, 255
Danger, catastrophizing, 31, 33–34, 44,
62, 92–*94, 113,* 160
Danger, detecting, 30–34, 41, 53, 62, 93,
160, 162–164
Death, fear of, 24, 37, 39, 46
Depersonalization, 229, *232,* 239
Depression
activities and, 283–284
affecting relationships, 283–284
anxiety-related, 3, 282
compassion and, 285
with GAD, 154–155
genetic predisposition to, 282
growing, 2
insomnia with, 259
medications for, 272–273

mood tracking and, 282–283
with OCD, 8, 120, 154
with panic disorder, 8, 87, 99
with PTSD, 9, 221, 225, 230
with SAD, 186
staying connected and, 283–284
suicide and, 286–288
symptoms of, 282
thoughts with, 285–286
volunteering and, 284
Derealization, 229, *232,* 239
Diabetes, 3
Diagnostic tests, 11, *289–300*
for agoraphobia, *289*
for GAD, *294–295*
for OCD, *290–292*
for PTSD, *298–300*
for SAD, *296–297*
Dichotomous thinking, 302
Diet, 263–268
Dirt, fear of, 3
Disability, 3
Disassociation, 236
Discomfort, 36–37, *51–52,* 99, 204, 254
Disorientation, 102, *113,* 154
Distrust, 252
Divorce, 4, 159, 190
Dizziness
anxiety creating, 34
diet and, 265
examples of, 106, 109–110
with GAD, 154
medications for, 274
natural, 92
with panic disorder, 87–89, *95,* 102,
105, *113*
with PTSD, 238–239
Drugs. *See* Medications; Substance abuse

E
Elevators, fear of, 1–3, 8, 31, 65–66,
73–76, 107, 109
Embarrassment, 25, 120, 187, 194, 220,
305
Embracing anxiety, 50–52, *51, 56,* 58–59
Emotions
avoiding/escaping behavior and,
160–161
detecting danger and, 31–34
diving into, 47–48
eliminating, 229
with GAD, 161, 167, 172–173, 178–
179, *183*
intelligence of, 305–310, *307*
journaling, 173, *183*
letting go and, 47–*49*
negative, *162*
observation of, 47

motivation to change, 70–71
needing certainty, 62, 81–82
observing, 74
operant conditioning of, 60
overcoming, 65, *85–86*
predictions and, 78–79
probabilities and, *43–44, 56*, 62, 81,
312
relapse of, 84
rituals of, 68–69
rules/beliefs for, 62–64, *85*
safety behaviors with, 62, 68–70, *69*,
72, 81
spreading, 71
statistics of, 57–58, 60
strategy for, 84
substance abuse with, 81
symptoms of, 58, 61, 65–66, 68–*69*, 72
thoughts with, *64, 80*
SSRI (Selective Serotonin Reuptake
Inhibitors) medications, 272, *274*
Starvation, fear of, *61, 63*
Strangers, fear of, *63*
Substance abuse
anxiety-related, 2–3, 10
with panic disorder, 99
with PTSD, 9, 220–222, 224, 227, 229,
243, 245
with SAD, 8–9, 186, 192, 194–195
specific phobias and, 81
Suffering, 249, 253
Suffocation, fear of, 91–92, 107
Suicide, 2, 186, 286–288
Superstition, 35, 68
Surrender, 41, 48–49
Survival
evolution and, 6, 15–16, 21, 23, 26,
38, 189
fears and, 20–21, 24, 58
genetics and, 15–16, 22
instincts, 6–7
mental, 223
social cooperation for, 23
Sweating
controlling, 35
fear hierarchies and, 72
with GAD, 163
medications for, 271
with panic disorder, 8, 34, 87–88, *113*
with PTSD, 223, 228
relaxation techniques for, 256
with SAD, 186, 190, 194, 201–202, 205
Symbolic thinking, 23

T
TCA (Tricyclic Anti-Depressant)
medications, 273, *275*

Temporary anxiety, 309
"Tense-and-release relaxation technique,
256–258
Tension, 1, 9, 68, 102, 154, 162, 179–180
Terrorism, 5
Theory of mind, 21–22, 121
Thought-action fusion, 123, *125*, 127,
130, 133
Thoughts
abnormal, 122, *125–127, 129*, 148
accepting, 143, *150*
all-or-nothing, 196
automatic, 80, 301, 312
catastrophizing, 196, 198, 314
of certainty, 122, *125*
challenging, 164, 209, 211–*213, 218*,
261, 314
controlling, 35–36, 122–*125*, 127, *129,
149*
costs/benefits of, 312, 316
dangerous, 122, 126–127
delay of, *152*
with depression, 285–286
diving into, 47–48
double standards and, 313
drifting of, 134, *151*
emotions and, 311
evaluating, *149*, 231–*233*, 285–286,
311–317
evidence for, 312–313
facts and, 311
fear of, 34, *64*
flooding of, 124, *151*, 177–178, *183*
fortune-telling/predicting and, 195,
198
with GAD, *170–171*, 176–178, 181–
183
identifying, 301–*304*
insomnia and, 14
interpreting, 123, 313
intrusive, *129*
irrational, 13, 119
letting go of, 47–*49*
logic of, 312
mind and, 31
mind reading and, 195, 198
modifying, *152*
monitoring, 126, *129*
as movie, 315
negative filter of, 195
neutralizing, 128–*129*
normal, 123
observing, 47, 53, 181–182, 231, *247*
obsessions and, 119
with OCD, 117, 122–130, *129*, 133–
134, 140, *149, 151*
with panic disorder, 97, 102–103

About the Author

Robert L. Leahy, Ph.D., is recognized as one of the most respected cognitive therapists in the world and is known internationally as a leading writer and speaker in this revolutionary field. He brings to *Anxiety Free* the accumulated knowledge of 25 years of helping people overcome anxiety. He holds a number of high-ranking positions in his field, including director of the American Institute for Cognitive Therapy, president of the International Association of Cognitive Psychotherapy, president of the Association for Behavioral and Cognitive Therapies, and president of the Academy of Cognitive Therapy. He is the author and editor of 15 books, including the best-selling *The Worry Cure*; and has been featured in *The New York Times Sunday Magazine, Forbes, Fortune, Newsweek, Psychology Today, Washington Post, Redbook, Shape, First for Women, Women's Health, Self,* and *USA Today Magazine*. He has also appeared on national and local radio and television including *20/20, Good Morning America*, and *The Early Show*.

Hay House Titles of Related Interest

YOU CAN HEAL YOUR LIFE, the movie,
starring Louise L. Hay & Friends
(available as a 1-DVD program and an expanded 2-DVD set)
Watch the trailer at: **www.LouiseHayMovie.com**

THE SHIFT, the movie,
starring Dr. Wayne W. Dyer
(available as a 1-DVD program and an expanded 2-DVD set)
Watch the trailer at: www.DyerMovie.com

❋ ❋ ❋

BE HAPPY! Release the Power of Happiness in YOU,
by Robert Holden, Ph.D.

CHANGE YOUR THOUGHTS—CHANGE YOUR LIFE:
Living the Wisdom of the Tao, by Dr. Wayne W. Dyer

IT'S THE THOUGHT THAT COUNTS: Why Mind Over
Matter Really Works, by David R. Hamilton, Ph.D.

LIFE SUPPORT: A Survival Guide for the Modern Soul,
by Derek Draper

MAXIMIZE YOUR POTENTIAL THROUGH
THE POWER OF YOUR SUBCONSCIOUS
MIND TO OVERCOME FEAR AND WORRY, by Dr. Joseph Murphy

❋ ❋ ❋

All of the above are available at your local bookstore,
or may be ordered by visiting:
Hay House UK: **www.hayhouse.co.uk;**
Hay House USA: **www.hayhouse.com®;**
Hay House Australia: **www.hayhouse.com.au;**
Hay House South Africa: **www.hayhouse.co.za;**
Hay House India: **www.hayhouse.co.in**

We hope you enjoyed this Hay House book.
If you would like to receive a free catalogue featuring additional
Hay House books and products, or if you would like information
about the Hay Foundation, please contact:

Hay House UK Ltd
292B Kensal Rd • London W10 5BE
Tel: (44) 20 8962 1230; Fax: (44) 20 8962 1239
www.hayhouse.co.uk

***

Published and distributed in the United States of America by:
Hay House, Inc. • PO Box 5100 • Carlsbad, CA 92018-5100
Tel.: (1) 760 431 7695 or (1) 800 654 5126;
Fax: (1) 760 431 6948 or (1) 800 650 5115
www.hayhouse.com

Published and distributed in Australia by:
Hay House Australia Ltd • 18/36 Ralph St • Alexandria NSW 2015
Tel.: (61) 2 9669 4299; Fax: (61) 2 9669 4144
www.hayhouse.com.au

Published and distributed in the Republic of South Africa by:
Hay House SA (Pty) Ltd • PO Box 990 • Witkoppen 2068
Tel./Fax: (27) 11 467 8904 • www.hayhouse.co.za

Published and distributed in India by:
Hay House Publishers India • Muskaan Complex • Plot No.3
B-2 • Vasant Kunj • New Delhi – 110 070.
Tel.: (91) 11 41761620; Fax: (91) 11 41761630.
www.hayhouse.co.in

Distributed in Canada by:
Raincoast • 9050 Shaughnessy St • Vancouver, BC V6P 6E5
Tel.: (1) 604 323 7100; Fax: (1) 604 323 2600

***

Sign up via the Hay House UK website to receive the Hay House
online newsletter and stay informed about what's going on with
your favourite authors. You'll receive bimonthly announcements
about discounts and offers, special events, product highlights,
free excerpts, giveaways, and more!
www.hayhouse.co.uk

JOIN THE HAY HOUSE FAMILY

As the leading self-help, mind, body and spirit publisher in the UK, we'd like to welcome you to our family so that you can enjoy all the benefits our website has to offer.

 **EXTRACTS** from a selection of your favourite author titles

 **COMPETITIONS, PRIZES & SPECIAL OFFERS** Win extracts, money off, downloads and so much more

 **LISTEN** to a range of radio interviews and our latest audio publications

 CELEBRATE YOUR BIRTHDAY An inspiring gift will be sent your way

 **LATEST NEWS** Keep up with the latest news from and about our authors

 **ATTEND OUR AUTHOR EVENTS** Be the first to hear about our author events

 **iPHONE APPS** Download your favourite app for your iPhone

 **HAY HOUSE INFORMATION** Ask us anything, all enquiries answered

join us online at **www.hayhouse.co.uk**

 Astley House, 33 Notting Hill Gate
London W11 3JQ
T: 020 3675 2450 E: info@hayhouse.co.uk